Theories in Second
Language Acquisition

Second Language Acquisition Research Theoretical and Methodological Issues
Susan M. Gass, Jacquelyn Schachter, and Alison Mackey, *Editors*

Schachter/Gass Second Language Classroom Research: Issues and Opportunities
Birdsong Second Language Acquisition and the Critical Period Hypotheses
Ohta Second Language Acquisition Processes in the Classroom: Learning Japanese
Major Foreign Accent: Ontogeny and Phylogeny of Second Language Phonology
VanPatten Processing Instruction: Theory, Research, and Commentary
VanPatten/Williams/Rott/Overstreet Form-Meaning Connections in Second Language Acquisition
Bardovi-Harlig/Hartford Interlanguage Pragmatics: Exploring Institutional Talk
Dörnyei The Psychology of the Language Learner: Individual Differences in Second Language Acquisition

Monographs on Research Methodology

Tarone/Gass/Cohen Research Methodology in Second Language Acquisition
Gass/Mackey Stimulation Recall Methodology in Second Language Research
Yule Referential Communication Tasks
Markee Conversation Analysis
Dörnyei Questionnaires in Second Language Research: Construction, Administration, and Processing

Of Related Interest

Gass Input, Interaction, and the Second Language Learner
Gass/Sorace/Selinker Second Language Learning Data Analysis, Second Edition
Gass/Selinker Second Language Acquisition: An Introductory Course, Second Edition
Mackey/Gass Second Language Research: Methodology and Design

Theories in Second Language Acquisition

An Introduction

Edited by

Bill VanPatten and Jessica Williams

LEA LAWRENCE ERLBAUM ASSOCIATES, PUBLISHERS
2007 Mahwah, New Jersey   London

Senior Acquisitions Editor: Cathleen Petree
Editorial Assistant: Erica Kica
Cover Design: Tomai Maridou
Full-Service Compositor: MidAtlantic Books & Journals, Inc.

This book was typeset in 10.5/12 pt Goudy Old Style, Italic, Bold, and Bold Italic. Headings were typeset in Americana, Bold and Italic.

Lawrence Erlbaum Associates, Inc., Publishers
10 Industrial Avenue
Mahwah, New Jersey 07430
www.erlbaum.com

CIP information for this volume can be obtained by contacting the Library of Congress.

ISBN   0-8058-5937-3 (case)
ISBN   0-8058-5738-9 (pbk)

Books published by Lawrence Erlbaum Associates are printed on acid-free paper, and their bindings are chosen for strength and durability.

Printed in the United States of America
10   9   8   7   6   5   4

Contents

Preface

This book focuses on a number of contemporary mainstream theories in second language acquisition (SLA) research that have generated attention among scholars. For several decades the field of SLA has struggled with the nature of theories, what they are, and what would be an "acceptable" theory of SLA. The first book to appear regarding theories was Barry McLaughlin's 1987 work, *Theories of SLA*, in which he reviewed a number of theories that were prevalent at the time. Since then other books have appeared that focus on specific theories—including books authored by the contributors to the present volume. In addition, there has been continued effort to offer overviews of theories, and scholars have continued to discuss in the journals the role of theories in SLA. Indeed, the present volume draws upon one particular publication by Michael Long in a special issue of the *TESOL Quarterly* in 1990 devoted to the construction of a theory in SLA. In that article Long discusses the nature of what a theory needs to be in SLA and also summarizes the research in order to establish "the least" a theory of SLA needs to explain. We borrow from Long's article in our first chapter to outline the challenges to contemporary theories and list ten observations that need to be accounted for on theoretical grounds.

One might ask why there are so many competing theories in SLA. Why isn't there just one theory that accounts for SLA? What is it about SLA that invites a diffusion of theoretical perspectives? To understand this, one might consider the parable about the four blind men and the elephant. These sightless men chance upon a pachyderm for the first time and one, holding its tail, says, "Ah! The elephant is very much like a rope." The second one has wrapped his arms around a giant leg and says, "Ah! The elephant is like a tree." The third has been feeling along side the elephant's massive body and says, "Ah! The elephant is very much like a wall." The fourth, having seized the trunk, cries out, "Ah! The elephant is very much like a snake." For us, SLA is a big elephant that researchers can easily look at from different perspectives. SLA is, after all, an incredibly complex set of processes, and if you have been introduced to the field via any of the excellent overviews of SLA, this most likely is your conclusion. Thus, researchers have grabbed onto different parts of the elephant as a means of coming to grips with the complex phenomenon. This does not mean, however, that researchers and scholars have gone poking around SLA blindly and without thought; the present chapters should convince you otherwise. Unlike the blind men of our fable, researchers understand that in order to understand the whole of SLA, they may need to concentrate on the smaller parts first. In the end, we may even need multiple theories that complement one another in order to account for different observed phenomena of SLA. As you complete the readings in your book, you might ask yourself, "Just what part of the elephant is each theory examining?"

The present book came about as a perceived need to have a comprehensive yet readily accessible set of readings for the beginning student of SLA. Each of us has taught introductory courses on SLA to students in TESOL and applied linguistics, and we have felt that a good introduction to theories is beneficial. At the same time, we know that it is easy for authors who don't work in a particular theory to reduce the theory to the point that students misinterpret it or to misinterpret the theory themselves and pass on this misinterpretation to students. To this end, we decided that a collection of chapters written by the experts who work in the theories would best suit our needs as well as those of our students. We are pleased to present this volume for the beginning student of SLA.

ACKNOWLEDGMENTS

Since its inception, this volume has been developed with the novice reader in mind—the beginning student of SLA who may not have much background in linguistics or even SLA. Keeping that novice reader in mind has been a challenge for us and no less for the various contributors whose theories you will read here. The process of getting this volume into final form was long and demanded considerable effort on the part of the contributors to present some very complex notions in an accessible and consistent format. We know this often tried the patience of our authors. We took them away from their research and teaching duties in order to answer our numerous queries and revise their chapters—sometimes more than they anticipated. That they stuck with us to the end is demonstration of their commitment and dedication to the profession and to its newest members. They have our heartfelt thanks.

We also thank the folks at Lawrence Erlbaum Associates for their help in making this volume come about: Cathleen Petree and the rest of the LEA staff. Thanks also go to Susan Gass, Jacquelyn Schachter, and Alison Mackey for supporting our idea since its conception.

Theories in Second Language Acquisition

1

Introduction:
The Nature of Theories

Bill VanPatten and Jessica Williams
University of Illinois, Chicago

Almost everyone has heard of Einstein's Theory of Relativity. People have also heard of things such as the Theory of Evolution and the Atomic Theory. What is common to all these theories is that they are theories about what scientists call *natural phenomena*, things that we observe everyday. Theories are a fundamental staple in science, and all advances in science are, in some way or another, advances in theory development. If you ask scientists, they would tell you that the sciences could not proceed without theories. And if you ask applied scientists (such as those who develop medicines or attempt to solve the problem of how to travel from Earth to Mars), they would tell you that a good deal of their work is derived from theoretical insights.

Theories are also used in the social and behavioral sciences, such as psychology, sociology, and economics. As in the natural sciences, social sciences attempt to explain observed phenomena such as why people remember some things better than others under certain conditions or why the stock market behaves the way it does.

In the field of SLA research, theories have also come to occupy a central position. Some would even say that the only way SLA could advance as a research field is to be theory driven. The purpose of the present book is to introduce the reader to current theories in SLA and to provide a background for continued in-depth reading of the same. As a starting point, we will need to examine the nature of theories in general.

WHAT IS A THEORY?

At its most fundamental level, a theory is a set of statements about natural phenomena that explains why these phenomena occur the way they do. In the sciences, theories are used in what Kuhn (1996) calls the job of "puzzle solving." By this Kuhn means that scientists look at observable phenomena as puzzles or questions to be solved. Why does the earth revolve around the sun and not fly off into space? Why are humans bipedal but the other primates are knuckle-walkers? These are all questions about things that confront us everyday, and it is the job of scientists to account for them.

In short, then, the first duty of a theory is to *account for* or *explain* observed phenomena. But a theory ought to do more than that. A theory also ought to make predictions about what would occur under specific conditions. Let's look at three examples: one familiar, the other two perhaps less so. In the early part of the 19th century, scientists were already aware of the presence of micro-organisms in the air and water, and they had an idea about the connection be-tween the organisms and disease. However, they had no idea of how they came into existence; indeed, belief in the spontaneous generation of these organisms was widespread. "Bad air" was thought to cause disease. Careful experimentation by Louis Pasteur and other scientists demonstrated that microbes, though carried by air, are not created by air. Living organisms come from other living organisms. These discoveries led to the development of the *germ theory of disease*, which proposed that disease was caused by microorganisms. The acceptance of this theory had obvious important applications in public health, such as the development of vaccines, hygienic practices in surgery, and the pasteurization of milk. It not only could *explain* the presence and spread of disease, it could also *predict*, for example, that doctors who delivered babies without washing their hands after performing autopsies on patients who had died from childbirth fever would transmit the disease to new patients. Even more important, the same theory could be used to *connect* phenomena that on the surface appeared unrelated, such as the transmittal of disease, fermentation processes in wine and beer production, and a decline in silkworm production.

Now let's take an example from psychology. It is an observed phenomenon that some people read and comprehend written text faster and better than others. As researchers began to explore this question, a theory of individual differences in working memory evolved. That theory says that people vary in their ability to hold information in working memory (defined, roughly, as that mental processing space in which a person performs computations on information at lightening speed). More specifically, the theory says that people vary in their working memory *capacity*: some have greater capacities for processing incoming information compared with others, but capacity is limited in some way for everyone. Initially used to account for individual differences in reading comprehension ability in a person's first language, the theory also accounts for a wide range of seemingly unrelated phenomena, such as why people remember certain sequences of numbers and not others, why they recall certain words that have been heard, why people vary on what parts of sentences they remember best, why certain stimuli are ignored and others attended to, and why some students are good note takers and others are not, among others. A theory of working memory, then, allows psychologists to unify a variety of behaviors and outcomes that on the surface do not necessarily appear to be related. There are even attempts to apply the theory to SLA to explain why some people learn faster and better than others.

Let's take a final example, this time from language. In one theory of syntax (sentence structure), a grammar can allow movement of elements in the sentence. This is how we get two sentences that essentially mean the same thing as in

(1)   Mary said what?

(2)   What did Mary say?

In this particular theory, the *what* is said to have moved from its position as an object of the verb *said* to occupy a place in a different part of the sentence. At the same time, this theory also says that when something moves it leaves a hidden *trace*. Thus, the syntactician would write (2) like (3).

(3)   What$_i$ did Mary say t$_i$?

In (3) the t stands for the empty spot that the *what* left and the i simply shows that the *what* and the t are "co-indexed"; that is, if there happens to be more than one thing that moves, you can tell which trace it left behind.

To add to the picture, the theory also says that ts, although hidden, are real and occupy the spot left behind. Thus, nothing can move into that spot and no contractions can occur across it. Armed with this, the syntactician can make a variety of predictions about grammatical and ungrammatical sentences in English. We might predict, for example, that (4) is a good sentence but (5) is bad and not allowed by English grammar.

(4)   Should I have done it?

(5)   *Should I've done it?

The reason for this is that *should* has moved from its original spot and left a t behind as illustrated in (6):

(6) I should have done it. → Should$_i$ I t$_i$ have done it?

At the same time, the syntactician would predict restrictions on the contraction of *want to* to *wanna*. Thus, (7) is fine because there is no trace intervening where a contraction wants to happen.

(7)   Who$_i$ do you want to invite t_i to dinner? → Who do you wanna invite to dinner?

All English speakers would agree, however, that (8) is awful.

(8)   *Who do you wanna take Susie to the prom next month?

You could probably work this out yourself, but the reason (8) is bad is that the *who* has moved and left a *t* that blocks a possible contraction. Compare (7) and (8) redone here as (9) and (10)

(9)   Who$_i$ do you want to invite t_i to dinner? → Who do you wanna invite to dinner?

(10) Who$_i$ do you want t_i to take Susie to the prom next month? → *Who do you wanna take Susie to the prom next month?

Be careful not to pronounce *wanna* like *want tuh*; *want tuh* is not a contraction and is merely the schwaing of the vowel sound in *to*. *Want tuh* sounds okay in sentence (8) precisely because it is not a contraction.

Thus, the theory unifies constraints on contractions with modals (*should, would, will, may, might*), with auxiliaries (*do, have*), with copular verbs (*be*), with the verb *want*, and with pronouns (*I, you, he,* and so on). It makes predictions about good and bad sentences that perhaps we have never seen or heard, some of which, like silkworms and beer, don't seem to have much in common.

To summarize so far, a theory ought to account for and explain observed phenomena and also make predictions about what is possible and what is not. In addition, when accounting for and predicting things, most theories—good ones, that is—also tend to unify a series of generalizations about the world or unify a series of observations about the world. In the brief view of syntactic theory here, the few generalizations made about how syntax works unifies a variety of observations about contractions and not just contractions with *should*. All contractions conform to the generalizations.

For SLA, then, we will want a theory that acts like a theory should. We will want it to account for observable phenomena (something we turn our attention to later in this chapter). We want the theory to make predictions. And, ideally, we want it to unify the generalizations we make as part of the theory. In other words, we want a single theory to bring all of the observed phenomena under one umbrella. Whether this is possible at this time has yet to be determined and is something that this book will explore.

WHAT IS A MODEL?

Many people confuse theories and models. A model describes processes or sets of processes of a phenomenon. A model may also show how different components of a phenomenon interact. The important word here is *how*. A model does not need to explain *why*. Whereas a theory can make predictions based on generalizations, this is not required of a model. The problem is that in the real world—and in SLA as a research discipline—this distinction is not always maintained. You will find as you read further in the field that researchers often use *model* and *theory* interchangeably. Thus, although in principle it would be a good idea to distinguish between these two terms as they do in the natural sciences, in practice many of us in SLA do not do so.

WHAT IS A HYPOTHESIS?

Distinct from a theory, a hypothesis does not unify various phenomena; it is usually an idea about a single phenomenon. Some people use theory and hypothesis interchangeably, but in fact they are distinct and should be kept separate. In science we would say that a theory can generate hypotheses that can then be tested by experimentation or observation. In psychology, for example, there are theories regarding memory. You may recall the theory about working memory and capacity discussed earlier. The theory says (among many other things) that working memory is limited in capacity. This means that people can only pay attention to only so much information at a given time before working memory is overloaded. The theory also says that there are individual differences in working memory and in how people use what they have. Some people have X amount of working memory capacity as they attend to incoming information whereas others have more or less. A hypothesis that falls out of this, then, is that working memory differences among individuals should affect reading comprehension: Those with greater working memory capacity should be faster readers or they should comprehend more. This is a testable hypothesis. We ought to add here that the only valuable hypotheses for a theory are those that are testable, meaning some kind of experiment can be run or some kind of data can be examined to see if the hypothesis holds up. Another example of a hypothesis comes from SLA: the Critical Period Hypothesis. There is a theory in neurolinguistics that states that the brain begins to specialize at an early age; specific brain functions become increasingly associated with specific areas of the brain. In addition, some functions may be developmentally controlled; that is, they turn on and—more important for language learning—turn off at specific points in development. The Critical Period Hypothesis is a direct consequence of this theory. It states that the ability to attain native-like proficiency in a language is related to the initial age of exposure. If language learning begins after a certain age (and there is a considerable controversy over what this age is as well as whether there even is a critical period—see the various papers in Birdsong, 1999), the learners will never reach a level of proficiency or competence comparable to a native speaker's. A corollary to this hypothesis is that language-learning ability declines with age after this point. Again, both of these are testable hypotheses. Recall that earlier we said we wanted a theory to make predictions. Predictions are actually hypotheses. When we make a prediction based on a theory, we are in effect making a hypothesis.

CONSTRUCTS

All theories have what are called *constructs*. Constructs are key features or mechanisms that the theory relies on; they must be definable in the theory. In the theory about disease transmission, *germ* is a construct. In the theory about working memory, *capacity* is a construct; and in the theory about syntax, a *trace* is a construct.

In evaluating any theory, it is important to understand the constructs upon which the theory relies, otherwise it is easy to judge a theory one way or another—that is, as a good or bad theory—without a full understanding of the underpinnings of the theory. For example, without an understanding of the construct *germ*, it would have been easy to dismiss germ theory. But given that the construct *germ* was easily definable and identifiable, dismissal of germ transmission and diseases was not so facile. To fully understand something like relativity, one must have a thorough grasp of the constructs *time*, *space*, and others.

In SLA we see that constructs that are in need of definitions abound. For example, take the term *second language acquisition*. Each word is actually a construct; you can ask yourself what does *second* mean, what does *language* mean, and how do we define *acquisition*? In SLA theorizing, most people use the term *second* to mean any language other than one's first language. It makes no difference what the language is, where it is learned, or how it is learned. This suggests, then, that any theorizing about SLA ought to apply equally to the person learning Egyptian Arabic in Cairo without the benefit of instruction as well as to the person learning French in a foreign-language classroom in the United States. Defining *second* in an all-encompassing way has an effect on the scope of the theory. If the construct *second* were not defined this way, then it would have limited scope over the contexts of language learning. For example, some people define *second* language to refer to a language learned where it is spoken (e.g., immigrants learning English in this country, an American learning Spanish in Costa Rica), whereas *foreign* is used to refer to situations in which the language is not commonly spoken outside of the classroom (e.g., German in California). Thus, if *second* were defined in the more restricted way, a theory of SLA would be limited to the first context of learning.

The term *language* is deceptively simple as a construct, but have you ever tried to define it? Does it mean speech? Or does it mean the rules that govern speech production? Or does it mean the unconscious knowledge system that contains all the information about language (e.g., the sound system, the mental dictionary, syntactic constraints, rules on word formation, rules on use of language in context)? Thus, any theory about SLA needs to be clear on what it means by *language*. Otherwise the reader may not fully grasp what the theory claims, or worse, may misinterpret it.

In summary, here are key issues discussed so far:

- Theories ought to explain observable phenomena.
- Theories ought to unify explanations of various phenomena where possible.
- Theories are used to generate hypotheses that can be tested empirically.
- Theories may be explanations of a *thing* (such as language) or explanations of *how* something comes to be (such as the acquisition of language).
- Theories have constructs, which in turn are defined in the theory.

WHY ARE THEORIES AND MODELS EITHER GOOD OR NECESSARY FOR SLA RESEARCH?

We have explored what theories are but only indirectly addressed why they might be useful. Certainly they help us to understand the phenomena that we observe. Consider again the Critical Period Hypothesis. It has often been observed that speakers who begin the process of SLA later in life usually have an accent. A theory about the loss of brain plasticity during natural maturation may help explain this phenomenon. The same theory might predict that learners who begin foreign language study in high school will be less likely to approach a native-like standard of pronunciation than those learners who have access to significant amounts of target language input much earlier in life. These kinds of predictions have clear practical applications; for example, they suggest that foreign language learning should begin at a young age.

Let's look at another concrete example. In one theory of SLA, producing language (usually called *output*) is considered an important element in structuring linguistic knowledge and anchoring it in memory. In another theory, in contrast, output is considered unimportant in developing second language knowledge. Its role is limited to building control over knowledge that has already been acquired. These differences in theory have clear and important consequences for second language instruction. In the first case, output practice would have a significant role in all aspects of instruction. In the second case, it would be most prominent in fluency practice.

So far we have explored the utility of theories from a practical, real-world perspective. Theories are also useful in guiding research, which may not always have the immediate practical purposes of the instruction example. If we step back for a moment and consider the theories previously mentioned, we have looked at:

- A theory that explains/predicts constraints on contraction in English.
- A theory that explains/predicts foreign accents in adult learners.
- Theories that predict the role of output in the second language acquisition process.

You may notice that they are not all the same. The first is a theory of *what* is to be acquired, that is, the unconscious mental representation of constraints on language. It is not enough to say, for example, that learners are acquiring English, for this begs the questions what is English? and how is it different from Spanish or Chinese? Clearly, a dictionary of the English language is not the language itself, so memorizing a dictionary is not equivalent to acquiring English. Nor would it be sufficient to study a big grammar book and commit all its rules to memory. It is very unlikely that any grammar book includes the *wanna* rule that appeared earlier in this chapter, for example. And what about the sound system and constraints on syllable formation (e.g., no syllable in English can start with the cluster *rw*, but such a syllable initial cluster is possible in French)? In short, English, like any other language, is complex and consists of many components. You may recall that we touched on this issue when we noted that *language* itself is a construct that a theory needs to define. Once the theory defines what it means by language, it can better guide the questions needed to conduct research.

The second two items on the list above are not really about the target of acquisition; rather, they address the factors that affect learning outcomes (e.g., the Critical Period position), or they address *how* learning takes place—in other words, processes learners must undergo. These processes may be internal to the learner (such as what might be happening in working memory as the learner is attempting to comprehend language and how this impacts learning) or they may be external to the learner (such as how learners and native speakers engage in conversation and how this impacts learning). Theories regarding factors or processes are clearly different from theories about the *what* of acquisition, but they, too, can guide researchers conducting empirical research.

Finally, research can return the favor to theorists by evaluating competing theories. For example, one theory of learning, including language learning, maintains that humans are sensitive to the frequency of events and experiences, and that this sensitivity shapes their learning. Within this theory, linguistic elements are abstracted from exposure to language and from language use. What look like rules in a learner's grammar are really just the result of repeated exposure to regularities in the input. A competing theory maintains that language learning takes place largely by the interaction of innate knowledge (that is, human specific and universal linguistic knowledge) and data gathered from the input. Within this theory, frequency may have some role in making some aspects of language more noticeable, but it is not a causal factor as it is in the first theory. Each of these two theories can generate predictions, or hypotheses, about how language acquisition will take place under specific conditions. These hypotheses can then be tested against observations and the findings of empirical studies.

WHAT NEEDS TO BE EXPLAINED BY THEORIES IN SLA?

As we mentioned at the outset of this chapter, one of the roles of theories is to explain observed phenomena. Examples we gave from the sciences were the observation that Earth revolves around the sun and doesn't fly off into space, and that humans are bipedal while our closest relatives are knuckle-walkers. Theories in science attempt to explain these observations—that is, tell *why* they exist.

In the field of SLA research, a number of observations have been catalogued (e.g., Long, 1990), and what follows is a condensed list of them. At the end of the chapter are references for more detailed accounts of these observations.

Observation # 1. Exposure to input is necessary for SLA. This observation means that acquisition will not happen for learners of a second language unless they are exposed to input. Input is defined as language the learner hears (or reads) and attends to for its meaning. For example, a learner hears "open your books to page 24" in a second language. The learner is expected to comprehend the message and open his or her book to page 24. Language the learner does not respond to for its meaning (such as language used in a mechanical drill) is not input. Although everyone agrees that input is necessary for SLA, not everyone agrees that it is sufficient.

Observation # 2. A good deal of SLA happens incidentally. This observation captures that various aspects of language enter learners' minds/brains when they are focused on communicative interaction (including reading). In other words, with incidental acquisition the learner's *primary* focus of attention is on the message contained in the input, and linguistic features are "picked up" in the process. Incidental acquisition can occur with any aspect of language (e.g., vocabulary, syntax, morphology [inflections], phonology).

Observation # 3. Learners come to know more than what they have been exposed to in the input. Captured here is the idea that learners attain unconscious knowledge about the second language (L2) that could not come from the input alone. For example, learners come to know what is ungrammatical in a language, such as the constraints on *wanna* contraction that we saw earlier in this chapter. These constraints are not taught and are not evident in the samples of language that learners hear. Another kind of unconscious knowledge that learners attain involves ambiguity. Learners come to know, for example, that the sentence *John told Fred that he was going to sing* can mean either John will sing or Fred will sing.

Observation # 4. Learner's output (speech) often follows predictable paths with predictable stages in the acquisition of a given structure. Learner's speech shows evidence of what are called "developmental sequences." One example involves the acquisition of negation in English. Learners from all language backgrounds show evidence of the following stages:

Stage 1: no + phrase: No want that.

Stage 2: subject + no + phrase: He no want that.

Stage 3: *don't, can't, not* may alternate with *no*: He can't/don't/not want that.

Stage 4: Negation is attached to modal verbs: He can't do that.

Stage 5: Negation is attached to auxiliaries: He doesn't want that.

In addition to developmental sequences, there are such things as "acquisition orders" for various inflections and small words. For example, in English –*ing* is mastered before regular past tense, which is mastered before irregular past tense forms, which in turn are mastered before third-person (present tense) –*s*. This observation also captures that learners may pass through "U-shaped" development. In such a case, the learner starts out doing something correctly, then subsequently does it incorrectly, and then "re-acquires" the correct form.

A classic example comes from the irregular past tense in which learners begin with *came, went* (and similar forms), then may begin to produce *camed, goed/ wented,* and then later produce the correct *went, came,* and other irregular forms.

Observation # 5. Second language learning is variable in its outcome. Here we mean that not all learners achieve the same degree of unconscious knowledge about a second language. They may also vary in speaking ability, comprehension, and a variety of other aspects of language knowledge and use. This may happen even under the same conditions of exposure. Learners under the same conditions may be at different stages of developmental sequences or be further along than others in acquisition orders. What is more, it is a given that most learners do not achieve native-like ability in a second language.

Observation # 6. Second language learning is variable across linguistic subsystems. Language is made up of a number of components that interact in different ways. For example, there are the sound system (including rules on what sound combinations are possible and impossible as well as rules on pronunciation), the lexicon (the mental dictionary along with word-specific information, such as verb "X" cannot take a direct object or it requires a prepositional phrase, or verb "X" can only become a noun by the addition of *–tion* and not *–ment*), syntax (what are possible and impossible sentences), pragmatics (knowledge of what a speaker's intent is—say, a request versus an actual question), and others. Learners may vary in whether the syntax is more developed compared with the sound system, for example.

Observation # 7. There are limits on the effects of frequency on SLA. It has long been held that frequency of occurrence of a linguistic feature in the input correlates with whether it is acquired early or late. However, frequency is not an absolute predictor of earliness or lateness. In some cases, something very frequent takes longer to acquire than something less frequent.

Observation # 8. There are limits on the effect of a learner's first language on SLA. Evidence of the effects of the first language on SLA has been around since the beginning of contemporary SLA research in the early 1970s. It is clear, however, that the first language does not have massive effects on either processes or outcomes, as once thought. (We will review one particular theory in chapter 2.) Instead, it seems that the influence of the first language is somehow selective and also varies across individual learners.

Observation # 9. There are limits on the effects of instruction on SLA. Teachers and learners of languages often believe that what is taught and practiced is what gets learned. The research on instructed SLA says otherwise.

First, instruction sometimes has no effect on acquisition. For example, instruction has not been shown to cause learners to skip developmental sequences or to alter acquisition orders. Second, some research has shown that instruction is detrimental and can slow down acquisition processes by causing stagnation at a given stage. On the other hand, there is also evidence that in the end, instruction may affect how fast learners progress through sequences and acquisition orders and possibly how far they get in those sequences and orders. Thus, there appear to be beneficial effects from instruction, but they are not direct and not what many people think.

Observation #10. There are limits on the effects of output (learner production) on language acquisition. Although it may seem like common sense that "practice makes perfect," this adage is not entirely true when it comes to SLA. There is evidence that having learners produce language has an effect on acquisition, and there is evidence that it does not. What seems to be at issue, then, is that whatever role learner production (i.e., using language to speak or write) plays in acquisition, there are constraints on that role just as there are on other factors as noted above.

Again, the role of a theory is to explain these phenomena. It is not enough for a theory to say the phenomena exist or to predict them; it also has to provide an underlying explanation for them. For example, natural orders and stages exist. But why do they exist, and why do they exist in the form they do? Why do the stages of negation look the way they do? As another example, why is instruction limited? What is it about language acquisition that puts constraints on it? Why can't stages of acquisition be skipped if instruction is provided for a structure? And if instruction can speed up processes, why can it?

As you read through the various theories in this volume, you will see that current theories in SLA may explain close to all, some, or only a few of the phenomena. What is more, the theories will differ in their explanations because they rely on different premises and different constructs.

ABOUT THIS VOLUME

In this volume, we have asked some of the foremost proponents of particular theories and models to describe and discuss them in an accessible manner for the beginning student of SLA theory and research. As they do so, the authors will address particular topics and questions so that readers may compare and contrast theories more easily. They will each address:

- The theory and its constructs.
- What counts as evidence for the theory.

- Common misunderstandings.
- An exemplary study.
- How the theory address the observable phenomena of SLA.

Specific interests and areas of expertise have led the authors to the linguistic and cognitive aspects of SLA. Thus, the theories and perspectives taken in the present volume will reflect such orientations. To be sure, there are social perspectives that can be brought to bear on SLA. However, such perspectives tend to focus on the *use* of the second language and only minimally address issues of acquisition that are of concern here. In excluding such perspectives from the present volume we do not suggest that they are unimportant for the field of SLA research as a whole. Instead, our intention is to gather those approaches that currently compete to explain the acquisition of a linguistic system (with primary emphasis on syntax, morphology, and, to a lesser degree, lexicon).

Chapter 2 provides historical context for current research in SLA and explores two theories that have had lasting impact on the field: behaviorism and Krashen's Monitor Theory. In chapter 3, White presents the most widely known and researched theory of language in the field, Universal Grammar (UG). Research within this generative perspective attempts to characterize the nature of interlanguage competence. This approach is described as *modular* because it considers language learning as different from other kinds of learning. It is motivated by the *poverty of stimulus* problem—that is, how learners come to know more than what they are exposed to in the input. White argues for an innate language faculty at the heart of both first and second language learning.

In chapter 4, Bardovi-Harlig explores one functional perspective on SLA: what she terms the concept-oriented approach. In contrast to UG, functional approaches maintain that language form follows language function, and that language development arises out of communicative need. Again, unlike UG, it does not privilege any linguistic level (e.g., syntax, semantics, phonology); rather, it investigates form–meaning mappings across linguistic levels.

Nick Ellis presents the Associate–Cognitive CREED in chapter 5. This perspective also contrasts with generative approaches in that it maintains that language learning is like other kinds of learning. Ellis argues that the ease and speed with which language learning takes place depends in large part on the frequency of specific items (called *constructions*) in the input; in other words, learning is an associative process. Each exposure of a form–meaning mapping increases its strength. Abstract generalizations (rules) do not exist in the mind apriori but emerge as a result of massive exposure to input.

In chapter 6, DeKeyser presents Skill Acquisition Theory, another cognitive perspective on SLA. Like the emergentist perspective presented by Ellis, this theory holds that language learning is like other forms of learning, moving from effortful, aware performance to fluent, skilled behavior. The process begins with the acquisition of knowledge about language. At this stage, execution requires the deliberate, piece-by-piece assembly of utterances. It then moves to a stage where a smoother execution is made possible by the assembly of ready-made chunks; in other words, there is a restructuring of the processing procedure. Practice leads to the final stage, automatization, during which performance becomes fluent.

Bill VanPatten draws on aspects of several theories for his Input Processing Theory in chapter 7. This theory seeks to explain why learners process input as they do, and in particular, why they make specific form–meaning connections. It focuses on initial stages of development when learners process input data during comprehension. This perspective assumes a limited processing capacity model of human cognition, common to many cognitive approaches, but also embraces the generative notion that language learning is unlike other forms of learning. Limited processing capacity, universal processing principles, and first language (L1) parsing strategies are used to explain how form–meaning connections are made.

In chapter 8, Pienemann presents Processability Theory, which like Input Processing, focuses on how learners process the formal properties of the language but the focus is on how learners process output. This theory rests largely on the language processing theory of William Levelt and on a theory of language that may be somewhat unfamiliar to readers, Lexical–Functional Grammar. Processability Theory maintains that learners will only produce structures that the language processor can handle at a given time. It presents a hierarchy of processing procedures that has strong predictive power for the emergence of structure in learners' output.

In chapter 9, Carroll presents one of the most complete and complex theories of SLA, which includes a theory of language and a theory of how language is processed. Most of the approaches and theories presented in this text make claims about only one or two of these. The primary mechanism for Carroll's Autonomous Induction Theory of language learning is failure—that is, when incoming input is processed unsuccessfully. This results in changes in the mental representation of language.

In chapter 10, Gass and Mackey address of some the most influential ideas in SLA. They explore the constructs of *input, output,* and *interaction,* and the important role that each plays in SLA. Their approach contains elements of Long's Interaction Hypothesis, Krashen's Input Hypothesis, and Swain's Output Hypothesis. The authors maintain that language learning is embedded in communication, and they examine the mechanisms that connect interaction to acquisition. These ideas form the basis for a good deal of current thinking about language teaching.

In chapter 11, Lantolf and Thorne present an approach that contrasts with the others in this volume: Sociocultural Theory. This perspective maintains that all learning, including language learning, is a socially mediated process. Learning takes place as a result of participating in cultural and social activity. Sociocultural Theory rejects any distinction between social and psychological development. Knowledge is seen not as an abstract system but as a socially constructed one in which the learner moves from other-regulated interactions to self-regulated learning and production.

Lourdes Ortega brings together the many themes in the volume in the last chapter. She distills the ten observations into five themes and then summarizes each theory's perspectives on the five themes in table format. She then discusses a number of issues she believes to be critical to advancement of theories in SLA, including the relationship between the theories and current work in cognitive science, the relationship between explicit and implicit learning, the comparison of SLA with bilingual research more generally, and the role of individual experience in acquisition. Her observations underscore the continued need for interdisciplinary work in L2 research.

An important point to mention is that the above perspectives are in large part reactions to earlier attempts to explain SLA. In general, theories often surface as reactions to other theories that are deemed inadequate or of lesser explanatory power; that is, they have difficulty explaining some or all observable phenomena and/or they make incorrect predictions. For our purposes, we would do well to examine two theories that had enormous impact on the early shaping of SLA research: behaviorism and Monitor Theory. These two perspectives will be the focus of chapter 2 as we examine them with an eye toward understanding how theories work in SLA research.

DISCUSSION QUESTIONS

1. In what ways do theories affect our everyday lives? Try to list and discuss examples from politics, education, and society.
2. Discuss a theory from the past that has been disproved. Also discuss a theory from the past that has stood the test of time. Do you notice any differences between theses theories in terms of their structure? Is one simpler than the other? Does one rely on non-natural constructs for explanation?
3. Theories are clearly useful in scientific ventures and may have practical applications. They have also become useful, if not necessary, in the behavioral and social sciences. In what way is the study of SLA a scientific venture rather than, say, a humanistic one?

4. Re-examine the list of observable phenomena. Are you familiar with all of them and the empirical research behind them? Is there an observable phenomenon in particular you would like to see explained? You may wish to consult some basic texts on this topic listed in the Suggested Further Readings section.

SUGGESTED FURTHER READINGS

Birdsong, D. (Ed.) (1999). *Second language acquisition and the critical period hypothesis.* Mahwah, NJ: Erlbaum.

Ellis, R. (1994). *The study of second language acquisition.* Oxford: Oxford University Press.

This volume is a comprehensive overview of the field that continues to be an excellent resource on many topics in the field.

Gass, S., & Selinker, L. (2001). *Second language acquisition: An introductory course* (2nd ed.). Mahwah, NJ: Lawrence Erlbaum Associates.

This is a basic introduction to the field in a form that is accessible to readers new to the field. It includes at the end of each chapter authentic data-based problems that help readers grapple with issues typical of SLA research.

Kuhn, T. S. (1996). *The structure of scientific revolutions.* 3rd edition. Chicago: University of Chicago Press.

Lightbown, P., & Spada, N. (1999). *How languages are learned* (2nd ed.). Oxford: Oxford University Press.

This volume is aimed at teachers and focuses on language acquisition in classroom settings.

Long, M. (1990). The least a second language acquisition theory needs to explain. *TESOL Quarterly 24,* 649–66.

VanPatten, B. (2003). *From input to output: A teacher's guide to second language acquisition.* New York: McGraw-Hill.

This is an introductory volume for teachers with little background in SLA. It focuses on how input data are processed, what the linguistic system looks like and how it changes, how learners acquire the ability to produce language, and other aspects of acquisition.

2

Early Theories in Second Language Acquisition

Bill VanPatten and Jessica Williams
University of Illinois, Chicago

Prior to the 1990s, explanation of second language acquisition (SLA) fell into basic two periods. The first period is marked by the use of behaviorism—a theory borrowed from psychology—to account for both first and second language acquisition, and by the use of structural descriptions of language. Subsequently, as empirical research on both first and second language acquisition demonstrated some major problems with the behaviorist account of language learning, the field of SLA entered a postbehaviorist era in which multiple theories appeared to account for SLA. There were many competing accounts and explanations of various aspects of SLA at that time (among others, Schumann's Acculturation Model, Tarone's Variable Competence Model, and Andersen's Nativization Model; see the suggested readings for further information on these). Some of them have been updated; others have faded from prominence. The dominant theory at that time, however, is one that retains considerable influence today: the Monitor Theory of Stephen Krashen. In this chapter, we will explore both behaviorism and Monitor Theory, two theories that have had the lasting impact on SLA, particularly for those concerned with classroom instruction.

BEHAVIORISM AND STRUCTURAL LINGUISTICS

Since its beginnings, the field of SLA has drawn theoretical inspiration from other fields. Indeed its origins lie in a practical orientation to language teaching. Before the field of SLA theory and research was established, notions of how people acquired non-primary languages (those not learned as a first language

17

in childhood) were closely tied to pedagogical concerns. An outgrowth of the U.S. "Army Method," the Audio-Lingual Method emerged in the 1950s and borrowed heavily from behavioral psychology and from structural linguistics. These two fields of scholarship, though developed separately, came to be closely associated during this period.

The Theory and Its Constructs

Behaviorism is a theory of animal and human behavior. It attempts to explain behavior without reference to mental events or internal processes. Rather, all behavior is explained solely with reference to external factors in the environment. You may be familiar with Pavlov's experiments with dogs. Many date the origins of modern behaviorism to this research. In one experiment, a tone sounded whenever the dogs were fed. Thus, when the dogs heard the sound (the *stimulus*), they anticipated a meal, and they would begin salivating (the *response*). What Pavlov demonstrated was that when the dogs heard the sound, yet no food appeared, they salivated anyway. Because of the repeated association of the sound with food, after a series of trials the sound alone caused the dogs to salivate. This is called *classical conditioning*. Specifically, this means that in a given context, two events are naturally connected (eating and salivating), and then a third event (the sound) is introduced. After a series of repetitions, the association of the third event alone can trigger the response. Salivating in the presence of food is a natural response for dogs; it is a reflex action. Behaviorists believed the same to be true for human behavior: They reasoned, for instance, that if a child cries and then is picked up by a caregiver, he will develop the *habit* of crying in order to summon the caregiver. If his cry brings no response, he will abandon this strategy. This reliance on association to explain behavior is the hallmark of behaviorism.

In addition, there is a significant role for *frequency*. Each time the response is made to the stimulus, the association between them is strengthened. If the organism no longer receives the stimulus, the response behavior is expected to diminish, a process referred to as *extinction*. Continuous repetition, therefore, is an important factor in developing new behaviors. Finally, behaviorists claimed there could be an association among the responses themselves, which initially could be triggered by the external stimulus. For example, a mouse moving through a maze would respond to the initial stimulus of a piece of cheese. However, after several trials, the mouse's motor movements (e.g., first turn left, then right, then right again) would soon become associated with one another. In the same way, typists would associate certain letters with one another in a predictable sequence: *th* is more likely to be followed by *e* than *l*. Simply by typing the sequence *th*, the typist may end up typing a word like *the* without even thinking about it. Similarly, in language learning, after repeated "trials," a learner might come to associate the pronoun *nous* with the verb form *faisons* even after drilling has ceased.

Behaviorists took this idea a step further with the concept of *operant* or *behavioral conditioning*. This is a feedback system in which reinforcement and punishment can induce an organism to engage in new behaviors: Chickens can learn to dance, pigeons to bowl, and people to speak new languages. In operant conditioning, an organism can be conditioned to engage in a behavior even when the stimulus is no longer present if it has learned the relevant association through consistent feedback. For example, if a chicken is conditioned to dance in response to food, but the provision of food is also accompanied by a flashing light, eventually, the chicken will dance in response to the flashing light, even if no food is provided.

Behaviorists contended that mental processes were not involved in this process; it was purely a result of the association of events, a response to environmental stimuli and subsequent *reinforcement* or *punishment*. In effect, these are both responses to the response. Reinforcement encourages continuation of the response behavior whereas punishment discourages continuation of the response. A rat that engages in a behavior (e.g., running on a wheel) and then receives food is more likely to engage in this behavior again. If it receives a shock, it is more likely to stop the behavior. These ideas were soon applied to human behavior, along with the notion that thoughts, feelings, and intentions are not necessarily involved in human behavior, which, like animal behavior, is seen as set of responses to external stimuli. This concept is central to behaviorism and contrasts sharply with approaches to learning that followed it.

Within the behaviorist theory, all learning—including language learning—is seen as the acquisition of a new behavior. The environment is the most—indeed, perhaps the only—important factor in learning. Learning consists of developing responses to environmental stimuli. If these responses receive positive reinforcement, they will become habits. If the responses receive punishment (in this case error correction), they will be abandoned. And so the process goes on, with the child learning language through habit formation. A child learns a language by imitating sounds and structures that she hears in the environment. If she produces an utterance that brings a positive response, she is likely to do so again. If there is no response or a negative response, repetition is less probable. Thus, language learning is seen as similar to any other kind of learning, from multiplication to yodeling: imitation of models in the input, practice of the new behavior, and the provision of appropriate feedback.

According to behaviorism, SLA occurs in a similar fashion. To learn a second language (L2), one must imitate correct models repeatedly. Learning of novel forms can also occur through *analogy*; for example, learners of English can acquire plural marking on nouns by analogy to previously learned forms: duck:ducks → cat:cats. Positive reinforcement of accurate imitations and correction of inaccurate imitation facilitates the learning process. It is important to note the important role for output in this theory. Good habits required repeated engagement in the target behavior—in this case, the production of the L2. Active participation by the learner was considered a crucial element of the learning process.

The salient characteristic of SLA that differentiates it from child language learning is that L2 learners already have a set of habits—a first language (L1)—that must be overcome in the process of acquiring a second language, which is seen as a new set of habits. This process is a difficult one but can be facilitated by appropriate instruction. Learning conditions are ideal when models are plentiful and accurate, and when feedback is immediate and consistent. Such a position has clear consequences for L2 instruction. Learners should be exposed to a large number of target examples of language; they should imitate these models repeatedly and receive appropriate feedback—positive feedback for accurate imitations, and correction of inaccurate ones. This process should be repeated until these behaviors have become a habit.

Behaviorism was not the only impetus behind this kind of approach to language learning and teaching at this time. It was closely linked to *structural linguistics*, which offered a compatible theory of language. Structural linguistics presented language as based on a finite set of predictable patterns. Language could be analyzed as a series of building blocks, beginning from the sound system all the way to sentence structure. The goal of structural linguistics was entirely descriptive. Explanation—why the language operates as it does—was not seen as within the purview of linguistics. Because structural linguistics portrayed language as based on a discrete and finite set of patterns, it blended easily with behaviorism, which viewed learning as the acquisition of a discrete set of behaviors. Thus, combining the insights of behaviorism and structural linguistics, applied linguistics at this time viewed a L2 learner's task as the imitation and internalization of these patterns.

Behaviorism offered several constructs, such as *conditioning, reinforcement,* and *punishment,* that remain important today. These are not directly observable; rather, they must be inferred from observation. For example, one can observe a stimulus, a response, and feedback. However, one can only infer that a response is conditioned or that a behavior has been reinforced. Some of these constructs have specific applications to SLA. As we have noted, the acquisition of an L2 was seen as the acquisition of a new set of habits, a process that was obstructed by first language habits. These L1 habits had to be overcome in order for SLA to be successful. Obviously, SLA is not always immediately—or even ultimately—successful. This lack of success was blamed in part on *transfer,* an important construct in SLA at that time, one with direct behaviorist roots. Transfer was said to occur when habits from the L1 were used in at-tempting to produce the L2.

Transfer could have either beneficial or negative consequences, depend-ing on the distance between the L1 and L2. These differences were determined via *Contrastive Analysis*. This tool was used to compare languages, structure by structure and sound by sound, in order to predict learner difficulty. Wherever languages were similar, there would be *positive transfer*; that is, learners would have little difficulty because they would simply be able to use their old habits in a new context. If the two languages were different—or two seemingly com-parable structures were different—there would be *negative transfer*, resulting in learner difficulty and error. This type of transfer is often referred to as *inter-ference*, another important construct. The habits of the L1 were seen as inter-fering with the acquisition of a new set of habits. Thus, errors were seen as evidence of lack of learning, primarily the result of L1 interference. An im-portant goal of language teaching was help learners avoid these interference errors, lest they become habits. Repetitions of correct models, as well as im-mediate and consistent negative feedback, or error correction, were seen as the best way to eradicate errors before learners developed bad habits. And because habit formation was considered the result of response to external stimuli rather than of internal processes, there was little need for learners to think about what they were doing. They needed only listen and repeat.

There are several important implications of this position. First, the L1 (specifically, the extent of the difference between it and the target language) was considered that primary source of learner difficulty and error. This leads to a second significant implication: Difference is related to difficulty. Where the L1 and L2 differ only slightly, relatively little difficulty would be expected; where the contrast between the two languages is greater, greater difficulty and, consequently, more error would be predicted. The implications for lan-guage teaching were also clear: provision of correct models, massive repeti-tion without learner reflection, avoidance of error, and provision of appropri-ate feedback.

What Counts as Evidence for the Theory

There is, in fact, no real evidence for the behaviorist explanation of SLA. Little actual research was done in SLA to confirm empirically what was claimed by behaviorist theories; therefore, no exemplary study is presented here, as in the next section of this chapter and in later chapters. Nor was there much effort to explain evidence that fell outside of their predictions. Indeed, the goal of behaviorist research was to describe what was directly observable and not to explain the processes behind them. At the time, the primary proof that researchers adduced was indirect: the influence of the L1. They reasoned that any evidence of L1 influence was proof that learners were using earlier habits. The importance of the L1 in SLA seems apparent to the layman and experienced teacher alike. Many of the errors that learners make appear traceable to their L1s. For example, L2 learners of Spanish whose L1 is English may rely on English in attempting to speak Spanish:

> I am eleven.
>
> *Yo soy once.*

Yet the fact that the L1 is an important factor in SLA does not in itself constitute an argument for behaviorism. In addition, early researchers often assumed that because errors like these are so common, influence of the L1 on SLA was clear and direct. Indeed, this is what occurred during this period in applied linguistics. Subsequent research has shown that its influence is far more nuanced and complex.

How the Theory Addresses the Observable Phenomena of SLA

Of the observable phenomena listed in chapter 1, behaviorist approaches could be used to explain the following:

Observation # 1. Exposure to input is necessary for SLA.   Within behaviorist theory, the environment was seen as the controlling factor in any kind of learning. Given that language learning was seen a process of imitation and repetition of what was heard, it could not proceed without input. In particular, behaviorism stressed the use of target language input as a stimulus for habit formation. In classrooms, language was provided by teachers who modeled the correct behavior, which students were directed to imitate. However, it should be noted that the language provided by teachers normally wouldn't qualify as input by today's standards because it was not intended to communicate meaning but simply to model language.

Observation # 2. Much of SLA happens incidentally.   Language learning, just as any process of habit formation, was thought to occur outside of consciousness. Behaviorists claimed that mental processes were not involved at all in learning; it was purely a response to external stimuli. Thus, all learning occurred as a byproduct of the organism's interaction with its environment. Deliberate efforts to learn might facilitate the process.

Observation # 5. Second language learning is variable in its outcome. This observation can also be explained by behaviorist accounts in that learning context affects the outcome of SLA in two ways:

(1) Learners with different L1s may experience different outcomes because their L1–L2 differences may vary.
(2) Learners who experience different environmental stimuli will experience different levels of eventual attainment.

For example, if learners have different levels of exposure to target models, or if they receive different levels of feedback, they may also differ in their level of attainment. If conditions are ideal, theoretically, all L2 learners with the same L1 should experience similar outcomes. This claim was never tested empirically, however.

Thus, behaviorism can explain some of these observed phenomena, and others, in only a limited way. Indeed, when the first major empirical studies of SLA were done in the 1970s, their findings did not support behaviorist claims. Error correction often did not improve learner performance. Teaching did not always result in learning. Many errors that were predicted by Contrastive Analysis did not occur, and many errors that did occur could not be explained by appealing to L1 influence. Thus, although most SLA researchers would concede the importance of L1 influence on SLA, the difference between the behavioral view of language learning and views more widely held today cannot be overemphasized. The L1 is now considered one of many interacting factors involved in the learning process and its influence is neither simple nor direct. Yet the abandonment of behaviorism does not mean that all of the factors privileged by the theory have also been discarded. We will encounter some of them again, in particular the role of practice and input frequency, in later chapters in this book (see chapters by Ellis and DeKeyser).

Finally, it is important to note the change in attitude toward error since the behaviorist period. With the appearance of the seminal 1967 paper by S. Pitt Corder, "The significance of learners' errors," errors came to be viewed as evidence of learning in progress—indeed, a necessary step in the language learning process—rather than one to be avoided.

THE CHALLENGE OF FIRST AND SECOND LANGUAGE ACQUISITION RESEARCH

In the 1960s and 1970s, throughout the wider fields of psychology and linguistics there was widespread rejection of behavioral approaches to learning (and teaching). First language acquisition research in the early 1960s very quickly began to demonstrate that children could not possibly internalize a linguistic system according to the tenets of operant conditioning. The linguistic system was far too complex, and children's utterances showed evidence of processes beyond imitation and analogy. Instead, children were seen to bring to the task of language acquisition an innate facility that guided their learning of language that was unaffected by the kinds of conditioning that were the basis of behaviorism. For example, children produce utterances that they could not have heard in the input, like *Don't giggle me* and *I love cut-upped eggs* (Pinker, 1994). They also acquire very complex rules that could not have been learned through mere imitation or analogy. Children can interpret the questions such as *When did Billy say he hurt himself?* as having two possible answers (*while he was skateboarding* or *He told us while we were eating dinner*), but *How did Billy say he hurt himself?* as having only one (*skateboarding*). Furthermore, they seem to acquire grammatical features in fixed orders that do not vary according to child, context, caregiver behavior, or any other external influence, as behaviorist accounts would predict. Finally, research documented learners' passage through these predictable stages in the acquisition, making only certain kinds of errors and not the range of theoretically possible errors. For example, one might expect a child to make an error such as *He did his homework* → **He didn't his homework*. This utterance might be constructed on the analogy of other utterances in which *did* is negated with the form *didn't*. Yet, children do not make this error. Neither is it the case that learners always find the simplest solution. In forming a question from the sentence *That girl who is in your kindergarten class is coming over to play tomorrow*, several possibilities present themselves. If we assume that in sentences containing the verb *be*, question formation involves moving the verb to the front, which *is* should be fronted? The simplest solution would simply be to move the first one: **Is that girl who in your kindergarten class is coming over to play tomorrow?* However, children never make this error. From an early age, they unerringly choose the correct verb to front in forming a question. How do they know this? Linguists came to believe that much of this knowledge is innate and that language learning is guided by a specific mental faculty. In this way, language learning came to be viewed as unique, different from other kinds of learning.

These insights influenced researchers in SLA, and similar work with L2 learners soon followed. The results demonstrated that neither behaviorism nor Contrastive Analysis could predict or explain learner errors. They also suggested that L2 learners, too, acquired many grammatical structures in relatively consistent sequences, and furthermore that many of the errors that they made were similar to those made by children learning their mother tongue. These findings led researchers to claim that all language acquisition is internally driven and that SLA is largely unaffected by the L1. In short, they claimed that SLA is very much like first language acquisition. This view has been referred to as the Creative Construction Hypothesis (Dulay & Burt, 1975). In direct contrast to behaviorist claims, the Creative Construction Hypothesis maintained that language learning is a creative process in which the learner makes unconscious hypotheses on the basis of input. The processing of input is in turn controlled by innate mechanisms, the same ones that operate in first language acquisition. This idea would form the cornerstone of Monitor Theory, to which we now turn.

MONITOR THEORY

One of the most ambitious and influential theories in the field of SLA, and one that is probably the most familiar to language instructors, is *Monitor Theory*, developed by Stephen Krashen in the 1970s and early 1980s. It was the first theory to be developed specifically for SLA. It has been particularly influential among practitioners and also laid the foundation for important ideas in contemporary theorizing within SLA. Its broader success rests in part on its resonance with the experience of language learners and language teachers. An understanding of this theory is crucial to understanding the field of SLA theory and research as a whole.

The Theory and Its Constructs

Monitor Theory is the first theory in the field that is broad in scope and attempts to relate and explain a variety of phenomena in language learning, ranging from the effect of age on SLA to the apparently uneven effects of instruction. Unlike behaviorism, it proposes a language specific model of learning, although the actual processes involved in learning are not explained; thus, labeling the Monitor Theory a theory of learning may be somewhat overstated. Although not articulated in Krashen's writing, Monitor Theory seems to be connected to Chomsky's theory of language (see White, chapter 3 this volume), which states that humans are uniquely endowed with a specific faculty for language acquisition. Much of what we consider linguistic knowledge is, in fact, part of our biological endowment. In other words, children come to the task of language already knowing a great deal; they simply need the triggering data in the input in order for language acquisition to take place. Krashen maintains that a similar process occurs in SLA—that is, that child and SLA processes are essentially the same.

Within Monitor Theory, the driving force behind any kind of acquisition is the comprehension of meaningful messages and the interaction of the linguistic information in those messages with the innate language acquisition faculty. According to Krashen, Monitor Theory can explain why what is taught is not always learned, why what is learned may not have been taught, and how individual differences among learners and learning contexts is related to the variable outcome of SLA.

Monitor Theory consists of five interrelated hypotheses. These in turn rest on several important constructs, key concepts that are inferred but are not directly observable.

The Acquisition–Learning Hypothesis.   Perhaps the most important hypothesis in Monitor Theory is the acquisition–learning distinction. Krashen maintains that acquisition and learning, constructs within the theory, are two separate ways of gaining knowledge. Once gained, these types of knowledge are stored separately. *Acquisition* takes place naturally and outside of awareness; it emerges spontaneously when learners engage in normal interaction in the L2, where the focus is on meaning. Neither instruction nor the intention to learn is necessary. The theory claims that learners draw on acquired unconscious knowledge in spontaneous language use, and in this regard, Krashen would argue, SLA is much like first language acquisition. Typically, learners are not be able to articulate this knowledge and are said to operate "by feel" rather than "by rule."

Learning, on the other hand, involves gaining explicit knowledge about language such as its rules and patterns. It occurs when the L2 is the object but not necessarily the medium of instruction. Gaining and using this knowledge are conscious and effortful processes that are undertaken intentionally. The crucial and most controversial part of the distinction is that these two knowledge stores—the acquired system and the learned system—can never interact. In other words, knowledge that is learned may not be converted into acquired knowledge via some kind of practice and become available for spontaneous use. For this reason, Monitor Theory is referred to as a *non-interface* model. This is why learners may "know" rules—that is, they may be able to articulate them but may nevertheless be unable to use them in spontaneous production. Conversely, a learner may use a structure accurately and spontaneously yet be unable to verbalize the rule for its use. Both learners and teachers are all too familiar with this phenomenon, making the theory an intuitively appealing one. Thus in Monitor Theory, even if learners formally study the grammar rules, they will not be able to draw on that knowledge in spontaneous communication because it has not been acquired. For this reason, Krashen argues, the effects of formal instruction on SLA, including feedback on errors, are peripheral, suggesting that such pedagogical approaches should be abandoned in favor of one based on the provision of copious input and the opportunity for meaningful interaction. The acquisition–learning distinction is the central hypothesis in Monitor Theory.

The Monitor Hypothesis. Within Monitor Theory, it turns out that learned knowledge is not terribly useful. Its primary function is editing acquired knowledge during language production. What this means is that learners can draw on this knowledge—Krashen calls this construct *The Monitor*—when they have sufficient time to consult their rule knowledge, for instance, in an untimed writing assignment. Krashen maintains that this is only likely, however, when the task also requires the learner to pay attention to accuracy, as would be likely, for example, in a fill-in-the-blank exercise. Since these kinds of activities are relatively unimportant in overall language use and are arguably only language-like behavior, the utility of learned knowledge within Monitor Theory is negligible. It follows that it is not worth spending precious instructional time on developing learned knowledge, as is typically the case in L2 classrooms.

The Natural Order Hypothesis. As we have noted, research in both first and second language acquisition had demonstrated that learners follow sequences in their acquisition of specific forms, such as the grammatical morphemes *–ing, –ed, –s*, and others. In addition, they appear to pass through predictable stages in their acquisition of grammatical structures such as questions, negation, and relative clauses. Collectively, these have been taken as evidence for the *Natural Order Hypothesis*. One study of the Natural Order is presented at the end of this section. Researchers claimed that these orders were independent of instructional sequences or even of the complexity of the structures to be acquired. For example, although the third person singular *–s* ending in English is relatively straightforward, it appears to be challenging for L2 learners, even those of fairly advanced proficiency. According to Monitor Theory, these regularities occur because all language acquisition is guided by the innate language acquisition faculty.

The Input Hypothesis. According to Monitor Theory, humans acquire language in only one way—by understanding messages in the L2 or, as Krashen says, by receiving *comprehensible input*, another central construct in the theory. This aspect of Monitor Theory is referred to as the *Input Hypothesis*. Comprehensible input contains language slightly beyond the current level of the learner's internalized language. In defining comprehensible input, Krashen introduces two more constructs: i, which he defines as a learner's current level of proficiency and $i+1$, which is a level just beyond the learner's current level. Krashen considers input that is $i+1$ to be the most valuable data for SLA. It is not clear in Monitor Theory exactly what 1 is, or how either 1 or i is identified. In practical terms, however, their precise definitions are unimportant since these levels of input are never isolated from the general input.

Krashen specifies that *roughly tuned input* will automatically include several levels of input including i, $i+1$ and probably $i-1$ and $i+2$, et cetera, as well. In other words, as long as a teacher or native speaker does not speak extremely quickly, using very complex language to a low-level learner, the presence of comprehensible input is probably assured. Learners will naturally access and use what they need, allowing acquisition to take place spontaneously as long as they are exposed to this rich and comprehensible input. This is most likely to occur when communication consistently focuses on meaning rather than form. This means instruction is not only about grammatical rules of little use but also, according to this theory, output (production) activities are not of much value either. Production is considered the result rather than the cause of acquisition. Forcing learners to produce before they are ready can even inhibit the acquisition process by taking learners' focus away from comprehension and processing of input. Rich input, combined with the power of the language acquisition faculty, is all that is needed to promote successful language acquisition. Indeed, Krashen has claimed that comprehensible input is not just a necessary condition for SLA, it is the sufficient condition. In the presence of comprehensible input, SLA is an inevitable result.

The Affective Filter Hypothesis.   It is also important for learners to be comfortable and receptive to the input in their learning environment. To characterize this, Krashen posits another construct, *the affective filter*. Learners who are comfortable and have a positive attitude toward language learning have their filters set low, allowing unfettered access to comprehensible input. In contrast, a stressful environment, one in which learners are forced to produce before they feel ready, raises the affective filter, blocking the learners' processing of input. The affective filter, according to Krashen, can help explain the variable outcome of SLA across L2 learners, including differences in the learners' ages and in classroom conditions.

Most evidence in support of the theory is indirect. Krashen has primarily marshaled general evidence in support of his theory. For example, he maintains that the overall positive outcome of language immersion programs, particularly in Canada, and the widespread mediocre results of foreign language instruction in the United States are evidence of the central importance of comprehensible input and the relatively minor impact of direct instruction. He offered evidence from studies in which students who received massive amounts of comprehensible input through pleasure reading outperformed those who received traditional grammar-based instruction, as well as those individual learners in acquisition-poor environments who failed to acquire in spite of instruction.

AN EXEMPLARY STUDY: LARSEN-FREEMAN (1974)

During the 1970s and early 1980s, there were many studies that demonstrated consistent acquisition orders for grammatical morphemes for both children and adults. Krashen claimed that the results of these studies provided evidence for Monitor Theory, specifically, the Natural Order Hypothesis. One such study, "The acquisition of grammatical morphemes by adult ESL students," is described here in some detail.

In Larsen-Freeman (1975) a study was designed to test whether the order that had been established for the acquisition of grammatical morphemes in previous studies would also be found using other elicitation tasks. Specifically, it tested whether the order would remain the same if skills other than speaking were tested. The answer to these questions were sought in terms of the acquisition order of ten grammatical morphemes: –ing, be-auxiliary, short plural (–s), long plural (–es), 3rd person singular –s, past regular, past irregular, possessive –s, be-copula, and articles. The choice of these particular morphemes was based on work done earlier with children and adults learning their second language that had found a consistent order of acquisition. However, most of these studies had used the same instrument to elicit data from the participants: the Bilingual Syntax Measure (BSM), a series of cartoon pictures showing a variety of scenes. Larsen-Freeman's study was an effort to determine whether previous findings had been an artifact of this elicitation device or whether the orders were independent of task conditions. She also wished to confirm earlier results that suggested learners' L1 backgrounds made little difference regarding the order in which they acquired grammatical morphemes. She made no formal hypotheses regarding the outcome of the study.

The participants in this study were 24 beginning adult L2 learners of English. The participants came from four different language backgrounds: Arabic, Farsi, Japanese, and Spanish. Data containing the ten grammatical morphemes were elicited from the participants as they performed several different tasks: (a) the BSM, the instrument that had been used in previous research; (b) a forced-choice[1] listening task; (c) a forced-choice reading task; (d) a fill-in-the-blank writing task; and (e) and an elicited imitation task.

When Larsen-Freeman compared all four language groups, she found fairly consistent results across four of the tasks (the exception was the reading task). However, comparing two languages at a time, there was not always a significant correlation in the orders that she found. The BSM was the only the only task that yielded consistently significant correlations for all language groups. In further analysis of these data, she found that where a language group varied

---

[1]Participants had to choose among sentences that contained the grammatical appropriately supplied, inappropriately supplied, or not supplied.

from the expected order, the deviation could generally be explained in terms of L1 features. In spite of these smaller differences, taking her results as a whole, Larsen-Freeman concluded that "language background does not seem to radically influence the way in which learners order English morphemes" (p. 417).

In her analysis of the tasks themselves, Larsen-Freeman also found some consistency in the ranking of morphemes (particularly within the BSM and elicited imitation tasks) but by no means the rigid order that has been proposed in previous studies that had used the BSM as the sole elicitation device. Again, she concluded that overall there was "some consistency in the ranking of certain morphemes across all five tasks" (p. 417), but she cautioned that the differences she did find across tasks required further investigation. She suggested that factors such as modality differences or specific task or skill differences might explain her findings.

Krashen later explained these findings within Monitor Theory. What differences Larsen-Freeman did find were greatest in the writing and particularly the reading tasks. He reasoned that these "unnatural" orders occurred when learners were able to monitor their output—in other words, to draw on their learned knowledge. He specifically pointed to the fact that certain morphemes that ranked low in the natural order tended to rise in rank when learners where able to monitor their production. These morphemes, such as 3rd person singular –s and regular past tense, were the morphemes that were more easily learned but not so easily acquired. The task conditions for the reading and writing elicitations in the Larsen-Freeman's study were, according to Krashen, precisely those conditions conducive to the use of the Monitor: They required learners to focus on form and provided ample time for them to reflect on their learned knowledge.

This and other morpheme studies were important milestones in the development of SLA as an independent field and one of the cornerstones of Krashen's Monitor Theory. The generally stable order found in the production of learners across different L1s suggested an internally guided process. The perturbations in the order that were found in tasks performed under specific conditions provided support for Krashen's separate learning and acquisition processes and separate knowledge stores.

How the Theory Addresses the Observable Phenomena of SLA

Of the observed phenomena listed in chapter 1, Monitor Theory can be used to explain the following:

Observation # 1. Exposure to input is necessary for SLA. The role of input—specifically, comprehensible input—in Monitor Theory is clear and explicit. Input is the driving force behind acquisition. Input is not only necessary for SLA, it is sufficient. In the presence of comprehensible input, SLA is inevitable. In its absence, SLA is impossible. The reason for this, according to Monitor Theory, is that L2 learners make use of the special language acquisition faculty in their brain similarly to child L1 learners.

Observation # 2. A good deal of SLA happens incidentally. According to Monitor Theory, acquisition takes place naturally and spontaneously when the learner is focused on meaning. It is not necessary for learners to have the intention to learn in order for acquisition to take place. Again, this falls out of Monitor Theory relying on a special language faculty that responds to data in the input.

Observation # 4. Learner's output (speech) often follows predictable paths with predictable stages in the acquisition of a given structure. As noted, this is one of the cornerstones on which Monitor Theory rests. Because all language learning is guided by internal and presumably universal processes, there are common routes of acquisition for all learners, as evidenced by the staged development in children and adults of diverse L1 backgrounds. However, Monitor Theory cannot explain the actual orders themselves (e.g., why –*ing* precedes past tense, which precedes third-person –*s*).

Observation # 5. Second language learning is variable in its outcome. Cross-learner variation can be explained by Monitor Theory, according to Krashen. He attributes variation in outcome to differential access to comprehensible input. In some cases, this may be a result of different settings of the affective filter, which can limit learners' access to comprehensible input. If the learning context is such that a learner's filter is set high, or such that little comprehensible input is available, learning outcomes may fall short of expectations.

Observation # 8. There are limits on the effect of a learner's first language on SLA. Because all acquisition is guided by universal internal processes, according to Monitor Theory, the effects of the L1 are minimal. All learners use the same strategies in learning an L2, as demonstrated by the similarity of errors committed by learners with a variety of different language backgrounds.

Observation # 9. There are limits on the effects of instruction on SLA. This is related to observation #2. Acquisition will take place naturally in the presence of comprehensible input, which is the only type of data that is useful to internal processors responsible for language acquisition. Pedagogy based on direct instruction generally contains little comprehensible input. Such instruction can only contribute to learned knowledge, which is of limited use. In fact, it can get in the way of acquisition by limiting learner access to comprehensible input. Again, the limits of instruction are due to a specialized language faculty in the mind that is unaffected by direct instruction.

Observation #10. There are limits on the effects of output (learner production) on language acquisition. According to Monitor Theory, production is the result of acquisition and cannot contribute in any direct way to it. The internal processors that drive acquisition can only use one form of linguistic data: comprehensible input. When learners speak or write, they are generally using language they have already acquired.

Monitor Theory has come in for considerable criticism over the years. Each of its hypotheses has been seen as problematic is some way. Indeed, there have been few empirical studies actually testing any of the aspects of Monitor Theory. One reason is that there are problems in what researchers call *operationalization* of the constructs, specifically, that they are vaguely defined, making empirical testing difficult. For example, there is no independent way of confirming which knowledge source—acquired or learned—a learner is using as the basis of use. When presented with evidence of spontaneous and error-free production by L2 learners who have only been exposed to formal instruction in which comprehensive input is scarce, Krashen has claimed that learners have developed parallel language stores. Their acquired knowledge has simply "caught up" with the learned knowledge. Such a contention is difficult to prove, at best; Krashen's detractors maintain that he has failed to do so.

Krashen's use of the natural order as evidence for Monitor Theory has also been criticized as circular. Predictable acquisition orders are both explained by and proof of an innate language faculty. In addition, beyond the general rationale that the order is the result of the interaction of input with an internal acquisition device, Monitor Theory does not provide an explanation for the specific findings. Why, for example, should *–ing* precede *–s* in the order? (Subsequent studies did tackle this question. See Ellis's discussion of Goldschneider & DeKeyser, chapter 5 this volume.) Similarly, the affective filter has been criticized because, while an intuitively appealing notion, it is difficult to determine without circularity when the filter is high or low. If learners fail to progress, it can be attributed to a high affective filter, but then evidence of the filter's high setting is often learner's failure to acquire. Although a valuable metaphor, the construct does not tell us a great deal about language learning processes. Finally, critics have commented that the construct $i+1$ cannot be operationalized. If we wanted to do research, for example, to see if the provision of $i+1$ in the input really does push acquisition along, how do we define i, and how do we subsequently operationalize $i+1$? More detailed criticisms of the theory can be found in some of the suggested readings (see McLaughlin, 1987).

Yet, for many practitioners the most convincing evidence for Monitor Theory is their own experience: What is taught is not always learned, and what has apparently been mastered in drills and other controlled exercises seems to disappear in activities that call for spontaneous language use. This, coupled with the many instances of successful SLA in the absence of instruction, is enough to persuade many observers of the validity of the Input Hypothesis and particularly of the acquisition–learning distinction. There is no denying that teachers and learners alike experience this curious disjunction of knowledge. We will encounter subsequent attempts to explain it and a similar distinction between implicit and explicit knowledge in other theories in this volume. The strict noninterface position, however, remains unique to Monitor Theory.

DISCUSSION QUESTIONS

1. Behaviorism emphasized the environment and the learner's observable experience with the environment to explain learning and human development. Can you cite a clear example of a human behavior that is learned through a stimulus–response type of experience? Can you cite a clear example that is not?

2. Select one of the observed phenomena that behaviorism cannot account for. In what way does it pose a challenge to the theory?

3. One criticism of Monitor Theory is that it is more descriptive of acquisition than explanatory in nature. That is, positing a natural order hypothesis merely describes the phenomenon in need of explanation. Do you think this is true of the acquisition–learning distinction? The input hypothesis?

4. Typically, a theory replaces another because of the latter's inadequacy. That is, the latter cannot account for observed phenomena and/or makes incorrect predictions about something. Why do you think Monitor Theory supplanted behaviorism? Later you will read about other theories. Why might they supplant Monitor Theory?

5. In what ways are behaviorism and Monitor Theory in direct opposition to each other? (Hint: Consider the issue of what mental apparatus learners take to the task of acquisition.)

SUGGESTED READINGS

Andersen R. (Ed.) (1983). *Pidginization and creolization as language acquisition.* Rowley, MA: Newbury House.

This volume addresses some of the similarities in the processes involved in language acquisition and pidginization/creolization.

Dulay, H., & Burt, M. (1975). Creative construction in second language learning and teaching. In M. Burt & H. Dulay (Eds.), *On TESOL, '75: New directions in second language learning, teaching and bilingual education* (pp. 21–32). Washington, DC: TESOL.

This article lays out the claims and research that formed the foundation of the Creative Construction Hypothesis.

Hatch, E. (Ed.). (1978). *Second language acquisition: A book of readings.* Rowley, MA: Newbury House.

This volume is a collection of the early empirical studies from the post-behaviorist era of SLA.

Krashen, S. (1981). *Second language acquisition and second language learning.* Oxford: Pergamon Press.

Krashen, S. D. (1982). *Principles and practice in second language acquisition.* Oxford: Pergamon Press.

Krashen, S. D. (1985). *The input hypothesis: Issues and implications.* London: Longman.

These three volumes expand on Krashen's views and the Monitor Theory introduced in this chapter.

Lado, R. (1957). *Linguistics across cultures.* Ann Arbor: University of Michigan Press.

This is the most important single volume the behaviorist–Contrastive Analysis tradition. It offers the insights of this perspective for second language learning and teaching.

Robinett, B., & Schachter, J. (Eds.) (1983). *Second language learning: Contrastive analysis, error analysis, and related aspects.* Ann Arbor: University of Michigan Press.

This collection contains a variety of very early studies in the field, including several that demonstrate the use of Contrastive Analysis.

Schumann, J. H. (1978). *The pidginization hypothesis: A model for second language acquisition.* Rowley, MA: Newbury House.

This volume is a book-length treatment of Schumann's idea about the role of social and affective factors in SLA.

Selinker, L. (1972). Interlanguage. *International Review of Applied Linguistics, 10,* 209–231.

This article was a pioneering attempt to establish learner language, which Selinker termed interlanguage as an independent linguistic system.

Tarone, E. (1988). *Variation in interlanguage*. London: Edward Arnold.

This is a book length look at explanations of variation within individual interlanguages (ILs). Tarone connects IL variation to theories of variation within sociolinguistics.

REFERENCES

Corder, S. P. (1967). The significance of learners' errors. *International Review of Applied Linguistics, 5*, 161–169.

Larsen-Freeman, D. (1975). The acquisition of grammatical morphemes by adult ESL students. *TESOL Quarterly, 9*, 409–419.

McLaughlin, B. (1987). *Theories of second language learning*. London: Arnold.

Pinker, S. (1994). *The language instinct*. New York: William Morrow.

3

Linguistic Theory, Universal Grammar, and Second Language Acquisition

Lydia White
McGill University

THE THEORY AND ITS CONSTRUCTS

The Linguistic Competence of Native Speakers and L1 Acquirers

Generative linguistic theory aims to provide a characterization of the linguistic competence of native speakers of a language and to explain how it is possible for child first language (L1) acquirers to achieve that competence. The generative perspective on second language (L2) acquisition has parallel goals, namely to account for the nature and acquisition of interlanguage competence (see Gregg, 1996; White, 1989, 2003).

In this framework, language use (comprehension and production) is assumed to be based upon an abstract linguistic system, a mental representation of grammar (syntax, phonology, morphology, and semantics). The knowledge of language represented in this way is unconscious. Furthermore, much of this unconscious knowledge does not have to be learned in the course of L1 acquisition; rather, it is derived from Universal Grammar (UG). This claim is motivated by the so-called *logical problem of language acquisition* or the problem of *the poverty of the stimulus*, in other words the mismatch between the input that children are exposed to and their ultimate attainment (e.g., Chomsky, 1986b). Our knowledge of language goes beyond the input in numerous ways. For instance, children and adults can understand and produce sentences that they have never heard before, they know that certain structures are ungrammatical without being taught this, and they know that certain interpretations of sentences are not possible in certain contexts.

Consider the following example, from de Villiers, Roeper and Vainikka (1990) and Roeper and de Villiers (1992). Imagine a scenario where a boy climbs a tree in the afternoon and falls out of it and hurts himself. In the evening, he tells his father about what happened. Now consider the questions in (1), uttered in this context.

(1)   a. When did the boy say (that) he got a bruise?
      b. When did the boy say how he got a bruise?

In this context, a question like (1a) is ambiguous; it can be a question about the time that he got hurt (in the afternoon) or the time that he told his father about the incident (in the evening). Question (1b), on the other hand, is not ambiguous. Even though it differs by only one word (the embedded clause being introduced by *how*), this question can only have an answer that related to the time of telling, such as *in the evening* or *when he was in the bath*. In other words, it must be construed as a question about the main clause; the embedded clause interpretation is ungrammatical, even though it is perfectly acceptable and available in the case of (1a). De Villiers and colleagues conducted a series of experiments using such scenarios and found that young children acquiring English as their mother tongue are highly sensitive to the difference between these two sentence types, allowing both interpretations in the case of (1a) but only one interpretation (the matrix clause one) in the case of (1b).

How do children know this? It is most unlikely that children are explicitly told that certain sentences are ambiguous, while others (which are superficially very similar) are not. Nor does this kind of information seem to be inducible from the language that children hear, given that children will be exposed to a range of grammatical *wh*-questions, involving simple and embedded clauses. In other words, the input *underdetermines* the child's linguistic competence. Hence, it is argued, children must bring innate, built-in knowledge to bear on the task of first language acquisition. In this case, a principle of UG, one of a number of so-called *island constraints* (Ross, 1967), restricts *wh*-movement in particular ways. Effectively, these constraints state that certain constituents form islands, from which phrases cannot escape.[1] The embedded clause in (1b) is a *wh*-island, headed by a question phrase (*how*), whereas the

---

[1]The situation is more complex than described here. There is a complex interaction depending on whether the *wh*-phrases are arguments or adjuncts, differences that are accounted for in terms of another constraint, the Empty Category Principle (ECP) (Chomsky, 1981).

embedded clause in (1a) is not. The *wh*-phrase *when* can "escape" only in the case of (1a), passing through a position which is not available in the case of (1b), since it is already filled by *how*. The alternative interpretation is possible in both cases because *when* is construed with the main clause; hence, no extraction from an embedded clause (island or otherwise) is involved.

A related effect of island constraints is that sentences involving *wh*-movement out of islands are ungrammatical in English, as shown in (2a). Here, *what* has been extracted out of an embedded *wh*-clause, an extraction that is impossible for the same reason that the embedded clause interpretation of (1b) is impossible. In contrast, (2b) is acceptable because the embedded clause is not an island.

(2)   a. *What$_i$ does John wonder [who bought t_i]?
       b. What$_i$ does John think [t_i that Mary bought t_i]?

Once again, on learnability grounds, it is implausible to suppose that L1 acquirers of English arrive at knowledge of the ungrammaticality of sentences like (2a) on the basis of English input alone. Instead, constraints of this kind must derive from UG. In other words, acquisition of *wh*-movement (and many other properties of language) is constrained by innate principles; language is acquired presupposing such knowledge, with the consequence that L1 acquirers do not have to learn when certain kinds of sentences are ungrammatical or when there can or cannot be certain kinds of structural ambiguity.

Interlanguage Competence

Given that linguistic theory offers a model of the linguistic competence of native speakers, it may be able to provide a characterization of nonnative competence as well. This is the assumption of researchers working on SLA from the generative perspective. It has long been observed that the language of L2 learners is systematic and rule-governed (e.g., Corder, 1967). The term *interlanguage*, coined by Selinker (1972), has been widely adopted to refer to the linguistic competence of L2 learners and L2 speakers (henceforth L2ers). L2 researchers working in the generative paradigm assume that interlanguage grammars, like native speaker grammars, involve unconscious mental representations, although they do not necessarily agree as to the precise nature of these representations, for example, the nature and degree of influence of the L1 and the status of UG constraints.

While the operation of UG in L2 acquisition cannot be taken for granted, considerations of learnability (the logical problem of L2 acquisition) apply in L2 acquisition as they do in L1 (e.g., White, 1989). That is, if it can be shown that L2ers acquire abstract and subtle properties that are underdetermined by the L2 input, this suggests that interlanguage competence must be subject to the same constraints as native competence.

Consider *wh*-movement once again. The fact that (1a) is ambiguous whereas (1b) is not, and the fact that (2a) is ungrammatical, in contrast to (2b), constitutes an L2 learnability problem, parallel to the problem faced by L1 acquirers. There is no reason to suppose that the L2 English input is any more informative about *wh*-questions than the L1 English input, unless L2ers receive specific instruction on this property, which seems highly unlikely. In other words, in the case of successful acquisition of this kind of abstract knowledge, island constraints must be implicated in L2 as well as L1.

However, if it turns out that L2ers indeed demonstrate the same kind of subtle knowledge as native speakers, a reasonable objection would be that the source of this knowledge is not UG directly; rather it is the mother tongue grammar (see, for example, Bley-Vroman, 1989; Schachter, 1990). In other words, the L2er might show knowledge of island constraints because these have been activated in the L1 grammar and not because interlanguage grammars are UG-constrained as such. Hence, in order to eliminate this possibility, it is necessary to investigate cases where the L1 and L2 differ in such a way that the mother tongue grammar could not provide the learner with the necessary knowledge. In the case of *wh*-questions, this would be achieved if the L1 is a language with so-called *wh-in-situ* instead of *wh*-movement, such as Chinese, Japanese, or Korean. In these languages, in contrast to English, *wh*-phrases do not move but remain in their underlying positions. This is true of simple *wh*-questions, as in the Chinese example in (3a), and *wh*-questions from embedded clauses, as in (3b).[2,3]

(3) a. ni xihuan shei?
        you   like who
        'Who do you like?'

     b. Zhangsan xiangxin shei mai-le shu?
        Zhangsan believe   who buy-ASP books
        'Who does Zhangsan believe bought books?'

In (3a), there is no *wh*-fronting; rather, the *wh*-phrase (*shei* 'who') remains in object position within the clause. The same is true of (3b), where *shei* remains in subject position in the embedded clause.

---

[2]Tones are omitted from the Chinese examples.

[3]Chinese examples in (3) and (5) come from Huang (1982). Thanks for Chen Qu for the examples (and judgments) in (4).

Now consider Chinese equivalents of (1). In (4a), the *wh*-phrase (*shenmoshihou* 'when') does not move out of the embedded clause. Consequently, and in contrast to its English equivalent, this question is not ambiguous: it can only be a question about the time the boy got hurt (the embedded clause reading), not the time of telling (the main clause reading). To ask a question about the time of telling, *when* must be in the main clause, as in (4b). Again, this question is not ambiguous. In other words, in Chinese, each interpretation is reflected in a different word order—namely, (4a) versus (4b)—in contrast to English, where one word order can have two meanings, as in (1a).

(4) a. nanhai shuo ta shenmoshihou nong qing
       boy   say he when   got bruise
       'When did the boy say that he got a bruise?'
    b. nanhai shenmoshihou shuo ta nong qing
       boy   when   say he got bruise
       'When did the boy say that he got a bruise?'
    c. nanhai shenmoshihou shuo ta zenyang nong qing
       boy   when   say he how   got bruise
       'When did the boy say how he got a bruise?'

In the case of (4c), *when* again unambiguously requires the matrix interpretation. In other words, in Chinese there is no contrast in ambiguity equivalent to the contrast found in English between (1a) and (1b). Thus, if L2 learners come to know that English sentences like (1a) are ambiguous whereas sentences like (1b) are not, this would suggest not only that they have acquired *wh*-movement but also that they have knowledge of constraints on *wh*-movement that could not have come from the L1.

We have also seen that sentences like (2a), involving *wh*-movement out of islands, are ungrammatical in English. In contrast, the Chinese sentence in (5) is grammatical because no *wh*-movement out of an island has taken place, due to *wh*-in-situ.

(5) ni xiang-zhidao shei mai-le   shenme?
    you wonder   who buy-ASP what
    'What is the thing such that you wonder who bought it?'
    (cf. *What do you wonder who bought?)

To summarize so far, the linguistic competence of native speakers of a language includes knowledge of ambiguity and of ungrammaticality, as exemplified by the above restrictions on *wh*-movement. Given that the input alone is insufficient to account for how such knowledge could have been acquired, children acquiring their mother tongues must have an innate specification for language, UG, which guides and limits their hypotheses about the form of the grammar that they are acquiring. If L2 learners of English come to know similar restrictions on *wh*-movement, especially if these could not be derived from the L1 grammar, this provides evidence for the continuing functioning of UG constraints in interlanguage grammars as well.

Universal Grammar: Principles and Parameters

The precise nature and content of UG is the domain of linguistic theory; proposals change and are refined as the theory develops. Nevertheless, broadly speaking, the following assumptions hold true across different versions of generative grammar, such as Government and Binding (GB) Theory (Chomsky, 1981) or Minimalism (Chomsky, 1995).

Principles of UG constrain the form of grammars as well as the operation of linguistic rules. The island constraints discussed above are examples of such principles; they specify universal restrictions on *wh*-movement, the idea being that all cases of *wh*-movement will be subject to such constraints. As we have seen, the claim is that language acquirers do not have to learn these principles—they are built into UG. *Parameters*, on the other hand, account for certain circumscribed differences across languages; the idea is that these differences are encoded in UG, so that language acquirers can easily determine what kind of language they are acquiring. Input data are said to *trigger* the appropriate parametric choice for the language being acquired (Lightfoot, 1989). In other words, the input determines the choice between parameter values made available by UG. As an example of a parameter, consider the case of *wh*-movement again. As we have seen, the position of *wh*-phrases differs across languages. This difference is attributed to a parameter, namely ±*wh*-movement. Languages divide into two main types, those with *wh*-in-situ, such as East Asian languages, and those with *wh*-movement, such as Germanic, Romance, and Slavic languages. In this case, input in the form of simple *wh*-questions will be enough to trigger the appropriate parameter value (see Crain & Lillo-Martin, 1999). The child acquiring English will be exposed to questions like (6a), with a fronted *wh*-phrase, indicating *wh*-movement, whereas the child acquiring Chinese will be exposed to sentences like (6b), indicating lack of movement.

(6) a. What do you want?
     b. ni xihuan shei?
         you like   who

TABLE 3.1.
Parameters and Constraints Relating to *wh*-Expressions

	Parameters	Constraints
English	+*wh*-movement	Island constraints activated
Chinese	−*wh*-movement	Island constraints inactive

Universal principles do not necessarily operate in all languages but only in that subset of languages that exhibit the relevant properties. In languages with overt wh-movement, movement is subject to UG principles in the form of island constraints. In other words, movement is not totally free; rather, there are certain kinds of constituents from which a *wh*-phrase cannot escape, as we have seen. These are *islands*, and it is UG that specifies which domains form islands.[4] In *wh*-in-situ languages, on the other hand, island constraints are irrelevant, due to lack of movement.[5]

Table 3.1 summarizes the relevant differences between Chinese and English. If interlanguage competence is UG-constrained, then once L2ers reset the ±*wh*-movement parameter, *wh*-movement in the interlanguage grammar should be subject to island constraints.

WHAT COUNTS AS EVIDENCE?

It must be understood that linguistic competence is an abstraction; it is impossible to "tap" linguistic competence directly. The generative perspective on L2 explores the nature of interlanguage competence by adopting a variety of performance measures to try to discover the essential characteristics of underlying mental representations. One problem that is frequently encountered is that it can be difficult to construct tasks that relate to unconscious knowledge, as opposed to conscious knowledge learned explicitly in the classroom. Ideally, performance data from a variety of sources should be brought to bear on

---

[4]While the precise characterization/definition of the relevant principles has changed over time, the essential issues remain the same. In GB theory, islands were defined in terms of bounding nodes (e.g., Chomsky 1981) or barriers (Chomsky 1986a). In Minimalism, UG specifies universal computations (*merge, move*), which are subject to economy principles yielding the same effects (Chomsky 1995).

[5]Many people argue that *wh*-in-situ languages have movement, but at the level of logical form (LF) (e.g., Huang 1982). There is considerable debate as to the extent to which LF movement is subject to constraints (see, for example, Huang 1982 versus Xu 1990).

the question of interlanguage competence. Relevant data can be classified into three types: *production data, comprehension data,* and *intuitional data.* The appropriateness of a particular elicitation task will depend on what the researcher is trying to discover.

Spontaneous production data might seem to provide an obvious source of information as to the nature of interlanguage competence. However, usage does not necessarily provide an accurate reflection of knowledge or acquisition; production data can result in an underestimation of an L2er's overall linguistic competence. For example, Lardiere (1998) shows that an L2er whose use of appropriate tense and agreement morphology is very infrequent in spoken English at the same time shows mastery of complex syntax. It is also possible that production data might lead one to overestimate a learner's competence. That is, L2ers may appear to be highly proficient, even native-like, and yet have non-native grammars. In other words, sentences that superficially appear to be identical to those produced by native speakers might in fact have different underlying representations (e.g., Hawkins & Chan, 1997).

Furthermore, when researchers are interested in phenomena that might not show up readily in production, alternatives are required. In the case of the island constraints discussed above, the ambiguity of sentences like (1a) and lack of ambiguity of sentences like (1b) are unlikely to be observable in production. Similarly, it is unlikely that L2ers will produce sentences like (2a). However, failure to find violations of island constraints in production cannot be taken as evidence of ungrammaticality because their absence might be due to an accident of data sampling. Because a major research question in this framework is whether interlanguage grammars are constrained by UG, it is essential to discover whether forms ruled out by UG constraints are in fact ungrammatical in the interlanguage grammar. One potential means of establishing this is through elicited production (Crain & Thornton, 1998). If a task is set up so that a certain structure might be expected and this structure is avoided by L2ers, this suggests, indirectly, that the structure is ungrammatical for the learner. As we shall see, White and Juffs (1998) use this technique to investigate island constraints in L2.

The most commonly used task to determine knowledge of L2 (un)grammaticality is the grammaticality judgment task. This kind of task allows the researcher to investigate whether sentences that are disallowed for native speakers because of principles of UG are also prohibited in the interlanguage grammar. Consider island constraints once again. Another kind of island is formed by a complex noun phrase (NP), a noun phrase containing a relative clause or a complement clause. Extraction of a *wh*-phrase from a complex NP is ungrammatical in English, as shown in (7a). In contrast, sentences like (7b) are grammatical because no such extraction has taken place.

(7)   a. *Whose life did you read a biography that described?
           (cf. I read a biography that described someone's life.)
       b. Whose life did you read about?

Suppose that you wish to determine whether an L2 learner of English knows that sentences like (7a) are ungrammatical—in other words, whether their grammar is subject to island constraints. In order to establish whether L2 learners know this constraint, a grammaticality judgment task is appropriate, in which learners are given a set of grammatical and ungrammatical sentences relevant to the structure in question and are asked to indicate whether or not the sentences are grammatical. If interlanguage grammars are constrained by UG, and provided that *wh*-movement has been acquired, then L2ers are expected to reject sentences like (7a) while accepting grammatical equivalents. Hence, by using grammaticality judgments, the experimenter can (indirectly) investigate aspects of interlanguage competence that may not otherwise be amenable to inspection. Again, White and Juffs (1998) use such a task to explore island effects in interlanguage grammars.

There is no one methodology that is appropriate for investigating all aspects of linguistic competence. If questions of interpretation are being investigated, grammaticality judgments can be totally uninformative. Consider, once again, the ambiguity of sentences like (1a), contrasted with the lack of ambiguity of (1b). If L2ers were asked to judge such sentences and indicated that both sentences are grammatical, this would not help to determine how they were interpreting the sentences (i.e., whether *when* was being construed as a question about the embedded clause or the main clause). For this reason, in testing whether L1 acquirers of English know the relevant properties, de Villiers and colleagues adopted a comprehension task: children were shown pictures and asked the test question; their responses indicated how they had interpreted that question.

COMMON MISUNDERSTANDINGS

Here we will consider four common areas of misunderstanding about generative SLA research. These relate to (a) the scope of the theory, (b) lack of native-like "success" in L2, (c) transfer, and (d) methodology.

The theory described in this chapter does not seek to account for all aspects of L2 acquisition. On the contrary, the theory is deliberately circumscribed, concentrating on description and explanation of interlanguage competence, defined in a technical way. In other words, the focus is on how the L2er represents the L2 in terms of a mental grammar. The theory does not aim to account for second language use, nor does it aim to account for all of the observable phenomena. (See next section.)

It is important to understand that UG is a theory of constraints on representation, as shown by the examples discussed above; this is true both of L1 acquisition (e.g., Borer, 1996) and L2 (White, 2003). UG determines the nature of linguistic competence; principles of UG (constraints) guarantee that certain potential analyses are never in fact adopted. This says nothing about the time course of acquisition (L1 or L2) or about what drives changes to the grammar during language development. Similarly, the theory of parameter setting does not, in fact, provide a theory of language development even though it is often seen as such. The concept of parameter resetting in L2 presupposes that some kind of change takes place in the interlanguage grammar, from the L1 parameter value to some other parameter value (for example, the change from –wh-movement to +wh-movement). In other words, interlanguage grammars at different points in time may be characterized in terms of different parameter settings. However, the precise mechanisms that lead to such grammar change are not part of the theory of UG. Rather, the theory needs to be augmented in various ways (Carroll, 2001; Gregg 1996).

A common misconception is that if UG constrains interlanguage grammars, this necessarily predicts a successful outcome in SLA such that the end-state grammars of L2ers should not differ in significant respects from those of native speakers. However, the claim that interlanguage grammars are UG-constrained is a claim that the linguistic representations of L2ers are subject to principles of UG, like other natural languages. It is not a claim that L2ers will necessarily achieve the same grammar as a native speaker would. Thus, UG does not dictate that wh-movement must be acquired (because it is not acquired by L1 acquirers of wh-in-situ languages)—only that, if acquired, it must be constrained by the relevant principles, such as island constraints. Many factors come into play in L2 that simply do not arise in L1 acquisition—including prior knowledge of another language and possible deficiencies in the input—which might prevent native-like attainment.

A related misconception is that the L1 should play a relatively trivial role in L2 acquisition if UG is involved. In other words, according to some, strong L1 influence is somehow incompatible with the claim that UG is implicated in L2 acquisition. In fact, many proponents of generative SLA incorporate the L1 grammar as an integral part of the theory. In particular, the Full Transfer Full Access Hypothesis (FTFA) and its precursors claim that the initial state of L2 acquisition consists of the steady state grammar of L1 acquisition (Schwartz & Sprouse, 1996; White, 1989). In other words, L2ers initially adopt the L1 grammar as a means of characterizing the L2 data. This constitutes *full transfer*. Subsequently, in the light of L2 input, revisions to the grammar may be effected. Such revisions are assumed to be UG-constrained, hence *full access*. Transfer may be persistent or not, depending on particular linguistic properties and particular language combinations (see observable phenomena, later in this chapter). In the event that L2ers fail to arrive at properties of the L2, interlanguage grammars are nevertheless expected to fall within the range permitted by UG; that is, they will be subject to constraints, like any natural language. It is also conceivable that L2ers arrive at analyses that are found in other languages, neither the L1 nor the L2 (e.g., Finer, 1991).

Continuing with our *wh*-movement examples, this implies that prior to acquiring *wh*-movement, learners whose L1 is a *wh*-in-situ language would be expected to treat the L2 as *wh*-in-situ as well. In support of this, evidence for *wh*-in-situ in the L2 English of speakers of Hindi (a *wh*-in-situ language) is reported by Bhatt and Hancin-Bhatt (2002). Furthermore, even when L2ers appear, superficially at least, to have abandoned a *wh*-in-situ analysis of the L2, they may not have acquired *wh*-movement, instead generating *wh*-phrases as clause initial topics, analogous to other topics in the L1 (Hawkins & Chan, 1997; Martohardjono & Gair, 1993; White, 1992). Consequently, island constraints would be nonoperative for the same reason that they are not operative with *wh*-in-situ, because movement has not taken place.

Finally, there are misconceptions relating to methodology. It has been claimed (Carroll & Meisel, 1990; Ellis, 1991) that researchers working in the UG paradigm take grammaticality judgment tasks to have some kind of privileged status such that they provide a direct reflection of linguistic competence. In fact, judgment data are recognized as being performance data, on a par with other data (White, 1989, 2003). The only privilege that grammaticality judgment tasks offer is a relatively straightforward way of assessing knowledge of ungrammaticality. As described in the section on evidence, different kinds of data provide different kinds of evidence and the suitability of any particular task (and the performance data gathered by means of it) will depend on the precise issue that the researcher is trying to investigate.

AN EXEMPLARY STUDY: WHITE AND JUFFS (1998)

White and Juffs (1998) address the question of whether the interlanguage grammars of adult L2 learners are constrained by principles of UG, in particular, island constraints. The study examines the case of native speakers of Mandarin Chinese, a *wh*-in-situ language, acquiring *wh*-movement in L2 English. If L2 acquisition is UG-constrained, and if these learners have acquired *wh*-movement, they are expected to observe constraints on English *wh*-movement even though these constraints are not activated in the L1.

Participants included 16 adult native speakers of Chinese who had never been outside the People's Republic of China (PRC). Their first significant exposure to English was as adults, at university in the PRC; prior to that they had received limited formal instruction in English in high school. Nineteen native speakers of English served as controls.[6]

Participants were tested on two tasks. The first was a timed grammaticality judgment task consisting of 30 grammatical and 30 ungrammatical sentences displayed one at a time on a computer. Participants were asked to read each sentence and make a judgment by pressing a key (green for possible sentences, red for impossible). Twenty-four of the test items were ungrammatical sentences violating island constraints (complex NPs, including noun complements and relative clauses, as well as subject and adjunct islands) and 18 were grammatical sentences of equivalent complexity (involving extractions from embedded clauses that are not islands). The rationale for this task was to investigate whether L2ers know that certain sentences are ungrammatical in English (i.e., island violations) while at the same time knowing that long distance *wh*-extraction is possible in principle. Accurate performance on both sentence types (acceptances of grammatical sentences and rejections of ungrammatical ones) would indicate the acquisition of *wh*-movement and constraints on such movement. Examples of test items are given in (8), where (8a) illustrates a case of grammatical *wh*-movement out of an embedded clause and (8b) shows ungrammatical *wh*-movement out of an island.

(8)   a. Which man did Jane say her friend likes?
       b. *Which article did you criticize the man who wrote?

The second task involved elicited production. Participants were presented with a set of 19 declarative sentences, each of which included an underlined word or phrase. They were asked to question the underlined word or phrase. Some of the sentences were constructed to result in grammatical *wh*-questions involving extraction from embedded clauses whereas others would result in island violations. The rationale here is that participants whose grammars are UG constrained will word their questions to avoid producing island violations, instead finding other ways to form the questions. Examples of test items are given in (9); potential responses are given in (10). Given a stimulus like (9a), the hypothesis is that L2ers will produce a grammatical response like (10a). On the other hand, given a stimulus like (9b), they will not produce the response (10b) (even though this is what a literal following of the instructions would dictate) because this violates an island constraint; instead, they should

---

[6]A second group of Chinese-speakers tested in Canada will not be discussed here.

avoid the ungrammatical response and provide a grammatical alternative, such as (10a).

(9)   a. Tom claimed that Ann stole <u>his car</u>.
      b. Sam believes the claim that Ann stole <u>his car</u>.
(10) a. What did Tom claim that Ann stole?
      b. *What does Sam believe the claim that Ann stole?

Results from both tasks suggest that the L2ers observe island constraints in their L2 English. In the case of the grammaticality judgment task, they reject ungrammatical sentences while accepting grammatical ones. Mean accuracy on this task is given in Table 3.2. The L2 group shows a high level of rejection of ungrammatical sentences, which does not differ significantly from the native speaker controls. (Their somewhat lower accuracy on the grammatical sentences is reflected in independent properties of some of these sentences; see White & Juffs, 1998, for discussion.)

The results from the question formation task (for sentences targeting complex NP islands, subject and adjunct islands) are given in Table 3.3. While L2ers produce some ungrammatical questions (15% of all responses), these mostly involved failure to produce subject-auxiliary inversion. For example, they would produce questions like *What Tom claimed that Ann stole?* There are few violations of island constraints (6% of all responses). Instead, like native speakers, the L2 group avoids producing violations by finding other ways of formulating a grammatical question.

Other studies have reported that L2 learners with Chinese, Japanese, or Korean as mother tongues accept violations of island constraints in grammaticality judgment tasks (e.g., Johnson & Newport, 1991; Schachter, 1990). I have suggested elsewhere that such results reflect a failure to represent *wh*-questions in terms of *wh*-movement (White, 1992; see also Hawkins & Chan, 1997; Martohardjono & Gair, 1993). In contrast, the results of the present study, using both grammaticality judgments and elicited production data, suggest that island constraints are active in the interlanguage grammars of L2ers once *wh*-movement is acquired. This is the case even when the L1 is

TABLE 3.2.
Grammaticality Judgment Task: Mean Accuracy (in percent)

	Acceptance of grammatical sentences	*Rejection of ungrammatical sentences*
Native speakers	92.5	94.0
L2ers	76.0	87.5

TABLE 3.3.
Question Formation Task: Response Types (in percent)

	Violations	Other ungrammatical	Grammatical avoidance
Native speakers	2.0	1.5	96
L2ers	6.0	15.0	78.0

wh-in-situ and when exposure to the L2 is as adults in a country where the L2 is very much a foreign language. In other words, the results are consistent with the claim that parameters of UG can be reset (in this case from –wh-movement to +wh-movement) and that interlanguage grammars are subject to principles of UG (in this case, island constraints).

EXPLANATION OF OBSERVED FINDINGS IN SLA

In seeking to characterize the unconscious underlying linguistic competence of L2 learners, the generative perspective on L2 acquisition cannot and does not aim to account for all of the observable phenomena discussed in this volume. Nevertheless, this perspective does offer insights into several of them.

Observation #1. Exposure to input is necessary.   According to UG theory, there are certain aspects of grammar that are not learned through exposure to input, namely knowledge of universal constraints. Nevertheless, UG does not operate in a vacuum: Universal principles and language-specific parameter settings must be triggered by input from the language being acquired. In the case of our examples, learners acquiring an L2 with wh-movement will require input to motivate the +wh-movement value of the parameter. However, once they have established that the L2 involves wh-movement, they will NOT require input to determine that island constraints operate; these come for free, so to speak.

Observation #3. Learners come to know more than they have been exposed to in the input.   This is the central observation that the theory aims to account for. The main motivation for the proposal that L1 language acquisition is constrained by UG is precisely the fact that native speakers come to know more than they have been exposed to. Generative SLA researchers make the same claim in the case of L2 acquisition: L2ers come to know very subtle properties of the L2 (such as ambiguity and ungrammaticality) that are underdetermined by the L2 input, both naturalistic input and classroom instruction (and that cannot be explained in terms of the L1 grammar either).

Observation #7. There are limits on the effects of frequency on SLA.
The claim of UG theory is that certain properties of language are not subject
to frequency effects. Indeed, the idea is the opposite: UG allows learners to acquire properties quite unrelated to frequency; children achieve certain kinds
of knowledge on the basis of little or no input. For example, consider the case
of so-called parasitic gaps, illustrated in (11). In (11a), the sentence is ungrammatical because the verb *correcting* requires an overt direct object pronoun
(i.e., *them*). Example (11b), a yes/no question, is ungrammatical for the same
reason. But (11c), a *wh*-question, is significantly better, even though *correcting*
still lacks an overt object.

(11)   a. *By mistake, I filed the papers without correcting.
       b. *Did you file the papers without correcting?
       c. Which papers did you file without correcting?

The grammaticality of (11c) is a consequence of properties of *wh*-movement
that are encoded in UG. Native speakers of English acquire the distinction
between these sentence types, even though sentences like (11a) and (11b)
will not be exemplified in the input (because they are ungrammatical), while
sentences like (11c) are presumably relatively rare. In other words, frequency
does not appear to play a role in such cases. The same claim would apply
in L2: certain properties of the L2 are expected to be acquired regardless of
frequency.

Observation #8. There are limits on the effects of a learner's first language.
We have already seen that certain versions of generative SLA (e.g., FTFA) assume strong L1 influence, with the L1 grammar taken as the starting point
(the initial state) in L2 acquisition. Although this claim implies that all parameters are initially set at the L1 setting in the interlanguage grammar, it does
not imply that they will all be reset to the L2 value at the same time. Hence,
L1 effects may be quite fleeting in some cases but lasting in others. Depending
on the L1 and the L2 in question, triggering input may motivate resetting to
the L2 value extremely early, as Haznedar (1997) shows for the headedness
parameter (switching from head final L1 to head initial L2). In contrast, if the
L2 input does not provide suitable positive evidence to motivate resetting,
transfer effects will be much longer lasting, maybe even permanent. For example, as discussed above, some L2ers appear to take fronted *wh*-phrases in
L2 English not as evidence for *wh*-movement as such but rather as evidence
that *wh*-phrases can be topicalized (a possibility permitted in the L1). Once
such an analysis is adopted, it is not clear what evidence would lead them to
abandon this.

Observation #9. There are limits on the effects of instruction. Clearly, one cannot instruct L2ers as to UG constraints (nor does anyone attempt to do so). On the contrary, this kind of abstract, complex, and subtle knowledge is achieved without being taught. Nevertheless, it could be that instruction might be effective in providing L2 input necessary to trigger parameter resetting (for example, in providing evidence—in the form of *wh*-questions—for or against *wh*-movement). Attempts have been made to provide learners with triggering input in the classroom, with mixed results (see White 2003 for discussion).

CONCLUSION

This chapter presents the perspective offered by linguistic theory. The central tenet of the theory is that the linguistic competence of native speakers is underdetermined by the input that children are exposed to, hence that an innate Universal Grammar is implicated. Researchers with a generative perspective on SLA investigate whether the same holds true for L2 acquisition. If interlanguage competence goes beyond the L2 input and the L1 grammar in particular respects, then UG is implicated in non-native language acquisition as well.

DISCUSSION QUESTIONS

1. Like other researchers within a UG framework, White relies on the logical problem of learning and the poverty of the stimulus argument to posit an innate language faculty. What explanation might there be other than innateness for the problems White discusses?

2. If both L1 acquisition and SLA are constrained by UG, how would you explain the observed differential outcomes between L1 acquisition and SLA (e.g., L1 acquisition is universally successful while SLA is not; L1 learners all attain some kind of native pronunciation, whereas most L2 learners do not)?

3. What evidence does White use to suggest language acquisition is different from other kinds of learning? Do you agree with this evidence? If not, how would you explain the findings of UG research?

4. Research within the UG framework tends to ignore the social context of language learning. Why is this appropriate for the framework?

5. As a theory of linguistic competence, the crux of research on UG is how learners come to know more than what they are exposed to. What other mechanisms in the mind/brain would you suggest are necessary to ex-

plain language acquisition? For example, what *triggers* movement from one stage of acquisition to the next?

SUGGESTED FURTHER READING

Hawkins, R. (2001). *Second language syntax: A generative introduction*. Oxford: Blackwell.

   This book provides a clear and comprehensive introduction to L2 acquisition of syntax and morphology within a generative linguistic perspective.

White, L. (1989). *Universal grammar and second language acquisition*. Amsterdam: Benjamins.

   This book presents the logical problem of L2 acquisition and discusses research relevant to the debate over the availability of principles and parameters of UG in L2 acquisition.

White, L. (2003). *Second language acquisition and Universal Grammar*. Cambridge: Cambridge University Press.

   In this book, theories concerning role of Universal Grammar and the extent of mother-tongue influence are presented and discussed. Particular consideration is given to the nature of the interlanguage grammar at different points in development, from the initial state to ultimate attainment.

REFERENCES

Bhatt, R., & Hancin-Bhatt, B. (2002). Structural minimality, CP and the initial state in adult L2 acquisition. *Second Language Research, 18,* 348–392.

Bley-Vroman, R. (1989). What is the logical problem of foreign language learning? In S. Gass & J. Schachter (Eds.), *Linguistic perspectives on second language acquisition* (pp. 41–68). Cambridge: Cambridge University Press.

Borer, H. (1996). Access to Universal Grammar: The real issues. *Brain and Behavioral Sciences, 19,* 718–720.

Carroll, S. (2001). *Input and evidence: The raw material of second language acquisition*. Amsterdam: Benjamins.

Carroll, S., & Meisel, J. (1990). Universals and second language acquisition: Some comments on the state of current theory. *Studies in Second Language Acquisition, 12,* 201–208.

Chomsky, N. (1981). *Lectures on government and binding*. Dordrecht: Foris.

———. (1986a). *Barriers*. Cambridge, MA: M.I.T. Press.

———. (1986b). *Knowledge of language: Its nature, origin, and use*. New York: Praeger.

———. (1995). *The minimalist program*. Cambridge, MA: M.I.T. Press.

Corder, S. P. (1967). The significance of learners' errors. *International Review of Applied Linguistics, 5,* 161–170.

Crain, S., & Lillo-Martin, D. (1999). *An introduction to linguistic theory and language acquisition*. Oxford: Blackwell.

Crain, S., & Thornton, R. (1998). Investigations in Universal Grammar: A guide to experiments on the acquisition of syntax. Cambridge, MA: M.I.T. Press.

de Villiers, J., Roeper, T., & Vainikka, A. (1990). The acquisition of long-distance rules. In L. Frazier & J. de Villiers (Eds.), *Language processing and language acquisition* (pp. 257–297). Dordrecht: Kluwer.

Ellis, R. (1991). Grammaticality judgements and second language acquisition. *Studies in Second Language Acquisition, 13*, 161–186.

Finer, D. (1991). Binding parameters in second language acquisition. In L. Eubank (Ed.), *Point counterpoint: Universal Grammar in the second language* (pp. 351–374). Amsterdam: Benjamins.

Gregg, K. R. (1996). The logical and developmental problems of second language acquisition. In W. Ritchie & T. Bhatia (Eds.), *Handbook of second language acquisition* (pp. 49–81). San Diego: Academic Press.

Hawkins, R., & Chan, C. Y.-H. (1997). The partial availability of Universal Grammar in second language acquisition: The "failed functional features hypothesis." *Second Language Research, 13*, 187–226.

Haznedar, B. (1997). L2 acquisition by a Turkish-speaking child: Evidence for L1 influence. In E. Hughes, M. Hughes, & A. Greenhill (Eds.), *Proceedings of the 21st Annual Boston University Conference on Language Development* (pp. 245–256). Somerville, MA: Cascadilla Press.

Huang, C.-T. J. (1982). Move WH in a language without WH movement. *The Linguistic Review, 1*, 369–416.

Johnson, J., & Newport, E. (1991). Critical period effects on universal properties of language: The status of subjacency in the acquisition of a second language. *Cognition, 39*, 215–258.

Lardiere, D. (1998). Case and tense in the "fossilized" steady state. *Second Language Research, 14*, 1–26.

Lightfoot, D. (1989). The child's trigger experience: Degree–0 learnability. *Brain and Behavioral Sciences, 12*, 321–375.

Martohardjono, G., & Gair, J. (1993). Apparent UG inaccessibility in second language acquisition: Misapplied principles or principled misapplications? In F. Eckman (Ed.), *Confluence: Linguistics, L2 acquisition and speech pathology* (pp. 79–103). Amsterdam: Benjamins.

Roeper, T., & de Villiers, J. (1992). Ordered decisions in the acquisition of wh-questions. In J. Weissenborn, H. Goodluck, & T. Roeper (Eds.), *Theoretical issues in language acquisition: Continuity and change in development* (pp. 191–236). Hillsdale, NJ: Lawrence Erlbaum Associates.

Ross, J. R. (1967). Constraints on variables in syntax. Unpublished PhD dissertation, M.I.T.

Schachter, J. (1990). On the issue of completeness in second language acquisition. *Second Language Research, 6*, 93–124.

Schwartz, B. D., & Sprouse, R. (1996). L2 cognitive states and the full transfer/full access model. *Second Language Research, 12*, 40–72.

Selinker, L. (1972). Interlanguage. *International Review of Applied Linguistics, 10*, 209–231.

White, L. (1989). *Universal grammar and second language acquisition*. Amsterdam: Benjamins.

———. (1992). Subjacency violations and empty categories in L2 acquisition. In H. Goodluck & M. Rochemont (Eds.), *Island constraints* (pp. 445–464). Dordrecht: Kluwer.

———. (2003). *Second language acquisition and Universal Grammar*. Cambridge: Cambridge University Press.

White, L., & Juffs, A. (1998). Constraints on wh-movement in two different contexts of non-native language acquisition: competence and processing. In S. Flynn, G. Martohardjono, & W. O'Neil (Eds.), *The generative study of second language acquisition* (111–129). Mahwah, NJ: Lawrence Erlbaum Associates.

Xu, L. (1990). Remarks on LF Movement in Chinese questions. *Linguistics, 28*, 355–382.

4

One Functional Approach to Second Language Acquisition: The Concept-Oriented Approach

Kathleen Bardovi-Harlig
Indiana University

THE THEORY AND ITS CONSTRUCTS

Functionalist approaches to language hold that language is primarily used for communication and does not exist without language users. Functionalism views language in terms of form-to-function and function-to-form mappings. Functional approaches to second language acquisition investigate such mappings in interlanguage and are especially interested in how these change over time in the developing interlanguage system. This chapter provides an overview of one functionalist approach to second language acquisition, the concept-oriented approach. Functionalist approaches to linguistics in general and to second language acquisition in particular are not common in North America, and readers might find the functionalist emphasis on meaning and function to be both exciting and unfamiliar.

The basic claim of functional approaches is the centrality of meaning and function in influencing language structure and language acquisition. Cooreman and Kilborn (1991) outline two major tenets: Language serves communication and form serves function. Functional approaches always work on multiple levels of language. As Cooreman and Kilborn state, "there is no formal separation of the traditionally recognized subcomponents in language, i.e., morphosyntax, semantics, and pragmatics" (1991, p. 196).

The concept-oriented approach begins with a learner's need to express a certain concept (such as time, space, reference, or modality) or a meaning within a larger concept (such as past or future time, within the more general concept of time) and investigates the means that a learner uses to express that concept. In this way the concept-oriented approach focuses on one direction of the form and function mapping, specifically the function-to-form mapping.[1]

A basic tenet of the concept-oriented approach to second language acquisition is that adult learners of second or foreign languages have access to the full range of semantic concepts from their previous linguistic and cognitive experience. Von Stutterheim and Klein argue that "a second language learner—in contrast to a child learning his first language—does not have to acquire the underlying concepts. What he has to acquire is a specific way and a specific means of expressing them" (1987, p. 194). Within the concept-oriented approach, the main construct is the concept that is being investigated, for example, futurity. The devices that are used to express the concept fall out from the orientation. For example, futurity in English is expressed by adverbs, modals (*will, going to*) and lexical futures (future oriented verbs, such as *want to* or *need to*).

Consistent with other functional approaches, the concept-oriented approach embraces a multi-level analysis, including lexical devices, morphology, syntax, discourse, and pragmatics. In other words, the concept-oriented approach includes all means of expression used by learners. As Long and Sato (1984, p. 271) note, "function to form analysis automatically commits one to *multi*-level analysis, since the entire repertoire of devices and strategies used by learners must be examined."

Thus, concept-oriented analyses are interested in the range of linguistic devices that speakers use to express a particular concept (von Stutterheim & Klein, 1987), the interplay of ways to express a meaning, and the balance of what is explicitly expressed and what is left to contextual information (Klein, 1995). From the concept-oriented perspective, Klein observes that a substantial part of language acquisition is the permanent reorganization of the balance among means of expression. The analysis seeks to explain how meanings within a larger concept are expressed at a given time, and how the expression of the concept changes over time.

As an example of interplay among means of expression and the changing balance, consider a learner's expression of past time. The earliest resources

---

[1]Such meaning-oriented studies in second language acquisition are known by a variety of names including the concept-oriented approach (von Stutterheim & Klein, 1987), the conceptual approach (Klein, 1995), the semantically-oriented approach (Giacalone Ramat, 1992), the functional–grammatical perspective (Skiba & Dittmar, 1992), the notional perspective (Berretta, 1995), and function-to-form studies (Long & Sato, 1984; Sato, 1990; see also Trévise & Porquier, 1986).

that learners have are their interlocutors' turns, which may provide a time frame on which a learner can build (this is called *scaffolding*), and universal principles such as chronological order, by which listeners assume that events in narratives are told in the same order in which they happened (chronological order). This is called the pragmatic stage (Meisel, 1987). In the next stage, the lexical stage, learners use temporal and locative adverbials as well as connectives (e.g., *and then*) to indicate time. Finally, learners may move to the morphological stage, in which tense indicates temporal relations. At the same time that past morphology develops, it also participates in structuring the narrative. The main story line (the foreground) is distinguished from the supporting information (the background) by high use of simple past in English (or preterit in Spanish, and passé compose in French).

Note that both the inventory and the balances change. The inventory changes as new forms are added: first lexical markers, then verbal morphology. The balance changes as the use of morphology becomes more reliable. In the early stages, adverbs are used in the absence of tense, whereas in the morphological stage, tense is used more than adverbials. However, as Schumann (1987) points out, adverbials persist in advanced interlanguage just as they do in the native speaker system.

The concepts of interplay and balance in a system also relate to the functionalist concept of *functional load*. Every linguistic device—whether a structure, morpheme, or word—has a function. For example, if an adverb such as *yesterday* is the only indicator in a sentence that an event happened in the past, then the functional load of the adverb is high. If the sentence also employs past-tense verb morphology to indicate the time frame, the functional load of both the adverb and the verbal morphology is less than either one occurring alone (Bardovi-Harlig, 1992).

One natural outcome of functionalism's interest in the interplay of linguistic resources and their change over time is an attempt to understand how interlanguage selects the first meaning-to-form mappings and how they expand. Andersen has captured this interest in the development of function-to-form and form-to-function mapping in two principles for SLA, the one-to-one principle and the multifunctionality principle (Andersen, 1984, 1990, 1993). The one-to-one principle states that an interlanguage system "should be constructed in such a way that an intended underlying meaning is expressed with one clear invariant surface form (or construction)" (1984, p. 79). As Andersen sums up, the one-to-one principle "is a principle of one *form* to one *meaning*" (1984, p. 79, emphasis in original). The multifunctionality principle comes into play at later stages and was formulated as follows:

(a) Where there is clear evidence in the input that more than one form marks the meaning conveyed by only one form in the interlanguage, try to discover the distribution and additional meaning (if any) of the new form. (b) Where there is evidence in the input that an interlanguage form conveys only one of the meanings that the same form has in the input, try to discover the additional meanings of the form in the input. (Andersen, 1990, p. 53)

The multifunctionality principle, then, allows multiple forms for a single meaning and multiple meanings for a single form.

As an illustration, consider the early expression of futurity by learners of English. Learners begin to express the futurity with *will* and only later under certain circumstances expand their repertoire to include the *going to* future (Bardovi-Harlig, 2004a, 2004b, 2005). Audiences often ask me why the learners do not just use the present progressive (*I'm going to Chicago*). The data show that the present progressive is used in less than 2% in learner expressions of the future. The explanation is rather straightforward functionally. The present progressive has the primary function of expressing ongoing action. In other words, it is involved in a one-to-one relationship with another meaning in the interlanguage. With time, learners do expand their systems beyond the initial stage described by the one-to-one principle and move into a stage characterized by multifunctionality, but at the outset they begin with a transparent, invariant, and simple association of futurity and *will*.

Adult learners use language in the service of communication, so making (and expressing) meaning is the main process underlying acquisition. Failure to convey the intended meaning is seen as an impetus to moving to the next acquisitional stage. Consider the three main stages in the expression of temporality: the pragmatic (such as use of chronological order or building on an interlocutor's discourse that provides temporal reference), the lexical (such as the use of temporal adverbials to establish a time orientation), and the morphological (the use of verb inflections to indicate time relations). Failure to convey the intended meaning using pragmatic means may drive learners to develop a more elaborate system, moving from the pragmatic to lexical stage, or from the lexical stage to greater lexical elaboration, or to the acquisition of verbal morphology in the final stage (Dietrich, Klein, & Noyau, 1995).

In contrast to the theories and models outlined in other chapters in this volume, the concept-oriented approach is neither a theory nor a model but rather a framework for analysis.[2] Although it does not make predictions or model the acquisition process as theories and models do, it does provide an orientation to second language acquisition research that guides research and

---

[2]That is not to claim that there are no functional theories, however, just that the particular approach discussed in this chapter is not one. For examples of classic functional theories see Functional Grammar (Dik, 1978), Role and Reference Grammar (Van Valin & Foley, 1980, Foley & Van Valin, 1984), and Cognitive Grammar (Langacker, 1987a, 1987b).

research questions. If one of the functions of a theory is to provide direction in identifying important research questions, this analytic framework satisfies that function. Klein (1995) compared the concept-oriented framework to a theory in the following way:

> A frame of analysis, such as the one used here, is not a theory that is meant to excel by the depth of its insights or by its explanatory power. Rather, it is an instrument designed for a specific purpose [to analyze language], and to serve this purpose, it should be simple, clear and handy. . . . A frame of analysis, if it is to be more than a temporary crutch, should also be flexible in the sense that it can easily be enlarged, refined and made more precise, whenever there is need to. (Klein, 1995, p. 17)

WHAT ARE THE ORIGINS OF THE APPROACH?

Functionalist approaches to SLA are related to functional linguistics more generally, a valuable resource for second language research. The interest in the function-to-form and form-to-function mapping is broader than the concept-oriented approach, and I will mention a few areas of investigation to give the reader a sense of the breadth of functionalist inquiry possible in L2 research.

Different approaches to functionalism explore different functions. Prague School functionalism pioneered work on functional sentence perspective (the role of information bearing elements, whether known or unknown, given or new) in determining word order (Firbas, 1979, 1981; Svoboda, 1974). This parallels a syntactic concern for word order but investigates it functionally. Similarly, research on topic (and topic-comment structure) in both L1 (Chafe, 1970; Kuno, 1972, 1980; Prince, 1981) and L2 (Hendriks, 2000; Huebner, 1983; Rutherford, 1983; Schachter & Rutherford, 1979) offer a second perspective on word order. Discourse concerns related to text type, specifically narratives, have been investigated crosslinguistically for a range of languages by Hopper (1979) and for L2 (Bardovi-Harlig, 1995, 1998; Flashner, 1989; Kumpf, 1984; von Stutterheim, 1991). Functionalist approaches can also be found in studies of processing and weighting of cues, most notably in the competition model (Bates & MacWhinney, 1981, 1982, 1987) that has influenced a number of L2 studies (Cooreman & Kilborn, 1991; Gass, 1987; Kilborn & Ito, 1989; MacWhinney, 1987). Functionalist accounts of first language acquisition (e.g., E. V. Clark, 1971; Clark & Clark, 1977) are also valuable resources for SLA.

The concept-oriented approach is particularly compatible with other meaning-oriented or function-oriented approaches to language and linguistic universals, such as semantic or notional typology, which investigates the expression of semantic concepts across the world's languages (Croft, 1995;

Palmer, 2001). The research on L2 temporality (the expression of time relations) has benefited greatly from crosslinguistic studies (e.g., Bybee, 1985; Bybee, Perkins, & Pagliuca, 1994; Dahl, 1985, 2000). Such inquiries inform second language acquisition researchers about both the range of expressions and the range of systems in which they appear that are possible in human language.

The concept-oriented approach to second language acquisition owes its articulation to von Stutterheim and Klein (1987). Subsequent longitudinal studies of groups of learners (rather than case studies) include the studies conducted by the European Science Foundation, led by Wolfgang Klein and Clive Purdue (e.g., Becker & Carroll, 1997; Dietrich, Klein, & Noyau, 1995, as well as many articles) and by American researchers (Bardovi-Harlig, 1992, 1994, 2004a, 2004b; Moses, 2002; Salsbury, 2000).

WHAT COUNTS AS EVIDENCE?

Studies in the concept-oriented framework typically take as evidence language used communicatively, a subset of what is generally called production data. Studies in this framework also prefer to observe production over time in what is called a longitudinal design. The tasks used to elicit data allow learners to construct meaning. The studies tend to observe learners' production (or output) in fairly natural situations. When speakers communicate, they encode particular meanings in various ways. Because the concept-oriented approach is interested in the way in which meanings or semantic concepts are expressed, communicative tasks or activities that have a clearly definable concept or purpose are used. Examples of some tasks that have been used include telling narratives (stories), retelling short excerpts of movies, and giving directions for the reenactment of an event. Telling or retelling stories allows researchers to study how events in the past are expressed. Asking learners to make predictions may reveal how they express the future, and also how they express certainty or uncertainty that is related to future events. Giving directions on how to perform an action naturally allows learners to encode both the order of events (what to do first, second, and third) and spatial relations (where to put what).

Studies conducted in this framework are typically longitudinal. This means that individual learners are observed for a relatively long time. The European Science Foundation sponsored a large multinational study that observed the same learners and the learning process for three years (e.g., Becker & Carroll, 1997; Dietrich, Klein, & Noyau, 1995).

Evidence of language processing is also valued in functional approaches (Cooreman & Kilborn, 1991). Evidence from processing studies suggest that in early stages, second language learners' reliance on adverbs to convey temporal relations is mirrored by their comprehension; learners use adverbs to understand temporal relations even when morphological indicators are present or when they conflict with the adverb (e.g., Boatwright, 1999; Lee, 1999; Lee, Cadierno, Glass, & VanPatten, 1997; Musumeci, 1989; Sanz & Fernández, 1992). In contrast to the concept-oriented studies, which rely on production tasks that are as close to spontaneous communication as possible, processing studies rely on highly controlled experimental designs, and the results are understood in terms of accuracy and rate of processing. What these different types of studies have in common, however, is their focus on investigating form-meaning associations. Any design that facilitates the investigation of such associations would be considered appropriate to a functional inquiry.

Because functionalist approaches do not seek to explain form for form's sake, or structure in the absence of function, functionalist inquiries, including concept-oriented studies, tend to avoid designs that focus on form rather than meaning, or that focus on form in the absence of meaning. Thus, tasks such as grammaticality judgments, which are used by other approaches, are not found in functionalist studies. Similarly, one would not expect to find sentence correction tasks if the sentences are isolated; however, if the sentences were part of a text and thus context and meaning are involved, it would be harder to rule out such a task a priori.

It is also important to consider what type of analysis would and would not be appropriate to the approach. Concept-oriented analyses report how learners use language and how they construct their language, but they typically do not report the findings in terms of whether the learners are correct or incorrect relative to the language being learned (what we call the *target language*). Consider that in a concept-oriented approach we would say that learners who use *goed (yesterday)* are using morphological inflection to express the past, but we would be unlikely to discount the form as ill-formed.

COMMON MISUNDERSTANDINGS

Ironically, although functionalist approaches are not very common, I do not think the concept-oriented approach is misunderstood, largely because few people think about this approach to interlanguage research and analysis. I think many people instinctively like the concept-oriented approach (and other functionalist approaches) because it is meaning-oriented, but when novice researchers attempt studies in this framework, they find it very difficult not to refer to form as the primary focus, or to describe learner production without evaluating accuracy based on what is expected in the target language. As an illustration, consider the concept of plurality, which is distinct from the plural morpheme (in English indicated by –s). Consider also the noun phrases *two boy, many friend,* and *three girls*. In a targetlike analysis only one noun phrase, *three girls*, correctly uses plural morphology; formally speaking, it is the only noun phrase that is "plural." In contrast, in a concept-oriented analysis, all three noun phrases express plurality. The interlanguage is seen to have three means of indicating plurality: quantifiers, numerals, and plural morphology. Over time, the balance will change and *–s* will become the dominant marker of plurality, co-occurring with the other markers.

Researchers who were trained in other traditions may regard the lack of formal separation of the traditionally recognized subcomponents in language (morphosyntax, semantics, and pragmatics) to be rather disconcerting and perhaps reflect "fuzzy thinking" as a syntactician suggested to me many years ago. However, to a functionalist, taking many levels into account at once leads to a more complete picture of language in the service of communication.

AN EXEMPLARY STUDY: BARDOVI-HARLIG (1994)

A concept-oriented approach typically begins with a concept to be investigated. It examines (a) how learners express the concept, (b) how the means of expression interact, and (c) how the expression changes over time. The study presented here, Bardovi-Harlig (1994), investigated the concept of reverse-order reports, or how learners conveyed events that are not in the order in which they happened.

Without evidence to the contrary, events in a series are understood to be in the order in which they happened, or *chronological order*. Narratives, for example, relate events in chronological order (Dahl, 1984). Any change from chronological order must be indicated, as Klein (1986, p. 127) states: "Unless marked otherwise, the sequence of events mentioned in an utterance corresponds to their real sequence." In spite of the strong tendency to report events in chronological order, narrators, including L2 learners, must also be able to deviate from chronological order. Compare example (1), which reports events in chronological order, with (2), which reports them in reverse order. The first event is labeled [1] and the second [2].

1. John graduated from high school in 1975 [1]. He went to college five years later [2].
2. John entered college in 1980 [2]. He had graduated from high school five years earlier [1].
3. The first one they met was a horse as thin as a stick, tied to an oak tree [2]. He had eaten the leaves as far as he could reach [1]. (Thompson, 1968, p. 2)
4. I ate my lunch [2] after my wife came back from her shopping [1]. (Leech, 1971, p. 43)

English signals reverse-order reports by tense (the pluperfect, as in 3), adverbials (4), and by a combination of both (2).

Method

This study is a longitudinal production study that followed 16 learners from 9 to 16 months. The learners were from four language backgrounds (Arabic, Japanese, Korean, and Spanish) and were low-level learners, as measured by their placement in level one out of six levels in an intensive English program. The intensive English classes met for 23 hours a week and provided instruction in listening and speaking, reading, writing, and grammar.

The data for the study came from two sources: primary language samples produced by the learners and teaching logs completed by participating grammar and writing instructors. The production data were comprised of the first three past-time texts from each half-month sampling period, resulting in 430 texts: 376 journal entries, 37 narratives from film retell tasks, and 17 essay exams and in-class compositions. Past-time texts were identified by the use of time adverbials that provided time frames (Bardovi-Harlig, 1992; Harkness, 1987; Thompson & Longacre, 1985) and program calendars.

Every verb supplied in past-time contexts was coded for its verbal morphology, and all adverbials were identified and coded (Harkness, 1987). Rates of appropriate use of past tense were calculated as the ratio of the number of different past tense forms (i.e., types) supplied to the number of obligatory environments. Next, the reverse-order reports (RORs) were identified and coded for verbal morphology and presence of other markers, namely adverbials, relative clauses, complements, and causal constructions.

The findings show that RORs are indeed marked as Klein predicted. RORs are marked by a variety of devices, fewer lexical and syntactic devices are used when specialized verbal morphology is used, and RORs seem to emerge when expression of the past has stabilized. The individual research questions are examined in turn.

How are RORs expressed? Of 103 RORs, 100 (94.2%) showed an explicit marker of reverse order, whereas only three (or 5.8%) did not. The explicitly marked RORs exhibited a variety of linguistic devices: morphological contrast (tense-aspect usage), adverbials (single and dual), and syntactic devices including causal constructions (especially the use of *because*), complementation (especially reported speech or thought), and relative clauses (see Table 4.1). Of 103 reverse-order reports, 63 exhibited a contrast in verbal morphology and 40 did not. Some of the reverse-order reports were indicated in multiple ways; thus, there are more markers of reverse-order reports than reverse-order reports themselves in Table 4.1.

TABLE 4.1.
Past-time Reverse-Order Reports

	No Morphological Contrast[1]	N	%	Morphological Contrast[2]	N	%
		Type of Contrast				
Devices						
No Marking	She said to me "Yes." [2] She didn't eat breakfast, lunch [1] so also she was hungry.	3	5.8	N/A		
Morphology only	N/A			John and I went to her building [2]. She had invited her friends.[1]	14	20.6
Single Adverb	My sister played piano very well. *Before* she played [2], we were very nervous [1]	13	25.0	*By the time* the baker caught her [2] she had run into our hero [1]. [Carlos T5.5]	23	33.8
Dual Adverb	*In level two* I studied many new things for me [2], I didn't study *before in the another school* [1]	11	21.2	*Today* morning my father called us. [2] He told us [3] that grand-mother has been sick *during two weeks* [1]	7	10.3
Relative Clause	Then the bolice [police] but [put] the girl [2] *which* stole the bread [1] on the lory with Charlie	7	13.5	In order to avoid mistakes and misunderstandings I had to review severals time [2] what I had done [1].	11	16.2
Because	Yesterday was a pusy [busy] day because I had to go to Indiana bell [2] *because* I didn't biad [paid] my bell [1] so I did.	12	23.1	I spent that time with my family [2] *because* I had been here since Ogust [1].	7	10.3
Complement	He thought [2] *that* I said "Coming" [1]	6	11.5	I thought about [2] how she had bought them and packed them [1].	6	8.8
	Total	52	100.1	Total	68	100.0

[1]N = 40
[2]N = 63

The morphological contrasts employed are often targetlike, and two-thirds of the sample showed a contrast between the simple past to indicate the second event and the pluperfect to indicate the first event. The remaining third is comprised of other contrasts including past [event 2] with present perfect or past progressive [event 1] and base forms [event 2] with past [event 1].

How do the means of expression interact?   When learners use verbal morphology to indicate reverse order reports, the use of other devices decreased (Table 4.1). The use of dual adverbials to show contrast declines by about half (21.2% to 10.3%). Learners also showed utterances that have neither lexical nor syntactic devices to indicate RORs *once verbal morphology marked RORs*, whereas this is very unusual when verbal morphology is not used: 20.6% of RORs with morphological contrast occur with no additional lexical or syntactic devices.

How does expression change over time?   Looking at language production over time shows that the learners exhibited variable rates of emergence for RORs. (*Emergence* refers to the earliest expression of a concept or a form.) Half of the learners began to use RORs within the first three months of observation, another four in the next three months, and another four between months seven and thirteen. Although calendar time does not present a consistent picture, emergence with respect to other features of the temporal system does. RORs emerge when learners show stable use of simple past tense, at about 80% appropriate use in past-time contexts.

Pluperfect, the grammatical form that serves to uniquely mark in the past-in-the-past, emerges even later. Whereas half of the learners showed use of RORs in the first three months, only half of those showed early use of the pluperfect. One learner showed emergent use by the end of the sixth month, and another two by the end of the seventh month. Three additional learners started to use the pluperfect in the corpus between months 9.5 and 12.5.

As predicted by Klein's principle of natural order, deviations from chronological order were signaled in interlanguage. The expression of RORs is delayed until the learner can use a marker to distinguish them from the surrounding narrative.

The finding that the acquisition of the pluperfect serves the expression of RORs but does not itself make RORs possible is an important result of employing a meaning-oriented approach to this inquiry. Both a form-focused approach (i.e., focusing on the acquisition of the pluperfect) and a meaning-oriented approach (focusing on the expression of RORs) could identify the acquisitional prerequisite of high appropriate use of past tense. However, focus on the form of the pluperfect alone would fail to capture the fact that the pluperfect moves into an established semantic environment. Through a meaning-oriented approach both prerequisites for the acquisition of pluperfect, high appropriate use of past tense and expression of RORs, are revealed.

EXPLANATION OF OBSERVED FINDINGS IN SLA

As noted at the beginning of this chapter, the concept-oriented approach is an analytic framework rather than a theory. It thus lacks the predictive power of a theory. It does, however, contribute to detailed descriptions of second language acquisition that take meaning as well as form in to account. Studies in the concept-oriented framework have contributed to a number of observations outlined in chapter 2, especially stages of acquisition, variable outcomes, influence of first language, and the effects of instruction. The longitudinal design that is favored by the concept-oriented studies permits the investigation of multiple learner variables. The functionalist approach offers accounts of two of the observations from chapter 2: predictable stages and the limitations of instruction.

Observation #4. Learners' output often follows predictable paths with predictable stages in the acquisition of a given structure. The overriding concern of functionalism is communication. Therefore, it is in keeping with its orientation for functionalism to explain major stages in those terms. More successful communication—resulting in conveying the speaker's meaning— propels learners to the next acquisitional stage. In the sequence from pragmatic to lexical to morphological expression of temporality, each stage affords a learner a greater range of expression and less dependence on interlocutors, resulting in an increasingly independent language user who speaks an interlanguage with ever-increasing communicative power.

Within the larger stages of development are multiple discrete stages. The morphological stage, for example, exhibits many substages in which different morphology emerges and enters into meaning to form mappings. One explanation for the order of acquisition of morphemes within the same subsystem is functional load. Meanings for which there are reasonable means of expression (i.e., grammatical and communicatively comprehensible) are less likely than others to promote acquisition of a new form. Take as an example the present perfect (e.g., *have gone*) and the pluperfect (e.g., *had gone*). Both are equally complex structurally, having both a tensed form of *have* plus a past participle. Longitudinal observation shows that the present perfect emerges noticeably earlier in adult second language acquisition, even when both are taught at the same time (Bardovi-Harlig, 2000). The difference between them is that the present perfect has no functional equivalent. In contrast, the meaning of the pluperfect (past in the past) can be expressed by the simple past plus an adverbial, as discussed earlier. This helps explain the order of emergence. It appears that an emergent interlanguage system puts greater store in range of expression (covering all the conceptual bases) than in redundancy.

Observation #9.   *There are limits on the effects of instruction on SLA.* Naturally, the explanation for instructional effects depends on the instructional effects that one sees. When I look at the results from instructional investigations of varying types, I see second language acquisition itself. If instructed and uninstructed learners are compared in the early period before instructed learners overtake uninstructed learners (Bardovi-Harlig, 2000), the stages are the same. As Gass (1989) argued, the fundamental psycholinguistic process of second language acquisition is the same whether learners enter classrooms or acquire language outside of them.

On the level of expression of individual concepts, instruction is also seen as having a limited role. The stage of acquisition of individual learners also interacts with instruction as Pienemann (1989, 1998) has argued. To better understand what leads to development in temporal expression, the study reported on earlier also collected instructional logs. Comparing the documented form-focused instruction with the emergence and use patterns of the pluperfect revealed that learners began to use the pluperfect at or following the time of instruction if they had already passed through the prerequisite stages for the pluperfect: stable use of past and expression of RORs. Learners who had not established a stable use of past, or who had not expressed RORs, did not show spontaneous use of pluperfect in their written texts.

This suggests that meeting these acquisitional prerequisites is a necessary step even when the pluperfect is available in instructional input, but it also shows that merely meeting the prerequisites at the time of instruction is not sufficient. This is consistent with Pienemann's teachability hypothesis, according to which the effects of instruction on the developing interlanguage are constrained by the learner's current stage of acquisition. However, even learners who apparently satisfy the acquisitional prerequisites for an instructionally targeted form may not immediately integrate that form into productive use.

The same learners show a similar lack of incorporation of a targeted form in instruction as seen in learners' delay in using *going to* in the expression of futurity. The presence of targeted forms in instructional input and the completion of acquisitional prerequisites within continued nonuse of the target form suggests that even in the presence of focused instruction, the one-to-one principle is at work. When learners have an established means of expressing a given concept in interlanguage (and especially when that form is communicatively clear and grammatical), they may be slow to expand their grammars even in the face of instruction.

CONCLUSION

The study of interlanguage development from a concept-oriented approach highlights the relationship of the various linguistic devices that learners may employ to express a given concept. In this chapter we saw how various linguistic means convey temporal reference, how they relate to each other, and how the balance changes over time. Because the concept-oriented approach investigates concepts rather than specific forms, the approach encourages the investigation of the interlanguage system from the very earliest stages, although it also allows investigation in advanced stages as well. It thus allows the SLA researcher to document premorphological stages, which importantly form part of the sequences of second language acquisition. The concept-oriented approach also emphasizes the investigation of the interlanguage system in its own right. This is important because target-language orientations, which are more common in the literature, often focus on the distance between a learner's interlanguage and the target language, rather than exploring the emergence, interplay, and balance of features of the interlanguage as a linguistic system.

DISCUSSION QUESTIONS

1. Compare and contrast White's approach with Bardovi-Harlig's. As a starting point you might consider the concepts of mental representation language and differentiated language levels as well as the distinction between a theory of language and a theory of language acquisition.
2. How does a functionalist approach explain staged development in SLA?
3. Identify a concept or question that you would like to investigate using a concept-oriented framework. How would you set up the study? Keep in mind that you need to determine how learners express the concept, how the various means of expression interact, and how the expression changes over time.
4. Functionalist approaches are useful for explaining the acquisition of many, if not all, meaning-based aspects of language. Can you think of areas of language acquisition that might pose a challenge for a functionalist approach?

SUGGESTED FURTHER READINGS

Bardovi-Harlig, K. (2000). *Tense and aspect in second language acquisition: Form, meaning, and use.* Oxford: Blackwell.

This book synthesizes research on the acquisition of tense and aspect from a variety of research perspectives, including concept-/meaning-oriented perspectives, across a variety of target languages. See especially, chapters 2 and 6.

Becker, A., & Carroll, M. (Eds.)(1997). *The acquisition of spatial relations in a second language.* Amsterdam: Benjamins.

For readers who would like to see how the concept-oriented framework is applied to areas beyond the expression of time, this European Science Foundation sponsored study (see also Dietrich et al.) reports on the expression of spatial concepts in five languages.

Cooreman, A., & Kilborn, K. (1991). Functionalist linguistics: Discourse structure and language processing in second language acquisition. In T. Huebner & C. A. Ferguson (Eds.) *Cross Currents in Second Language Acquisition and Linguistic Theory* (pp. 195–224). Amsterdam: Benjamins.

This article presents another view of functionalism in second language acquisition research including a comparison of functionalism and the competition model (Bates & MacWhinney, 1978; Bates & MacWhinney, 1982, 1984, 1987).

Dietrich, R., Klein, W., & Noyau, C. (1995). *The acquisition of temporality in a second language.* Amsterdam: John Benjamins.

Sponsored by the European Science Foundation, the study reported here is a masterful undertaking. The acquisition of temporal expression in five languages (English, French, German, Swedish, and Dutch) by adult learners is reported on from a concept-oriented approach. Summary introduction and conclusion chapters provide an overview of the procedures and results.

von Stutterheim, C., & Klein, W. (1987). A concept-oriented approach to second language studies. In C. W. Pfaff (Ed.), *First and second language acquisition processes* (pp. 191–205). Cambridge, MA: Newbury House.

This seminal article introduces the concept-oriented approach to the second language acquisition literature in English.

REFERENCES

Andersen, R. W. (1984). The one-to-one principle of interlanguage construction. *Language Learning, 34,* 77–95.

———. (1990). Models, processes, principles and strategies: Second language acquisition inside and outside the classroom. In B. VanPatten & J. F. Lee (Eds.), *Second language acquisition-foreign language learning* (pp. 45–78). Clevedon, UK: Multilingual Matters. (Reprinted from *IDEAL, 3,* 111–138.)

―――. (1993). Four operating principles and input distribution as explanations for underdeveloped and mature morphological systems. In K. Hyltenstam & Å. Viberg (Eds.), *Progression & regression in language: Sociocultural, neuropsychological, & linguistic perspectives* (pp. 309–339). Cambridge: Cambridge University Press.

Bardovi-Harlig, K. (1992). The use of adverbials and natural order in the development of temporal expression. *IRAL, 30,* 299–320.

―――. (1994). Reverse-order reports and the acquisition of tense: Beyond the principle of chronological order. *Language Learning, 44,* 243–282.

―――. (1995). A narrative perspective on the development of the tense/aspect system in second language acquisition. *Studies in Second Language Acquisition, 17,* 263–291.

―――. (1998). Narrative structure and lexical aspect: Conspiring factors in second language acquisition of tense-aspect morphology. *Studies in Second Language Acquisition, 20,* 471–508.

―――. (2000). *Tense and aspect in second language acquisition: Form, meaning, and use.* Oxford: Blackwell.

―――. (2004a). The emergence of grammaticalized future expression in longitudinal production data. In M. Overstreet, S. Rott, B. VanPatten, & J. Williams (Eds.) *Form and meaning in second language acquisition* (pp. 115–137). Mahwah, NJ: Lawrence Erlbaum Associates.

―――. (2004b). Monopolizing the Future OR How the *go*-future breaks into *will*'s territory and what it tells us about SLA. In S. Foster-Cohen (Ed.), *EuroSLA Yearbook* (pp. 177–201). Amsterdam: Benjamins.

―――. (2005). The future of desire: Lexical futures and modality in L2 English future expression. In L. Dekydtspotter, R. A. Sprouse, & A. Liljestrand (Eds.), *Proceedings of the 7th Generative Approaches to Second Language Acquisition Conference (GASLA 2004)* (pp. 1–12). Somerville, MA: Cascadilla Proceedings Project.

Bates, E., & MacWhinney, B. (1981). Second language acquisition from a functionalist perspective: Pragmatics, semantics and perceptual strategies. In H. Winitz (Ed.), *Annals of the New York Academy of Sciences Conference on Native Language and Foreign Language Acquisition* (pp. 190–214). New York: New York Academy of Sciences.

Bates, E., & MacWhinney, B. (1982). Functional approaches to grammar. In E. Wanner & L. Gleitman (Eds.), *Language acquisition: The state of the art* (pp. 173–218). New York: Cambridge University Press.

Bates, E., & MacWhinney, B. (1987). Language universals, individual variation, and the competition model. In B. MacWhinney (Ed.), *Mechanisms of language acquisition* (pp. 157–193). Hillsdale: Lawrence Erlbaum Associates.

Becker, A., & Carroll, M. (1997). *The acquisition of spatial relations in a second language.* Amsterdam: Benjamins.

Berretta, M. (1995). Morphological markedness in L2 acquisition. In R. Simone (Ed.), *Iconicity in language* (pp. 197–233). Amsterdam: Benjamins.

Boatwright, C. (1999, September). *On-line processing of time reference: Meaning before morphology.* Paper presented at the Second Language Research Forum, Minneapolis, MN.

Bybee, J. L. (1985). *Morphology: A study of the relation between meaning and form.* Amsterdam: Benjamins.

Bybee, J., Perkins, R., & Pagliuca, W. (1994). *The evolution of grammar: Tense, aspect, and modality in the languages of the world.* Chicago: University of Chicago Press.

Chafe, W. (1970). *Meaning and structure of language*. Chicago: The University of Chicago Press.

Clark, E. V. (1971). On the acquisition of the meaning of before and after. *Journal of Verbal Learning and Verbal Behavior, 10*, 266–275.

Clark, H., & Clark, E. (1977). *Psychology and language: An introduction to psycholinguistics.* New York: Harcourt Brace.

Cooreman, A., & Kilborn, K. (1991). Functionalist linguistics: Discourse structure and language processing in second language acquisition. In T. Huebner & C. A. Ferguson (Eds.), *Cross Currents in Second Language Acquisition and Linguistic Theory* (pp. 195–224). Amsterdam: Benjamins.

Croft, W. (1995).Modern syntactic typology. In M. Shibatani & T. Bynon (Eds.), *Approaches to language typology* (pp. 85–144). Oxford: Clarendon Press.

Dahl, Ö. (1984). Temporal distance: Remoteness distinctions in tense-aspect systems. In B. Butterworth, B. Comrie, & Ö. Dahl (Eds.), *Explanations for language universals* (pp. 105–122). Berlin: Mouton.

———. (1985). *Tense and aspect systems.* Oxford: Basil Blackwell.

———. (2000). *Tense and aspect in the languages of Europe.* Berlin: de Gruyter.

Dietrich, R., Klein, W., & Noyau, C. (1995). *The acquisition of temporality in a second language.* Amsterdam: Benjamins.

Dik, S. (1978). *Functional Grammar.* Amsterdam: North Holland.

Firbas, J. (1979). A functional view of 'ordo naturalis.' *Brno Studies in English, 13*, 29–59.

———. (1981). On the thematic and non-thematic section of the sentence. In H. Ringbom (Ed.), *Style and text* (pp. 317–334). Stockholm: Språkfölaget AB and Åba Akademi.

Flashner, V. E. (1989). Transfer of aspect in the English oral narratives of native Russian speakers. In H. Dechert & M. Raupach (Eds.), *Transfer in language production* (pp. 71–97). Norwood, NJ: Ablex.

Foley, W. A., & Van Valin, R. D., Jr. (1984). *Functional Syntax and Universal Grammar.* Cambridge: Cambridge University Press.

Gass, S. M. (1989). Second and foreign language learning: Same, different, or none of the above? In B. VanPatten & J. F. Lee (Eds.), *Second language acquisition/Foreign language learning* (pp. 34–44). Clevedon, UK: Multilingual Matters.

Giacalone Ramat, A. (1992). Grammaticalization processes in the area of temporal and modal relations. *Studies in Second Language Acquisition, 14*, 297–322.

Harkness, J. (1987). Time adverbials in English and reference time. In A. Schopf (Ed.), *Essays on tensing in English: Vol. 1. Reference Time, Tense and Adverbs* (pp. 71–110). Tübingen: Niemeyer.

Hendriks, H. (2000). The acquisition of topic marking in L1 Chinese and L1 and L2 French. *Studies in Second Language Acquisition, 22*, 369–397.

Hopper, P. J. (1979). Aspect and foregrounding in discourse. In T. Givón (Ed.), *Syntax and semantics: Discourse and syntax* (pp. 213–241). New York: Academic Press.

Huebner, T. (1983). *A longitudinal analysis of the acquisition of English.* Ann Arbor, MI: Karoma.

Kilborn, K., & Ito, T. (1989). Sentence processing strategies in adult bilinguals. In B. MacWhinney & E. Bates (Eds.), *The crosslinguistic studies of sentence processing* (pp. 257–291). Cambridge: Cambridge University Press.

Klein, W. (1986). *Second language acquisition.* (Rev. ed., Bohuslaw Jankowski, Trans.) Cambridge: Cambridge University Press. (Original work published 1984.)

————. (1995). The acquisition of English. In R. Dietrich, W. Klein, & C. Noyau (Eds.), *The acquisition of temporality in a second language* (pp. 31–70). Amsterdam: Benjamins.

Kumpf, L. (1984). Temporal systems and universality in interlanguage: A case study. In F. Eckman, L. Bell, & D. Nelson (Eds.), *Universals of second language acquisition* (pp. 132–143). Rowley, MA: Newbury House.

Kuno, S. (1972). Functional sentence perspective: A case study from Japanese and English. *Linguistic Inquiry, 3*, 269–320.

————. (1980). Functional syntax. In E. Moravcsik & J. Wirth (Eds.), *Current approaches to Syntax (Syntax and Semantics, vol. 13*; pp. 117–135). New York: Academic Press.

Langacker, R. W. (1987a). *Foundations of cognitive grammar: Theoretical Prerequisites.* Stanford: Stanford University Press.

————. (1987b). An overview of cognitive grammar. In B. Rudzka-Ostyn (Ed.), *Topics in cognitive linguistics* (pp. 3–48). Amsterdam: John Benjamins.

Lee, J. F. (1999). On levels of processing and levels of comprehension. In J. Gútierrez-Rexach & F. Martínez-Gil (Eds.), *Advances in Hispanic Linguistics* (pp. 42–59). Somerville, MA: Cascadilla Press.

Lee, J. F., Cadierno, T., Glass, W. R., & VanPatten, B. (1997). The effects of lexical and grammatical cues on processing past temporal reference in second language input. *Applied Language Learning, 8*, 1–23.

Leech, G. N. (1971). *Meaning and the English verb.* Harlow, Essex: Longman.

Long, M., & Sato, C. J. (1984). Methodological issues in interlanguage studies: An interactionist perspective. In A. Davies, C. Criper, & A. P. R. Howatt (Eds.), *Interlanguage* (pp. 253–279). Edinburgh: Edinburgh University Press.

MacWhinney, B. (1987). Applying the competition model to bilingualism. *Applied Psycholinguistics, 8*, 315–327.

Meisel, J. (1987). Reference to past events and actions in the development of natural language acquisition. In C. W. Pfaff (Ed.), *First and second language acquisition processes* (pp. 206–224). Cambridge, MA: Newbury House.

Moses, J. (2002). *The expression of futurity by English-speaking learners of French.* Unpublished doctoral dissertation, Indiana University, Bloomington.

Musumeci, D. (1989). *The ability of second language learners to assign tense at the sentence level.* Unpublished doctoral dissertation, The University of Illinois at Urbana-Champaign.

Palmer, F. R. (2001). *Mood and Modality.* Cambridge: Cambridge University Press.

Pienemann, M. (1989). Is language teachable? Psycholinguistic experiments and hypotheses. *Applied Linguistics, 10*, 52–79.

————. (1998). Language processing and second language development: Processability Theory. Amsterdam: Benjamins.

Prince, E. (1981). Toward a taxonomy of given-new information. In P. Cole (Ed.), *Radical pragmatics* (pp. 223–255). New York: Academic Press.

Rutherford, W. (1983). Language typology and language transfer. In S. Gass & L. Selinker (Eds.), *Language transfer in language learning* (pp. 358–370). Rowley, MA: Newbury House.

Salsbury, T. (2000). *The grammaticalization of unreal conditionals: A longitudinal study of L2 English.* Unpublished doctoral dissertation, Indiana University, Bloomington.

Sanz, C., & Fernández, M. (1992). L2 learners' processing of temporal cues in Spanish. *MIT Working Papers in Linguistics, 16*, 155–168.

Sato, C. J. (1990). *The syntax of conversation in interlanguage development.* Tübingen: Narr.

Schachter, J., & Rutherford, W. (1979). Discourse function in language transfer. *Working Papers in Bilingualism, 19,* 1–12.

Schumann, J. (1987). The expression of temporality in basilang speech. *Studies in Second Language Acquisition, 9,* 21–41.

Skiba, R., & Dittmar, N. (1992). Pragmatic, semantic, and syntactic constraints and grammaticalization: A longitudinal perspective. *Studies in Second Language Acquisition, 14,* 323–349.

Svoboda, A. (1974). On two communicative dynamisms. In F. Daneš (Ed.), *Papers on functional sentence perspective* (pp. 38–42). Prague: Academia Publishing, Czechoslovak Academy of Sciences.

Thompson, S. (1968). *One hundred favorite folktales.* Bloomington: Indiana University Press.

Thompson, S. A., & Longacre, R. E. (1985). Adverbial Clauses. In Timothy Shopen (Ed.), *Language Typology and Syntactic Description* (pp. 171–234). Cambridge: Cambridge University Press.

Trévise, A., & Porquier, R. (1986). Second language acquisition by adult immigrants: Exemplified methodology. *Studies in Second Language Acquisition, 8,* 265–275.

Van Valin, R. D., Jr., & Foley, W. A. (1980). Role and reference grammar. In E. A. Moravcsik & J. R. Wirth (Eds.), *Current approaches to syntax* (pp. 329–352). New York: Academic Press.

von Stutterheim, C. (1991). Narrative and description: Temporal reference in second language acquisition. In T. Huebner & C. A. Ferguson (Eds.), *Crosscurrents in second language acquisition and linguistic theories* (pp. 385–403). Amsterdam: Benjamins.

von Stutterheim, C., & Klein, W. (1987). A concept-oriented approach to second language studies. In C. W. Pfaff (Ed.), *First and second language acquisition processes* (pp. 191–205). Cambridge, MA: Newbury House.

5

The Associative–Cognitive CREED

Nick C. Ellis

The University of Michigan

THE THEORY AND ITS CONSTRUCTS

SLA has been actively studied from a *cognitive* perspective for the last two or three decades, and researchers within this tradition share basic goals, methods, and constructs. As in any active field of scientific enquiry, our theories are continuously measured against the observable phenomena, refined, and developed. The position outlined in this chapter is fairly typical of the beliefs shared by psychologists. The Associative–Cognitive CREED holds that SLA is Construction-based, Rational, Exemplar-driven, Emergent, and Dialectic. Some of these terms may be new to you but each will be explained in detail below, and it is worth sticking with them because of their currency in the different subdivisions of contemporary cognitive science.

A fundamental tenet of SLA is that we learn language in much the same way as we learn everything else. The cognitive content of language systems is special because the problem of representing and sharing meanings across a serial speech stream is unique to language, but the processes of learning are the same as those involved in the rest of human cognition. Thus SLA is governed by general laws of human learning, both *associative* (the types of learning first analyzed within the behaviorist tradition introduced in chapter 1) and *cognitive* (the wider range of learning processes studied within cognitive psychology, including more conscious, explicit, deductive, or tutored processes). You will see commonalities between this chapter and others in this volume by cognitively minded SLA researchers such as DeKeyser, VanPatten, Gass and Mackey, and Pienemann, although we clearly have different emphases too.

Construction Grammar

The basic units of language representation are *constructions*. These are form–meaning mappings, conventionalized in the speech community and entrenched as language knowledge in the learner's mind. Constructions are symbolic in that their defining properties of morphological, syntactic, and lexical form are associated with particular semantic, pragmatic, and discourse functions. Constructions are key components of cognitive linguistic and functional theories of language. These usage-based theories of language acquisition hold that we learn constructions by engaging in communication. Thus an individual's creative linguistic competence emerges from the combination of two things: the memories of all of the utterances encountered in communicative situations, and the induction of regularities in those utterances based on frequency (Ellis, 2002).

Many of the constructions we know are quite specific and are based on particular lexical items ranging from a simple "Wonderful!" to increasingly complex formulas like "One, two, three," "Once upon a time," or "Won the battle, lost the war." We have come to learn these patterns simply as a result of repeated usage. A major characteristic of the environments that are relevant to human cognition is that they are fundamentally probabilistic: every stimulus is ambiguous, as is any utterance or piece of language. Each of these examples of formulaic constructions begins with the sound "wʌn." At the point of hearing this initial sound, what should the appropriate interpretation be? A general property of human perception is that when a sensation is associated with more than one reality, unconscious processes weigh the odds, and we perceive the most probable thing. Psycholinguistic analyses demonstrate that fluent language users are sensitive to the relative probabilities of occurrence of different constructions in the speech stream. Since learners have experienced many more tokens (particular examples) of *one* than they have *won*, in the absence of any further information, they favor the interpretation of *one* over *won*.

The fact that high-frequency constructions are more readily processed than low-frequency ones is testament to associative learning from usage. Let's think about words, though the same is true for letters, morphemes, syntactic patterns, and all other types of construction. Through experience, a learner's perceptual system becomes tuned to expect constructions according to their probability of occurrence in the input, with words like one or won occurring more frequently than words like seventeen or synecdoche.

The learner's initial noticing of a new word can result in an explicit memory that binds its features into a realization of its whole form, such as the spoken sequence "wʌn" or the orthographic sequence *one*. As a result of this, a detector unit for that word, whose job is to signal the word's presence, or "fire," whenever its features are present in the input, is added to the learner's perception system. Every word detector has a resting level of activation and some threshold level that, when exceeded, will cause the detector to fire. When the component features are present in the environment, they send activation to the detector that adds to its resting level, thus increasing it. If this increase is sufficient to bring the level above threshold, the detector fires. With each firing of the detector, the new resting level is slightly higher than the old one—the detector is said to be *primed*. This means it will need less activation from the environment in order to reach threshold and fire the next time that feature occurs. Features that occur frequently acquire consistently high resting levels. Their resting level of activity is heightened by the memory of repeated prior activations. Thus our pattern-recognition units for higher-frequency words require less evidence from the sensory data before they reach the threshold necessary for firing.

The same is true for the strength of the mappings from form to interpretation. Each time "wʌn" is properly interpreted as *one* this connection is strengthened. Each time "wʌn" signals *won*, this is tallied too, as are the less frequent occasions when it forewarns of "wonderland." Thus the strengths of form-meaning associations are summed over experience. The resultant network of associations—a semantic network comprising the structured inventory of a speaker's knowledge of their language—is so tuned that the spread of activation upon hearing the formal cue "wʌn" reflects prior probabilities.

There are many additional factors that qualify this simple picture. The relationship between frequency of usage and activation threshold is not linear but follows a curvilinear "power law of practice" whereby the effects of practice are greatest at early stages of learning but diminish thereafter (see DeKeyser, chapter 6, this volume, for discussion of the power law of practice). The amount of learning induced from an experience of a form-function association depends upon the salience of the form and the functional importance of the interpretation. The learning of a form-function association is interfered with if the learner already knows another form that cues that interpretation (e.g., "Yesterday I walked"; see VanPatten's *Lexical Primacy Principle*, Chapter 7), or another interpretation for an ambiguous form (e.g., the preposition *a* in Spanish meaning *to* but also used as a direct object case marker). Some cues are much more reliable signals of an interpretation than others (e.g., word order is a more reliable cue to the subject role in English than is animacy). Knowing the most probable interpretation of individual cues is not sufficient; context is important too, with cue interpretation probabilities combining sequentially to qualify interpretation. Thus, for example, the interpretation of 'wʌn' in the context "Alice in wʌn . . ." is already clear.

Rational Language Processing

Indeed, it has been argued that such associative underpinnings allow language users to be *rational* in the sense that their understanding of the way language works is the best mental model possible, given their linguistic experience to date. The words that they are likely to hear next, the most likely senses of these words, the linguistic constructions they are most likely to utter next, the syllables they are likely to hear next, the graphemes they are likely to read next, the interpretations that are most relevant, and the rest of what is coming next across all levels of language representation, are made more readily available to them by their language processing systems. Their unconscious language representation systems are tuned to predict the linguistic constructions that are most likely to be relevant in the ongoing discourse context, optimally preparing them for comprehension and production (Ellis, 2006a).

Language learning is thus an intuitive statistical learning problem, one that involves the associative learning of representations that reflect the probabilities of occurrence of form-function mappings. Learners have to figure language out. Rational analysis shows that this figuring is achieved, and communication optimized, by considering the frequency, recency, and context of constructions. These are the factors that determine the likelihood of a piece of information being needed in the world. Frequency, recency, and context are likewise the three most fundamental influences on human cognition, linguistic and non-linguistic alike.

Exemplar-based Abstraction and Attraction

Although much of language use is formulaic, economically recycling constructions that have been memorized from prior use, we are not limited to these specific constructions in our language processing. Some constructions are a little more open in scope, like the slot-and-frame greeting pattern ["Good" + (time-of-day)], which generates examples like "Good morning," and "Good afternoon." Others are abstract, broad ranging, and generative, such as the schemata that represent more complex morphological (e.g., [NounStem-PL]), syntactic (e.g., [Adj Noun]), and rhetorical (e.g., the iterative listing structure, [the (), the (), the (), . . ., together they . . .]) patterns. Usage-based theories investigate how the acquisition of these productive patterns and other rule-like regularities of language are *exemplar-based*, with generalizations coming from frequency-biased abstraction of regularities from similar constructions.

Prototypes, the exemplars that are most typical of their categories, are those that are similar to many members of their category but not similar to members of other categories. People more quickly classify sparrows as birds than they do birds with less common features or feature combinations like geese or albatrosses. They do so on the basis of an unconscious frequency analysis of the birds they have known, with the prototype reflecting the central tendencies of the distributions of the relevant features. Although we don't go around consciously counting features, we nevertheless have very accurate knowledge of the underlying distributions and their most usual settings.

We are really good at this. Research in cognitive psychology demonstrates that such implicit tallying is the raw basis of human pattern recognition, categorization, and rational cognition. As the world is classified, so language is classified. As for the birds, so for their plurals. The sparrows, geese, and albatrosses examples illustrate similar processes in the acquisition of patterns of language. Psycholinguistic research demonstrates that people are faster at generating plurals for the prototype case that is exemplified by many types, and are slower and less accurate at generating irregular cases, those that go against the central tendency and that have few "friends" (e.g., exemplars similar in form that operate in similarly deviant manners; compare the plurals of moose, goose, and noose). These examples make it clear that there are no 1:1 mappings between cues and their outcome interpretations. Associative learning theory demonstrates that the more reliable the mapping between a cue and its outcome, the more readily it is learned. Consider an ESL learner trying to learn from naturalistic input what –s at the ends of words might signify. Plural –s, third person singular present –s, and possessive –s, are all homophonous with each other as well as with the contracted allomorphs of copula and auxiliary be. This is illustrated in Figure 5–1.

Connectionist models of language acquisition are used to investigate the representations that result when simple associative learning mechanisms are exposed to complex language evidence of this type. Connectionist simulations are massively parallel systems of artificial neurons that use simple learning processes. From the large numbers of stored exemplars, these processes abstract information (generalizations) based on frequency. Connectionist simulations show how the prototype case emerges as the prominent underlying structural

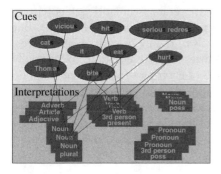

FIGURE 5–1.   The variety of contingencies between the –s morpheme in English and its functional interpretations make this a relatively low reliability cue.

regularity, and how minority subpatterns of inflection regularity—such as the English plural subpatterns discussed above—also emerge as smaller, less powerful generalizations. These generalizations are less powerful because they are less frequent; yet they are nonetheless powerful enough to attract friends that are structurally just like them (e.g., swim, swam, swum and drink, drank, drunk).

Emergent Relations and Patterns

Complex systems, such as the weather, ecosystems, economies, and societies, are those that involve the interactions of many different parts. These share the key aspect that many of their systematicities are *emergent*: They develop over time in complex, sometimes surprising, dynamic, adaptive ways. Meteorologists have developed rules and principles of the phenomena of the planet and its atmosphere that allow the prediction of weather. Geologists have outlined rules and principles to describe and summarize the successive changes in the Earth's crust. But these rules are the descriptions and heuristics of science. They describe emergent patterns. The rules themselves play no causal role in shifting even a grain of sand or a molecule of water. It is the interaction of water and rocks that smoothes the irregularities and grinds the pebbles and sand. Emergentists believe that many of the systematicities of language that are captured in linguistic analyses—for example, the parts of speech used to categorize different words, the syntactic roles used to describe different sentence parts, or the principles and parameters of UG—all play a similar role to the meteorologists' or geologists' descriptions of their field and have a similar causal status. They are phenomena to be explained. The emergentist study of language acquisition examines how these regularities emerge as learners' perceptual, cognitive, motor, and social functions induce structure.

Emergent language representation: From blank slate to language transfer. Our neural apparatus is highly plastic in its initial state. It is not entirely a blank slate, because there are broad genetic constraints on the usual networks of system-level connections and on the broad timetable of maturation and myelination. Nevertheless the cortex of the brain is broadly equipotent in terms of the types of information it can represent (Elman et al., 1996). But from this starting point, it quickly responds to the input patterns it receives, and through associative learning, it optimizes its representations to rationally model the particular world of experience of each particular individual. The term *neural plasticity* summarizes the fact that the brain is tuned by experience and that theories that rely heavily upon the inheritance of detailed knowledge representations are difficult to conceive of in neurological terms. Our neural endowment provides a general-purpose cognitive apparatus, embodied within the general human form that filters, constrains, and determines our experience, for each of us to learn about our particular world. In the first few years of life, the human learning mechanism optimizes its representations of first language from the cumulative sample of first language input. One result of this process is that the initial state for SLA is no longer a plastic system; it is one that is already tuned and committed to the L1. Transfer phenomena thus pervade SLA (James, 1980; Lado, 1957; Odlin, 1989).

Associative aspects of transfer: Learned attention and interference. Associative learning provides the rational mechanisms for first language acquisition from input analysis and usage, allowing just about every human being to acquire fluency in their native tongue. Yet although second language learners may be surrounded by language, not all of it "goes in," and SLA is typically much less successful than first language acquisitions (L1A). This is Corder's distinction between input (the available target language) and intake (that subset of input that actually gets in and that the learner utilizes in some way) (Corder, 1967). Does this mean that SLA cannot be understood according to the general principles of associative learning that underpin other aspects of human cognition? If L1A is rational, does this mean that SLA is fundamentally irrational? No, paradoxically perhaps, it is the very achievements of associative learning in first language acquisition that limit the input analysis of L2 and that result in the shortcomings of SLA. Associative learning theory explains these limitations too, because associative learning in animals and humans alike is affected by learned attention (Ellis, 2006b).

We can consider just one example here. Many grammatical meaning-form relationships are both low in salience as well as redundant in the understanding of the meaning of an utterance. It is often unnecessary to interpret inflections marking grammatical meanings such as tense because they are usually accompanied by adverbs that indicate the temporal reference: "If the learner knows the French word for 'yesterday', then in the utterance *Hier nous sommes allés au cinéma* (Yesterday we went to the movies) both the auxiliary and past participle are redundant past markers." (Terrell, 1991, p. 59; see also VanPatten, Chapter 7). This redundancy is much more influential in second rather than first language acquisition. Children learning their native language only acquire the meanings of temporal adverbs quite late in development. But second language learners already know about adverbs from their first language experience, and adverbs are both salient and reliable in their communicative functions while tense markers are neither. Thus, the second language expression of temporal reference begins with a phase where reference is established by adverbials alone, and the grammatical expression of tense and aspect thereafter emerges only slowly, if at all (Bardovi-Harlig, 2000).

This is an example of the associative learning phenomenon of "blocking," whereby redundant cues are overshadowed for the historical reasons that learners' first language experience leads them to look elsewhere for the cues to interpretation. Under normal L1 circumstances, usage optimally tunes the language system to the input; however, in the L2 situation, forms of low salience may be blocked by prior L1 experience, and all the extra input in the world may not result in advancement.

Dialectic

Associative L2 learning from naturalistic usage can thus fall far short of a native-like endstate. The usual social–interactional or pedagogical reactions to such non-nativelike utterances involve an interaction partner or instructor intentionally bringing additional evidence to the attention of the learner. In these ways, SLA can be freed from the bounds of L1-induced selective attention by some means of intervention that is socially provided (Lantolf & Thorne, chapter 11, this volume) and that recruits the learner's explicit conscious processing. Thus SLA is also *dialectic*, involving the learner in a conscious tension between the conflicting forces of their current interlanguage productions and the evidence of feedback, either linguistic, pragmatic, or metalinguistic, that allows socially scaffolded development.

Cognitive Contributions to SLA

Reviews of the experimental and quasi-experimental investigations into the effectiveness of explicit learning and L2 instruction (Ellis & Laporte, 1997; Spada, 1997), particularly the comprehensive meta-analysis of Norris & Ortega (2000), demonstrate that focused L2 instruction results in large target-oriented gains, that explicit types of instruction are more effective than implicit types, and that the effectiveness of L2 instruction is durable.

The Associative–Cognitive CREED is particularly concerned with the ways in which explicit and implicit learning processes interact in SLA. Ellis (2005) argues that the primary mechanism of explicit learning is the initial registration of pattern recognizers for constructions that are then tuned and integrated into the system by implicit learning during subsequent input processing.

WHAT COUNTS AS EVIDENCE?

Like other enterprises in cognitive science and cognitive neuroscience, the Associative–Cognitive CREED does not adhere to any specific research methodology or evidence. Data come from diverse approaches to research: educational experimental designs, psycholinguistic studies of sentence processing, analyses of learner production, and brain imaging and neuroscience. It is important that theories of SLA accord with what else we know about human learning. Thus, the CREED may draw upon evidence from studies related to comprehension, production, interaction, and computer simulations in order to build its case for the associative nature of L2 learning.

COMMON MISUNDERSTANDINGS

Broad frameworks, particularly those that revive elements of no-longer-fashionable theories such as behaviorism, open the potential for misunderstandings, of which we will mention a few here. Common misconceptions include that connectionism is the new behaviorism; that connectionist models cannot explain creativity and that connectionist models have no regard for internal representation; and that cognitive approaches deny influence of social factors, or motivational aspects, or—paradoxically—learners' beliefs, desires, or experiences of language learning on SLA. These misunderstandings are the result of focusing on one piece of the larger whole. The pieces of that whole interact, and when we acknowledge these interactions, we see how the separate components can limit each other, can mediate and moderate each other, and in other cases can even amplify each other in positive feedback relationships. A clear example of the interactions of frequency, salience, and reliability of mapping can be seen in the choice of an exemplary study that follows here. A more general moral is that it is important to adopt a complex systems framework that views SLA as a dynamic process in which regularities and system emerge from the interaction of people, their conscious selves, and their brains, using language in their societies, cultures, and world.

AN EXEMPLARY STUDY: GOLDSCHNEIDER
AND DEKEYSER (2001)

As introduced by VanPatten and Williams in chapter 2, SLA follows predictable and reliable developmental sequences. Goldschneider and DeKeyser (2001) wanted to determine the degree to which one well-attested order of acquisition, that concerning grammatical morphemes in English, is the result of aspects of the input such as frequency, perceptual salience, morphophonological regularity, and semantic complexity. Frequency, the reliability of the mappings between cues and their interpretations, and salience, as explained above, are essential determinants of associative learning in humans and animals alike. Therefore, can this aspect of SLA be equally understood in these terms?

Their study is a meta-analysis, a "study of studies." Meta-analysis is an important and powerful research tool that allows the systematic and replicable overview of findings relating to a particular question by means of the quantitative pooling of the sizes of the effects found in all of the relevant empirical studies. It is the best way to pull together the research data into one large body, review the findings, and summarize its trends (Norris & Ortega, 2006).

Goldschneider and DeKeyser (2001) analyzed 12 morpheme order studies that, in the 25 years following Brown (1973), investigated the order of L2 acquisition of the grammatical functors; progressive *–ing*; plural *–s*; possessive *–s*; articles *a, an, the*; third person singular present *–s*; and regular past *–ed*, and established a common order of acquisition for these structures in L2 that was broadly reliable across learners of different age and first-language backgrounds.

Brown (1973) had investigated the English L1 order of acquisition of grammatical morphemes in a naturalistic corpus of the speech of three children, Adam, Eve, and Sarah. Dulay and Burt (1973) followed this by investigating the order of acquisition in 151 Spanish-speaking children, aged 6–8, learning English as an L2 in the United States. Sentences were elicited via the Bilingual Syntax Measure (BSM), which involved cartoon descriptions to establish the percentage suppliance of different grammatical morphemes in obligatory contexts. Bailey, Madden, and Krashen (1974) subsequently tested the order of acquisition in 73 adults, 33 of whom were Spanish-speakers and the rest represented 11 other languages. These adult L2 learners showed similar orders for the acquisition of English morphemes, regardless of their mother tongue:

1. plural *–s*   "Books"
2. progressive *–ing*   "John go*ing*"
3. copula *be*   "John *is* here"/"John's here"
4. auxiliary *be*   "John *is* going"/"John's going"
5. articles *the/a*   "*The* books"
6. irregular past tense   "John *went*"
7. third person *–s*   "John likes books"
8. possessive *'s*   "John's book"

These and ten other studies showed remarkable commonality in the orders of acquisition of these functors across a wide range of learners of English as a second (and first) language. Although a number of possible explanations of these factors have been proposed, including frequency in the input, semantic complexity, grammatical complexity, phonological form, and perceptual salience, with input frequency being the favored major cause (Larsen-Freeman,

1975), nevertheless, Larsen-Freeman concluded that "[a] single explanation seems insufficient to account for the findings" (p. 419).

Goldschneider and DeKeyser (2001) pooled the studies, developed objective operationalizations of each of these aspects of the input, and analyzed their weights as individual independent causes of the observed acquisition order using multiple regression analysis.

Input frequency was assessed from a corpus of spoken English. Perceptual salience was composed from three subfactors: the number of phones in the functor (phonetic substance), the presence or absence of a vowel in the surface form (syllabicity), and the total relative sonority of the functor. As explained above, Goldschneider and DeKeyser's factor of morphophonological regularity relates to reliability of form-function mapping because conditioned phonological variation (for example, the [s, z, əz] allomorphs of plural –s, possessive –s, and third person singular –s) results in multiple forms of the cue and thus a less clear mapping between the interpretation and one particular cue, while homophony with other grammatical factors results in a less clear mapping between the cue and one particular interpretation. Semantic complexity measured the number of meanings expressed by a given form (e.g., third person singular –s expresses person, number, and present tense). Finally, syntactic category weighted the morphemes according to whether they were lexical or functional items, and within each of these groups whether they were free or bound morphemes (free morphemes are typically acquired before bound morphemes, again suggesting explanations in terms of salience).

Oral production data from the 12 studies, together involving 924 subjects, were pooled. On their own, each of these factors significantly correlated with acquisition order: perceptual salience $r = 0.63$, frequency $r = 0.44$, morphophonological regularity $r = -0.41$, syntactic category $r = 0.68$, and semantic complexity $r = -0.41$. When these five factors were combined in a multiple regression analysis, they jointly explain 71% of the variance in acquisition order, with perceptual salience having the highest predictive power on its own.

Each of the factors of frequency, reliability of form-function mapping, and perceptual salience is a significant predictor of acquisition order; together they explain a substantial amount of acquisition difficulty. That these stimulus factors are the major determinants of associative learning in animals (Rescorla & Wagner, 1972) strongly supports explanations in terms of associative learning from input analysis and usage-based acquisition.

Goldschneider and DeKeyser's analysis could not investigate the modulating effects of transfer from learners of different L1 backgrounds (Ellis, 2006b) because, as they explain themselves on p. 31, the original studies did not provide sufficient details of this. Nor, of course, could they look at the detailed sentence contexts of the morphemes as they had appeared in the learners' particular input histories.

EXPLANATION OF OBSERVED FINDINGS IN SLA

Observation # 1. Exposure to input is necessary for SLA.   The Associative–Cognitive CREED is input driven. As with other statistical estimations, a large and representative sample of language is required for the learner to abstract a rational model that is a good fit to the language data. Input is necessary, and it is sufficient for successful L1A but not for SLA. This is because the initial state for SLA is a no longer a blank slate: The learner's language representations, processing routines, and attention to language, are tuned and committed to the L1. The optimal solution for L2 is not the same as for L1, and the shortcomings of SLA stem from these various aspects of transfer and learned attention.

Observation # 2. A good deal of SLA happens incidentally.   The Associative–Cognitive CREED holds that the large majority of language learning is implicit. All of the counting that underpins the setting of thresholds and the tuning of the system to the probabilities of the input evidence is unconscious. So also is the emergence of structural regularities, prototypes, attractors, and other system regularities. At any one point we are conscious of one particular communicative meaning; yet meanwhile the cognitive operations involved in each of these usages are tuning the system, unconsciously, without us being aware of it (Ellis, 2002). We "know" far too many linguistic regularities for us to have explicitly learned them.

Observation # 3. Learners come to know more than what they have been exposed to in the input.   The Logical Problem of Language Acquisition argues that second language learners' grammars, like those of children learning their first language, are said to be underdetermined by the input, and some linguists therefore propose that learners have internal mental representations of how the language works (putative abstract rules that govern sentence structure) that contain information that could not have been learned by exposure. Productivity, abstraction, and generalization are natural features of connectionist systems—we have already seen how, like children, they produce overgeneralization errors such as *goed*. The processes of this generativity are demonstrable by simulation. The study of implicit human cognition shows that we know far more about the world than we are aware of or have been explicitly taught. Prototype effects are one clear and ubiquitous example of this: We have never seen the prototype deer but we will classify it faster and more accurately than examples further from the central tendency, and we will call it a deer, and not a horse, with great facility. Different notions, different constructions. VanPatten and Williams in chapter 1 cite the UG argument that the acquisition of *wanna* contractions shows that learners have abstract rules involving *wh*-traces, whereby contraction is not possible "across a trace," rules that are neither taught in ESL classes nor evidenced from the language that learners are exposed to. However, other linguists explain that transitive *want NP to* and intransitive *want to* are different lexicalized constructions, and *wanna* is only possible (or is very much more probable) as a contraction of the latter, a very natural shortening given that the sequence *want + to* happens much more frequently in the intransitive construction than in the transitive one (Bybee, 2002; Sag & Fodor, 1996). Again, different notions, different constructions. We do not have explanations of the emergence of all of the linguistic representations that play their part in UG accounts of language competence, any more than generativists have explained the inheritance and neural instantiation of these. The future will tell whether the logical problem will be solved better by inheritance or emergence. Meanwhile, it is clear that structure-dependence and hierarchical organization, factors which have been traditionally held up as unique and defining features of language, are actually properties of all sequential routines, scripts, and motor behaviors—they, at least, are naturally emergent properties.

Observation # 4. Learners' output (speech) often follows predictable paths with predictable stages in the acquisition of a given structure. As in first language acquisition, SLA is characterized not by complete idiosyncrasy or randomness but rather by predictable errors and stages during the course of development: Interlanguage is systematic. The Associative–Cognitive CREED believes that these systematicities arise from regularities in the input; for example, constructions that are much more frequent, that are consistent in their mappings and exhibit high contingency, that have many friends, and that are salient are likely to be acquired earlier than those that do not have these features. The Goldschneider and DeKeyser (2001) study featured earlier clearly demonstrates how such factors interact in determining the acquisition order of one specific SLA system. Connectionist simulations allow the investigation of how systematicities emerge from the conspiracy of such factors.

Observation # 5. Second language learning is variable in its outcome. Our linguistic systems are not dictionaries or grammars; they are not books or lists or reference tables, frozen in time. The notion of fixed cognitive categories, linguistic and non-linguistic both, is a myth: Conceptual categories are dynamically construed (Smith & Samuelson, 1997). Replace these static notions with those of activity, dance, and dynamic patterns of a large community of agents in patterns of activity that are context- and perspective-sensitive, reflecting both past and current activity of the language systems in interaction with the rest of the cognitive system (Ellis, 2005). For example, (a) priming effects show how learners are more likely to use constructions that have been recently used; (b) the more the working memory demands of a task, the more they will use memorized patterns and formulaic speech; the less the working memory load, the more creative their constructions might be; and (c) sociolinguistic and pragmatic factors spill over into the construction process. Different contexts, different dynamics. Each of the components of the system can affect the process and outcome success.

Observation # 6. Second language learning is variable across linguistic subsystems.   Language representation is diverse in its contents and spans lexicon, morphology, syntax, phonology, pragmatics, and sociolinguistics, among others. Within any of these areas of language, learners may master some structures before they acquire others. Such variability is a natural consequence of input factors such as exemplar type and token frequency, recency, context, salience, contingency, regularity, reliability, and the conspiracy of friends and enemies, along with the various other associative learning factors that affect the emergence of regularities.

Thus development, which is for the most part gradual and incremental, also evidences sudden changes in performance, suggesting occasional fundamental restructuring of the underlying grammar. Consider the first language acquisition of past tense marking. Learners initially fail to mark past tense; their first marking involves frequent irregular verbs such as *came* and *went*; next appear regular marking (addition of the default ending) in verbs such as *talked* and *cooked*, and the productivity of this schema is evidenced by the disappearance of irregulars from the interlanguage as they are replaced by overextensions (incorrect forms that have regular endings like *goed, wented*). The stage at which irregulars disappear and are replaced by regularized forms is sudden and suggests that learners' grammars are restructuring themselves to make everything regular even though such forms as *goed* are not part of the input. Eventually, of course, the irregulars reappear.

Observation # 7. There are limits on the effects of frequency on SLA.   Although there is no simple and direct correlation between input frequency and acquisition, broadly, high frequency elements are acquired earlier than low frequency elements. Frequency interacts with many other factors in language learning, such as salience, complexity, and individual differences. The study of associative learning concerns the factors that determine how much is acquired from each learning experience and how each increment is integrated into a representational system (Shanks, 1995).

Observation # 8. There are limits on the effect of a learner's first language on SLA.   At every level of language, there is evidence of L1 influence, both negative and positive. Although it is no longer considered the clear and direct influence proposed in the Contrastive Analysis Hypothesis, its significance in the language learning process seems incontrovertible. The Associative–Cognitive CREED considers how various cross-linguistic phenomena of learned selective attention—blocking, latent inhibition, perceptual learning, interference and other effects of salience, transfer, and inhibition—all filter and color the perception of the second language (Ellis, 2006a,b).

Observation # 9. There are limits on the effects of instruction on SLA. L1-tuned learned attention limits the amount of intake from L2 input, thus restricting the endstate of SLA. The cognitive and dialectic aspects of the CREED consider how attention to language form is sometimes necessary to allow learners to notice some blocked aspect of the language form. Reviews of the empirical studies of instruction demonstrate that tapping into learners' conscious and explicit learning processes can be effective.

However, instruction is not always effective. Any classroom teacher can provide anecdotal evidence that what is taught is not learned. But this observation can be made for all aspects of the curriculum, not just language. Explicit knowledge about language is of a different stuff from that of the implicit representational systems, and it need not impact upon acquisition from a large variety of reasons. Explicit instruction can be ill-timed and out of synchrony with development (Pienemann, 1998, chapter 8, this volume); it can be confusing; it can be easily forgotten; it can be dissociated from usage (Ellis, 1993), lacking in transfer-appropriateness and thus never brought to bear so as to tune attention to the relevant input features during usage; it can be unmotivating; it can fail in so many ways. Ineffective instruction is all too easy; the challenge is the reverse.

Observation # 10. There are limits on the effects of output (learner production) on language acquisition.   The CREED holds that there are a variety of mechanisms by which the demands of output can encourage creative construction. The conscious processes involved here allow a dynamic interface whereby explicit knowledge can influence implicit language learning (Ellis, 2005, section 4). Output is also a driving force of chunking, proceduralization, and automatization. There are thus a variety of roles of output in the SLA. However, you cannot learn a second language by output alone.

CONCLUSION

In the terms of chapter 1, the Associative–Cognitive CREED is perhaps too broad to qualify as a theory. But it does aspire to being a useful framework that relates many of the complex agents that underlie the dynamic nature of consciousness and the interface between explicit and implicit learning. No single

factor alone is a sufficient cause of SLA. Language is a complex adaptive system. It comprises the interactions of many players: people who want to communicate and a world to be talked about. It operates across many different
levels, different human configurations, and different timescales. Take out any
one of these levels and a different pattern emerges, a different conclusion is
reached. But nevertheless, like other complex dynamic systems, there are many
systematicities that, like observations 1–10, emerge to form the central phenomena of SLA.

DISCUSSION QUESTIONS

1. One critique of the type of approach Ellis takes is that it is an updated
   version of behaviorism. Do you agree with this criticism? How would
   Ellis respond?
2. Explain the difference between rule-based and rule-like behavior.
3. How does the Associative–Cognitive CREED address explicit and implicit learning and the nature of their interface?
4. Consider the case of the acquisition order of the present perfect and the
   pluperfect from Bardovi-Harlig (chapter 4). The functionalist approach
   offers one explanation for the order of emergence. How would the Associative–Cognitive CREED account for the order? What evidence might
   distinguish the two interpretations?
5. As we saw in chapter 3, the principle foundation of the approach White
   takes is the *poverty of the stimulus* (POS) situation or the *logical problem of
   language acquisition*. How does the Associative–Cognitive CREED view
   the POS? (You might want to review the examples in White's chapter
   before answering.)

SUGGESTED FURTHER READINGS

Croft, W., & Cruise, A. (2004). *Cognitive linguistics*. Cambridge: Cambridge
University Press.
    A comprehensive introduction to the fast-growing field of cognitive
linguistics.
Elman, J. L., Bates, E. A., Johnson, M. H., Karmiloff-Smith, A., Parisi, D., &
Plunkett, K. (1996). *Rethinking innateness: A connectionist perspective on
development*. Cambridge, MA: MIT Press.
    This book marked a sea change in our understanding of learning and
development. Six coauthors representing cognitive psychology, connection-

ism, neurobiology, and dynamical-systems theory synthesize a new emergentist framework for cognitive development with special focus on language acquisition.

Larsen-Freeman, D., & Ellis, N. C. (Eds.) (2006). *Language emergence: Implications for applied linguistics. Applied Linguistics, 27,* (4).

A special issue focusing on emergentist accounts of topics including complexity in interlanguage, the multilingual lexicon, the development of complex syntactic structures, bilingual language acquisition, metaphor in discourse, and language evolution, with commentaries from cognitive and sociocultural perspectives.

MacWhinney, B. (Ed.). (1999). *The emergence of language.* Mahwah, NJ: Lawrence Erlbaum Associates.

Proceedings of the founding conference for Emergentist Approaches to Language. Child language researchers, linguists, psycholinguists, and modelers using a range of formalisms present emergentist accounts of a wide range of linguistic phenomena.

Robinson, P. (Ed.). (2001). *Cognition and second language instruction.* Cambridge: Cambridge University Press.

Tutorial reviews of second language instruction and acquisition as seen from cognitive psychology. Topics include attention, memory, processing, learnability, connectionism and the competition model, and individual differences.

Robinson, P., & Ellis, N. C. (Eds.). (in press). *Handbook of cognitive linguistics and second language acquisition.* Mahwah, NJ: Lawrence Erlbaum Associates.

A handbook of cognitive linguistics. The first half brings together key figures in the development of cognitive linguistics as it relates to first language acquisition. The second half has second-language researchers develop these themes for SLA.

Tomasello, M. (2003). *Constructing a language.* Boston, MA: Harvard University Press.

A thorough account of child language acquisition from the perspectives of psychology and construction grammar.

REFERENCES

Bailey, N., Madden, C., & Krashen, S. (1974). Is there a 'natural sequence' in adult second language learning? *Language Learning, 24,* 235–243.

Bardovi-Harlig, K. (2000). *Tense and aspect in second language acquisition: Form, meaning, and use.* Oxford: Blackwell.

Brown, R. (1973). *A first language: The early stages*. Cambridge, MA: Harvard University Press.

Bybee, J. (2002). Phonological evidence for exemplar storage of multiword sequences. *Studies in Second Language Acquisition, 24*, 215–221.

Corder, S. P. (1967). The significance of learners' errors. *International Review of Applied Linguistics, 5*, 161–169.

Dulay, H. C., & Burt, M. K. (1973). Should we teach children syntax? *Language Learning, 23*, 245–258.

Ellis, N. C. (1993). Rules and instances in foreign language learning: Interactions of explicit and implicit knowledge. *The European Journal of Cognitive Psychology, 5*, 289–318.

———. (2002). Frequency effects in language processing: A review with implications for theories of implicit and explicit language acquisition. *Studies in Second Language Acquisition, 24*, 143–188.

———. (2005). At the interface: Dynamic interactions of explicit and implicit language knowledge. *Studies in Second Language Acquisition, 27*, 305–352.

———. (2006a). Language acquisition as rational contingency learning. *Applied Linguistics, 27*.

———. (2006b). Selective attention and transfer phenomena in SLA: Contingency, cue competition, salience, interference, overshadowing, blocking, and perceptual learning. *Applied Linguistics, 27(4)*.

Ellis, N. C., & Laporte, N. (1997). Contexts of acquisition: Effects of formal instruction and naturalistic exposure on second language acquisition. In A. M. DeGroot & J. F. Kroll (Eds.), *Tutorials in bilingualism: Psycholinguistic perspectives* (pp. 53–83). Mahwah, NJ: Lawrence Erlbaum Associates.

Elman, J. L., Bates, E. A., Johnson, M. H., Karmiloff-Smith, A., Parisi, D., & Plunkett, K. (1996). *Rethinking innateness: A connectionist perspective on development*. Cambridge, MA: MIT Press.

Goldschneider, J. M., & DeKeyser, R. (2001). Explaining the "natural order of L2 morpheme acquisition" in English: A meta-analysis of multiple determinants. *Language Learning, 51*, 1–50.

James, C. (1980). *Contrastive analysis*. London: Longman.

Lado, R. (1957). *Linguistics across cultures: Applied linguistics for language teachers*. Ann Arbor: University of Michigan Press.

Larsen-Freeman, D. (1975). The acquisition of grammatical morphemes by adult ESL students. *TESOL Quarterly, 9*, 409–419.

Norris, J., & Ortega, L. (2000). Effectiveness of L2 instruction: A research synthesis and quantitative meta-analysis. *Language Learning, 50*, 417–528.

Norris, J., & Ortega, L. (Eds.). (2006). *Synthesizing research on language learning and teaching*: Amsterdam: Benjamins.

Odlin, T. (1989). *Language transfer*. New York: Cambridge University Press.

Pienemann, M. (1998). *Language Processing and Second Language Development: Processability Theory*. Amsterdam: Benjamins.

Rescorla, R. A., & Wagner, A. R. (1972). A theory of Pavlovian conditioning: Variations in the effectiveness of reinforcement and nonreinforcement. In A. H. Black & W. F.

Prokasy (Eds.), *Classical conditioning II: Current theory and research* (pp. 64–99). New York: Appleton-Century-Crofts.

Sag, I. A., & Fodor, J. D. (1996). A traceless account of extraction phenomena. *Languages, 30*, 8–31.

Shanks, D. R. (1995). *The psychology of associative learning*. New York: Cambridge University Press.

Smith, L. B., & Samuelson, L. K. (1997). Perceiving and remembering: category stability, variability, and development. In K. Lamberts & D. Shanks (Eds.), *Knowledge, concepts and categories* (pp. 161–195). Hove, UK: Psychology Press.

Spada, N. (1997). Form-focused instruction and second language acquisition: A review of classroom and laboratory research. *Language Teaching Research, 30*, 73–87.

Terrell, T. (1991). The role of grammar instruction in a communicative approach. *The Modern Language Journal, 75*, 52–63.

6

Skill Acquisition Theory

Robert DeKeyser
University of Maryland

Skill acquisition theory accounts for how people progress in learning a variety of skills, from initial learning to advanced proficiency. Skills studied include both cognitive and psychomotor skills, in domains that range from classroom learning to applications in sports and industry. Research in this area ranges from quite theoretical (computational modeling of skill acquisition, the place of skills in an architecture of the mind) to quite applied (how to sequence activities for maximal learning efficiency in areas as diverse as teaching high school algebra, tutoring college physics, coaching professional basketball, or training fighter pilots).

The scientific roots of skill acquisition theory are found in various branches of psychology, but this research area has proven to be remarkably resilient through various developments in psychology, from behaviorism to cognitivism to connectionism. After all, the practical needs as well as the fundamental theoretical questions and the basic empirical facts remain, regardless of the continuous developments in psychological theory, methodology, and terminology.

THE THEORY AND ITS CONSTRUCTS

The basic claim of skill acquisition theory is that the learning of a wide variety of skills shows a remarkable similarity in development from initial representation of knowledge through initial changes in behavior to eventual fluent, spontaneous, largely effortless, and highly skilled behavior, and that this set of phenomena can be accounted for by a set of basic principles common to the acquisition of all skills. The terminology in the previous sentence was deliberately chosen to be nontechnical and theory-neutral; it will come as no surprise that a theory that has been applied to so many domains over such a long period of time has seen its share of technical terms, which have varied with the area of psychology researchers have worked in and the types of skills they have studied. Generally speaking, however, researchers have posited three stages of development, whether they called them cognitive, associative, and autonomous, as Fitts and Posner (1967); or declarative, procedural, and automatic, as Anderson (e.g., 1982; 1993; Anderson, Bothell, Byrne, Douglass, Lebiere & Qin, 2004); or presentation, practice, and production, as Byrne (1986).

These three stages are characterized by large differences in the nature of knowledge and its use, as reflected in various forms such as introspection, verbalization, and, most importantly, various aspects of behavior, especially under demanding conditions. Initially a student, learner, apprentice, or trainee may acquire quite a bit of knowledge about a skill without ever even trying to use it. That knowledge may be acquired through perceptive observation and analysis of others engaged in skilled behavior (e.g., learning a new dance move) but most often is transmitted in verbal form from one who knows to one who does not (as in a parent or driving instructor teaching a teenager how to drive a car) and often through a combination of the two, when the "expert" demonstrates the behavior slowly while commenting on the relevant aspects (e.g., teaching a child how to swim or play tennis).

Next comes the stage of acting on this knowledge, turning it into a behavior, turning "knowledge that" into "knowledge how" or, in more technical terms, turning declarative knowledge into procedural knowledge. This proceduralization of knowledge is not particularly arduous or time consuming. Provided that the relevant declarative knowledge is available and drawn on in the execution of the target behavior, proceduralization can be complete after just a few trials/ instances. Anderson et al. (2004, p. 1046), for instance, point out that, in a typical psychology experiment, the participant is converting, *during the warm-up trials*, from a declarative representation and a slow interpretation of the task (as set forth in the experimenter's instructions) to a smooth, rapid, procedural execution of the task (for an example in second language learning, see DeKeyser, 1997, who argues that proceduralization was essentially complete after the first 16-item block of practice items). Yet, proceduralized knowledge has a big advantage over declarative knowledge. It no longer requires the individual to retrieve bits and pieces of information from memory to assemble them into a "program" for a specific behavior; instead, that program is now available as a ready-made chunk to be called up in its entirety each time the conditions for that behavior are met.

Once procedural knowledge has been acquired, there is still a long way to go before the relevant behavior can be consistently displayed with complete fluency or spontaneity, rarely showing any errors. In other words, the knowledge is not yet robust and fine-tuned. A large amount of practice is needed to decrease the time required to execute the task (reaction time), the percentage of errors (error rate), and the amount of attention required (and hence interference with/from other tasks). This practice leads to gradual automatization of knowledge. Automaticity is not an all-or-nothing affair. Even highly automatized behaviors are not 100% automatic, as becomes clear when we stumble walking down the stairs, when we realize we are driving too fast when engaged in an exciting conversation with a passenger, or when we stumble over our words while uttering a simple sentence in our native language.

A central concept in the study of skill acquisition is the power law of learning. It has been observed many times, for skills as different as making cigars out of tobacco leaves or writing computer programs, that both reaction time and error rate decrease as a consequence of practice. This decrease follows a very specific mathematical function referred to as the power law (because the amount of practice is entered in the form of an exponent in the equation describing this law). If the learning curves for reaction time and error rate for such a variety of skills share this very specific shape (and not even a quite similar one like that of an exponential function), then this shape must contain the key to some fundamental learning mechanisms. Since Newell and Rosenbloom's (1981) seminal article, a variety of hypotheses have been formulated to explain this robust empirical phenomenon. This chapter is not the place to discuss the relative merit of these hypotheses (for more discussion see DeKeyser, 2001), but what they all have in common is that they posit a qualitative change over time, as a result of practice, in the basic cognitive mechanisms used to execute the same task. What superficially seems like a set of smooth quantitative changes (reaction time and error rate declining following a power function) in fact reflects a qualitative change in mechanisms of knowledge retrieval, quite radical for a while, and then gradually stabilizing without ever reaching an absolute endpoint (hence the power curve illustrated in Figure 6.1).

Probably the most widely accepted interpretation of this change is that it represents first a shift from declarative to procedural knowledge (achieved rather quickly, hence the rather steep initial section of the curve), followed by a much slower process of automatization of procedural knowledge. The term

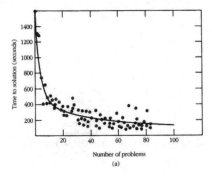

FIGURE 6–1. A sample graph of the power of learning curve.

automatization itself can be interpreted in various ways, ranging from a mere speed-up of the same basic mechanisms to a speed-up of a broader task through a qualitative change in its components. Again, we are not taking a position here on this point either (for more discussion see DeKeyser 2006, chapter 1), but we are using automatization in a more specific sense than just "improvement through practice" because we are reserving the term for the latter, flatter part of the learning curve, after the steep decline due to rapid proceduralization has taken place (see Figure 6–1).

Another point on which there is wide-spread agreement is that, regardless of the exact nature of the knowledge drawn on the later stages of development, this knowledge is much more specific than at the beginning and in fact so highly specific that it does not transfer well, even to what may seem quite similar tasks. A well-known example from the skill acquisition literature is reading versus writing computer programs (see Singley & Anderson, 1989), and an obvious parallel in the domain of language learning is comprehension versus production (DeKeyser, 1997; DeKeyser & Sokalski, 2001; Tanaka, 2001). Other examples, of course, would be transfer from speaking to writing, or from one situation to another (such as from orderly dialogue to argument with multiple interlocutors, or from the kitchen table to the board room). The implication for training is that two kinds of knowledge need to be fostered, both highly specific procedural knowledge, highly automatized for efficient use in the situations that the learner is most likely to confront in the immediate future, and also solid abstract declarative knowledge that can be called upon to be integrated into much broader, more abstract procedural rules, which are indispensable when confronting new contexts of use.

What is often overlooked is that this whole sequence of proceduralization and automatization cannot get started if the right conditions for proceduralization are not present (the declarative knowledge required by the task at hand, and a task set-up that allows for use of that declarative knowledge). Anderson, Fincham, and Douglass (1997), in particular, show convincingly that the combination of abstract rules and concrete examples is necessary to get learners past the declarative threshold into proceduralization. DeKeyser (2006) argues that this is precisely what is often lacking in language teaching in general and in preparing students for maximum benefit from a stay abroad in particular.

WHAT COUNTS AS EVIDENCE?

The oldest form of evidence in this area is behavioral in nature: reaction times, error rates, and differences in performance from one condition to another, such as interference from a secondary task. Any overview of the behavioral data should start with Newell and Rosenbloom (1981), not because theirs was the first study in this area but because the study was seminal in that it brought together empirical data from so many different studies about so many different forms of skill acquisition and proposed both a quantitative model (the power law) and a qualitative interpretation for this mountain of data. Some of the domains of learning included motor behavior, reading, decision-making, and problem-solving. For information on the individual studies included, see Newell and Rosenbloom's article. Major empirical studies since then include Anderson, Fincham, and Douglass (1997) on the role of rules and examples in the proceduralization of a simple reasoning task and Logan (1988, 1992, 2002) on the learning of a new form of arithmetic (with letters).

In the last 25 years, less direct evidence in the form of computational modeling has become very important in the study of skill acquisition, even more so than in other subfields of psychology. This line of evidence includes large amounts of work with a variety of computer models such as the various consecutive incarnations of ACT (see especially Anderson, 1993; Anderson & Lebiere, 1998; and Anderson et al., 2004), EPIC (Meyer & Kieras, 1997), SOAR (Newell, 1990), and 3CAPS (Just & Carpenter, 1992). In all such models, the aim is to show how a cognitive mechanism can work and with which implications for reaction time and error rate, but of course the model never proves that the processes taking place in the human mind are the same.

Only in the last 10 years or so have skill acquisition researchers begun to draw on what some would see as data that are even more direct than the behavioral data themselves, that is, neuro-imaging and other forms of neurological evidence such as evoked potentials (measures of electrophysiological activity in specific areas of the brain, experimentally linked to specific cognitive tasks).

Increasing use of techniques from cognitive neuroscience has yielded studies such as Raichle et al. (1994) using positron emission tomography (PET) to trace the effect of practice on the relative involvement of different brain areas in the same task (word generation), and Qin, Anderson, Silk, Stenger, and Carter (2004) using functional magnetic resonance imaging (fMRI) to investigate the effect of children's practice in algebra.

In sum, the behavioral data show the similarity in skill development across different cognitive domains (how reaction time and error rate develop as a result of practice); the neurological data show how different areas of the brain are involved to a different extent after different amounts of practice; and the computational models show the hypothetical inner workings of the mechanisms that cannot be observed directly through behavioral or neurological data.

As should be clear from the literature just cited, evidence for central constructs such as the power law, procedural knowledge, or automatization abounds in the psychological literature. What is harder to come by is empirical data that unambiguously point to a specific interpretation of these phenomena in terms of learning mechanisms. More importantly for our purposes here, very little research in the field of second language learning has explicitly set out to gather data from second language learners in order to test (a specific variant of) skill acquisition theory.

One of the reasons why research from a skill acquisition perspective is so rare in the field of second language acquisition is the methodology required. Experiments on skill acquisition typically involve rather large numbers of participants over rather long periods of time, yielding very large amounts of data for statistical analysis. Moreover, the collection of these data and the control required over the treatments and practice conditions requires a certain amount of investment in hardware and software.

This methodological challenge, combined with the fact that focus on form was out of fashion for a number of years in applied linguistics research, explains the small volume of directly relevant empirical research so far. The three studies that have tested the predictions of skill acquisition most directly are DeKeyser (1997), Robinson (1997), and de Jong (2005a,b). The former two each test one of two competing theories of skill acquisition with L2 data. DeKeyser (1997) found that the concepts of proceduralization, automatization, and specificity of procedural rules accounted well for the learning curves for reaction time and error rate during a semester of practice of a small number of grammar rules. Robinson (1997), on the other hand, found that his data on the learning of an ESL grammar rule did not fit the predictions of Logan's competing theory of automatization through retrieval of specific instances from memory instead of rules. Both of these studies are described in more detail in the Exemplary Study/ies section. Recent work by de Jong (2005a,b), with learners of Spanish as a second language provides further evidence for the skill specificity documented by DeKeyser (1997). She showed that extensive aural comprehension training, while increasing processing speed in comprehension, did not preempt a substantial number of errors in production and that, conversely, early production did not hinder acquisition.

Given the increasing sophistication of the technology as well as the research methodology at the disposal of second language researchers, along with a return to focus on form and explicit learning in recent years (see e.g. Doughty & Williams, 1998; Norris & Ortega, 2000) one can expect this area of research to pick up, especially as many researchers have begun to at least interpret existing findings from the second language literature within the framework of skill acquisition theory (de Bot, 1996; Healy et al., 1998; Lyster, 2004; Macaro, 2003; O'Malley & Chamot, 1990; Ranta & Lyster, 2006; Towell & Hawkins, 1994; Towell, Hawkins & Bazergui, 1996). Researchers do not need to be trained in computational modeling or neuroscience at all to contribute to research on skill acquisition. With a sophisticated approach to design, data collection, and data analysis, and using technology that is fairly easily available at research institutions, behavioral data still have much to contribute to this area.

COMMON MISUNDERSTANDINGS

Two kinds of misunderstanding about the contribution of skill acquisition theory to second language acquisition research are very common: the idea that skill acquisition either explains everything about second language acquisition or nothing—in other words that it competes with other theories to be the one and only valid explanation of the set of phenomena we call "second language acquisition"—and the idea that it is incompatible with a variety of empirical findings in the field. These two misunderstandings are, of course, related, as we will see below.

Because of its emphasis on the importance of explicit/declarative knowledge in initial stages of learning, skill acquisition theory is most easily applicable to what happens in (a) high-aptitude adult learners engaged in (b) the learning of simple structures at (c) fairly early stages of learning in (d) instructional contexts. That does not mean these four conditions all have to be fulfilled in order for skill acquisition theory to be applicable, but it does mean that the more the learning situation deviates from this prototypical situation in one of these four respects, the less likely it is that concepts from skill acquisition theory will account well for the data. If adults have below-average verbal aptitude, they may find it hard to form declarative representations of grammar rules (whether with the help of a teacher and textbooks or not). By the same token, children will not be able to conceptualize most grammar rules, which are of course inherently abstract. This problem is even worse when the rules are very complex. In that case even adults of above-average aptitude will find it hard to understand, and especially to proceduralize and automatize, the rule. Finally, as learners enter more advanced stages of learning (where they interact constantly and fluently with native speakers and are exposed to a large amount of oral and written input), the likelihood of implicit learning of frequent and relatively concrete patterns in the grammar increases substantially. That in turn does not mean that skill acquisition theory is of marginal relevance: A substantial amount of second/foreign language learning is done by adolescents and adults of above-average aptitude going through the initial stages of learning in a school context. Moreover, if the potential for learning in these initial stages is not maximized (because everything we know about cognitive skill acquisition is ignored), this will have repercussions, of course, for all learning thereafter.

Related to the just mentioned overgeneralization of skill acquisition theory to the situations where it does not apply well is the tendency to see the theory as incompatible with a number of empirical findings as well as theoretical positions in the field. Some will overinterpret the theory as predicting that any kind of construction can be learned, practiced, and automatized by anybody in any order, and that therefore it is incompatible with the literature on the natural order of acquisition (summarized, for instance, in Dulay, Burt, & Krashen, 1982; Goldschneider & DeKeyser, 2001; VanPatten & Williams, this volume, chapter 2). This reasoning actually combines a misreading of both skill acquisition theory and research on the natural order of acquisition because the latter never found an ordering for all or even most structures in the language, only for a few morphemes in some studies, or for a few closely related syntactic patterns in others. Also, most studies of order of acquisition were carried out with learners that had massive exposure to the language and/or were young learners, which means that they were largely implicit learners, and that the skill acquisition model (going from declarative/explicit to procedural/implicit knowledge) did not apply to them.

Similarly, skill acquisition theory should not be seen as being in competition with the theory underlying processing instruction (see especially VanPatten, 2004) as long as the latter is not seen as implying that practice in production is not important for full-fledged skill acquisition or the fine-tuning of declarative knowledge; in fact, processing instruction does for comprehension skills exactly what skill acquisition theory suggests should be done: take students from explicitly taught declarative knowledge, through careful proceduralization by engaging in the relevant task while the declarative knowledge is maximally activated, to (very initial stages of) automatization. Skill acquisition theory is not incompatible either with other contemporary tendencies in the way focus on form is implemented, such as task-based learning (see especially R. Ellis, 2003; Long & Norris 2000; Long & Robinson, 1998), because engaging in carefully sequenced tasks (from a psycholinguistic perspective) will again lead to proceduralization and potentially some degree of automatization provided that the requisite declarative knowledge is at the disposal of the learner during the task.

Finally, skill acquisition theory does not contradict the notion that implicit learning is important, or more specifically, that frequency plays an important role in various aspects of (second) language learning. While stressing the importance of implicit learning in general and frequency in particular, N. Ellis (see especially 2002, 2005; and chapter 5 this volume) makes it very clear that "many aspects of a second language are unlearnable—or at best acquired very slowly—from implicit processes alone" (2005, p. 307), and that "slot-and-frame patterns, drills, mnemonics, and declarative statements of pedagogical grammar . . . all contribute to the conscious creation of utterances that then partake in subsequent implicit learning and proceduralization" (2005, p. 308).

EXEMPLARY STUDY:
DeKEYSER (1997) AND ROBINSON (1997)

Two studies form the focus of discussion here, DeKeyser (1997) and Robinson (1997), because jointly they illustrate the application of the two most prominent variants of skill acquisition theory to the second language learning context: Anderson's theory of proceduralization and automatization of rules, and Logan's theory of automatization through retrieval of instances.

DeKeyser (1997) addressed one large question with several subcomponents. The overarching question was whether the learning of the grammar of a second language, between beginning and the end of practice (with practice beginning after the presentation and assimilation of declarative knowledge in the form of rules), would show a developmental pattern as predicted by Anderson's ACT-R model of skill acquisition and as observed for many other kinds of skills (evidence of fast proceduralization followed by slow automatization, both being highly skill-specific). More concrete questions serving as a proxy for this overarching question were whether data for both reaction time and error rate would follow a power function and whether the effect of comprehension and production practice for a given rule would be skill-specific or would transfer to the other skill.

Participants were 61 adults, mostly undergraduate students who had some amount of foreign language learning experience but who started learning an artificial language for this experiment. All teaching, practice, and testing was computer-administered over a period of one semester.

The participants were tested repeatedly for both reaction time and error rate over a period of 11 weeks. Testing for comprehension was in the form of choosing the right picture (from a set of four on the screen) corresponding to a given sentence in the artificial language; production was tested by having the participants complete the sentence in the artificial language that described what was happening in a picture presented on the screen. For both production and comprehension, applying the grammar rules that had been learned explicitly was essential for getting the test items correct. Four grammar rules (involving case and number marking on the noun, and gender and instrument marking on the verb) were taught, practiced, and tested. The participants were divided into three groups: some received comprehension practice for rules 1 and 2 and production practice for rules 3 and 4, some the other way around, and some received an equal amount of both production and comprehension practice for all rules. This way all participants received the same amount of teaching and practice for all rules and for both skills; the only thing that differed from group to group was which of the four rules were practiced, to what extent, and for which skill.

The data from all three groups of learners showed a gradual decrease in the form of a power function for both reaction time and error rate and for both comprehension and production. When participants were tested on a skill they had not practiced for the rule being tested, their performance was far worse, both for reaction time and error rate, than for participants who had practiced that rule for that skill; those participants, however, who had practiced all rules in both skills (but with half the number of items as the other learners) performed equally well as those that had had ample practice for the same item (in the skill tested only).

These data confirm the predictions of skill acquisition theory: Declarative knowledge followed by extensive practice led to increasingly robust knowledge, learned at a rate that can best be explained by fast proceduralization followed by slow automatization. Furthermore, the lack of transfer to the opposite skill is evidence for the skill-specificity of procedural knowledge, as claimed by skill acquisition theory.

Robinson (1997) posed several questions about the effectiveness of different instructional conditions along with the question that concerns us here: to what extent learning of specific instances as well as generalizations of a rule reflected the predictions of Logan's theory of automaticity as retrieval of instances. It was hypothesized that learners who had not learned rules but had only seen a set of examples (some occurring multiple times, with the frequency varying from example to example) would show results that reflected the frequency of these specific examples in the input, while learners who had a rule available to them as a result of training would follow that rule and hence not be sensitive to how often they had seen specific instances.

Participants were 60 adult Japanese learners of ESL who had received six years of formal high school education of English. The study was carried out in a laboratory context. All participants were required to read 55 stimulus sentences illustrating the rule used in the study (concerning constraints on dative alternation as in *John gave the cake to Mary/John gave Mary the cake*, but not *John donated the money to the church/*John donated the church the money*).

The participants were assigned to one of four training conditions (the instructed and enhanced conditions leading to rule learning; the implicit and incidental conditions not). After practice, reaction time and accuracy for all four groups were tested separately for previously encountered grammatical sentences as well as new grammatical and ungrammatical ones.

Learners in the instructed and enhanced conditions appeared to be able (to different degrees) to apply a rule to new examples while the learners in the implicit and incidental conditions were unable to do so. Most importantly for our purposes, the predictions of Logan's theory about the effect of frequency in the input were not borne out. Learners in all conditions were insensitive to the frequency of concrete instances, not just those who had learned a rule. Reaction time to previously seen sentences for the implicit, incidental, and enhanced conditions did not even follow the power law of practice (practice being quantified here as the number of times a specific instance had been encountered in the input).

The results suggest that the kind of knowledge acquired from exposure to examples alone without a rule being available is completely memory-based and therefore limited in its generalizability, and the lack of effect of the exact frequency of specific examples argues against Logan's theory of instance retrieval as an explanation of the power curve found in so many studies of skill acquisition.

EXPLANATION OF OBSERVED FINDINGS IN SLA

Observation #7. There are limits on the effects of frequency on SLA; Observation # 9. There are limits on the effects of instruction . . . ; and Observation #10. There are limits on the effects of output . . . The findings in chapter 1 that there are limits on the effects of frequency, on the effects of instruction, and on the effects of output are very easily explained in this framework: Factors such as whether students receive instruction, produce output, or are exposed to certain structures frequently play little role if (explicit) instruction and practice with input and output are not integrated in a way that makes sense according to this theory. Automatization requires procedural knowledge. Proceduralization requires declarative knowledge and slow deliberate practice. The acquisition of declarative knowledge of a kind that can be proceduralized requires the judicious use of rules and examples. These stages cannot be skipped, reversed, or rushed. Unfortunately, however, just about any kind of existing teaching methodology tends to do at least one of the three.

Observation #5. Second language learning is variable in its outcome; and Observation 6. Second language learning is variable across subsystems. The findings that second language learning is variable in its outcome and variable across linguistic subsystems are equally easy to explain in this framework. Different learners achieve very different levels of proficiency in a given area because of their different levels of ability to grasp the declarative knowledge, the widely differing amounts of practice of specific kinds that individual learners receive for specific structures, and, most importantly, the different sequencing of various kinds of explicit information, implicit input, and practice with input and output that different learners receive or create for themselves (which are influenced in turn by motivation, personality, and social context). Learners also show a large amount of intra-individual variation between the different linguistic domains because of differential aptitude, instruction, and practice. Even more importantly, skill acquisition theory easily explains the differences in performance from task to task that are so often observed for the same subcomponent of language in the same individual learner. Performance draws on procedural knowledge, which we saw is very specific and unevenly developed depending on the amount of practice of various elements of the language under various task conditions. In the same vein, skill acquisition theory explains the importance of learning activities and their sequencing, a factor that is not often addressed in the more linguistically oriented literature but that is of tremendous importance in the more applied literature. No amount of any activity means much if it does not fit into the right point of development of skill for a given individual.

Observation 4. Learners' output (speech) often follows predictable paths with predictable stages in the acquisition of a given structure. The fact that learners follow a predictable path in their development for a given structure also fits well with skill acquisition theory, especially if it is understood somewhat more broadly than in merely linguistic terms. Learners who are exposed to little or no instruction may learn different variants of a structure in a certain order through implicit mechanisms and may show little task variation at a given point in time. But learners who are carefully guided through the stages of skill acquisition for a given structure may show less developmental variation in that kind of structure but more developmental variation in speed and systematicity of use of this structure, including variation due to (even small variations in) task conditions. When such learners are forced to perform beyond the level of skill they have reached, they may or may not fall back on the same variants of structures used by implicit learners, depending on factors such as how much exposure they have received along with their systematic instruction and what age they are (the latter influence their relative susceptibility to implicit and explicit learning).

CONCLUSION

In this chapter, I have presented both major findings and methodological aspects of skill acquisition research, illustrated them with two studies from the second language domain, and explained how skill acquisition theory is quite compatible with many of the major findings from second language acquisition research and even explains some phenomena better than other theories. In closing, however, it is only fitting to take a somewhat broader view of how well explanations of second language acquisition phenomena based on skill acquisition theory fit into the larger enterprise of cognitive science; in our case that means trying to understand how the same mind that learns how to recognize the neighbors, play chess, appreciate music, ride a bicycle, program a computer, or use a native language also learns to understand and produce a second language.

An advantage of the approach illustrated in this chapter is definitely that it fits very well with other aspects of cognitive science. The same mechanisms, whether couched in psychological or neurological terms, are invoked to explain second language learning and a wide variety of other skills. Secondly, this approach to skill learning has itself proven to be quite robust over the decades, in spite of the obvious changes in emphases, methodology, and terminology.

Furthermore, research on skill acquisition, whether carried out with behavioral data or through neuro-imaging or computer modeling, is tremendously explicit in its procedures and claims. Power curves, computer programs, and brain scanners give precise answers to precise questions (even though interpreting the answers can still leave a lot of room for discussion). Most importantly of all, perhaps, research in this area is truly developmental. It does not take snapshots of learners at two or three points between initial learning and near-native proficiency, and does not speculate on how learners got from point "a" to point "b." It can document learning day after day, and show how rapid acquisition of declarative knowledge about some structures, rapid proceduralization of knowledge about others, and automatization of some elements of knowledge for specific uses all happen in parallel, while other elements never get automatized, or maybe not even proceduralized, or perhaps not even learned. The research may have less to say about which elements of language are going to be learned in what order than other more (psycho-)linguistically oriented approaches, but it is painstakingly precise and explicit about the big and small steps a learner takes in acquiring (a specific use of) a specific structure.

DISCUSSION QUESTIONS

1. Central to skill acquisition theory are the constructs of declarative knowledge, proceduralization, and automatization. Discuss each, paying particular attention to the difference in proceduralization and automatization as well as the context(s) in which automatization may occur.

2. Both DeKeyser and Ellis offer approaches that are cognitive in nature, that is, built on models/theories from psychology rather than, say, linguistics. How are the two approaches similar or different?

3. It is clear that skill acquisition theory is concerned with language behavior. Do you think that such an approach is incompatible with an approach that focuses on competence (e.g., White, chapter 3)?
4. One interpretation of skill acquisition theory is that it is better suited to
   explain tutored language acquisition as compared to nontutored language acquisition. Another is that it is better suited to explain adult
   SLA but not child L1A or child SLA. Do you agree?
5. Now that you have read about four different theories/models (chapters 3
   through 6), review the types of linguistic structures and features discussed in each. Do you notice any relationship between type of structure
   used as examples or described in research and the theories themselves?

SUGGESTED FURTHER READINGS

Anderson, J. R., Bothell, D., Byrne, M. D., Douglass, S., Lebiere, C., & Qin, Y.
(2004). An integrated theory of the mind. *Psychological Review, 111*,
1036–1060.

The latest overview of ACT-R theory with new emphases on neuro-
imaging data and the issue of modularity of the mind. Parts are very technical, others are very readable.

Carlson, R. (2003). Skill learning. In L. Nadel (Ed.), *Encyclopedia of cognitive
science* (pp. 36–42). London: Macmillan.

A short and readable presentation of skill acquisition theory from a
broad perspective, written by a prominent psychologist.

DeKeyser, R. (2001). Automaticity and automatization. In P. Robinson (Ed.),
Cognition and second language instruction (pp. 125–151). New York: Cambridge University Press.

The most thorough discussion to date of skill acquisition theory in general as it applies to second language learning.

———. (Ed.). (2006). *Practicing in a second language: Perspectives from applied
linguistics and cognitive psychology*. New York: Cambridge University Press.

A book that takes a broad view of practice, with many chapters drawing
on skill acquisition theory, applying it to issues from error correction in
the classroom to interaction with native speakers during study abroad.

Segalowitz, N., & Hulstijn, J. (2005). Automaticity in bilingualism and second
language learning. In J. F. Kroll & A. M. B. de Groot (Eds.), *Handbook
of bilingualism: Psycholinguistic perspectives* (pp. 371–388). Oxford: Oxford
University Press.

The most thorough discussion to date of automaticity and the process of
automatization as they apply to second language learning and bilingualism.

REFERENCES

Anderson, J. R. (1982). Acquisition of cognitive skill. *Psychological Review, 89,* 369–406.

————. (1993). *Rules of the mind.* Hillsdale, NJ: Lawrence Erlbaum Associates.

Anderson, J. R., & Lebiere, C. (1998). *The atomic components of thought.* Mahwah, NJ: Lawrence Erlbaum.

Anderson, J. R., Bothell, D., Byrne, M. D., Douglass, S., Lebiere, C., & Qin, Y. (2004). An integrated theory of the mind. *Psychological Review, 111,* 1036–1060.

Anderson, J. R., Fincham, J. M., & Douglass, S. (1997). The role of examples and rules in the acquisition of a cognitive skill. *Journal of Experimental Psychology: Learning, Memory and Cognition, 23,* 932–945.

Byrne, D. (Ed.). (1986). *Teaching oral English* (2nd ed.). Harlow, UK: Longman.

de Bot, K. (1996). The psycholinguistics of the output hypothesis. *Language Learning, 46,* 529–555.

de Jong, N. (2005a). *Learning second language grammar by listening.* Utrecht, The Netherlands, LOT (Landelijke Onderzoekschool Taalwetenschap).

————. (2005b). Can second language grammar be learned through listening? An experimental study. *Studies in Second Language Acquisition, 27,* 205–234.

DeKeyser, R. M. (1997). Beyond explicit rule learning: Automatizing second language morphosyntax. *Studies in Second Language Acquisition, 19,* 195–221.

————. (2001). Automaticity and automatization. In P. Robinson (Ed.), *Cognition and second language instruction* (pp. 125–151). New York: Cambridge University Press.

DeKeyser, R., & Sokalski, K. (2001). The differential role of comprehension and production practice. In R. Ellis (Ed.), *Form-focused instruction and second language learning* (pp. 81–112). Oxford: Blackwell.

Doughty, C., & Williams, J. (1998). Pedagogical choices in focus on form. In C. Doughty & J. Williams (Eds.), *Focus on form in classroom second language acquisition* (pp. 197–261). New York: Cambridge University Press.

Dulay, H., Burt, M., & Krashen, S. (1982). *Language two.* New York: Oxford University Press.

Ellis, N. (2005). At the interface: Dynamic interactions of explicit and implicit language knowledge. *Studies in Second Language Acquisition, 27,* 305–352.

Ellis, N. (2002). Frequency effects in language processing: A review with implications for theories of implicit and explicit language acquisition. *Studies in Second Language Acquisition, 24*(2), 143–188.

Ellis, R. (2003). *Task-based language learning and teaching.* Oxford: Oxford University Press.

Fitts, P., & Posner, M. (1967). *Human performance.* Belmont, CA: Brooks/Cole.

Goldschneider, J., & DeKeyser, R. (2001). Explaining the 'natural order of L2 morpheme acquisition' in English: A meta-analysis of multiple determinants. *Language Learning, 51,* 1–50.

Healy, A. F., Barshi, I., Crutcher, R. J., Tao, L., Rickard, T. C., Marmie, W. R., et al. (1998). Toward the improvement of training in foreign languages. In A. F. Healy & L. E. J. Bourne (Eds.), *Foreign language learning. Psycholinguistic studies on training and retention* (pp. 3–53). Mahwah, NJ: Lawrence Erlbaum Associates.

Just, M., & Carpenter, P. (1992). A capacity theory of comprehension: Individual differences in working memory. *Psychological Review, 99,* 122–149.

Logan, G. (1988). Toward an instance theory of automatization. *Psychological Review, 95*, 492–527.

———. (1992). Shapes of reaction-time distributions and shapes of learning curves: A test of the instance theory of automaticity. *Journal of Experimental Psychology, Learning, Memory and Cognition, 18*, 883–914.

———. (2002). An instance theory of attention and memory. *Psychological Review, 109*, 376–400.

Long, M., & Norris, J. (2000). Task-based teaching and assessment. In M. Byram (Ed.), *Encyclopedia of language teaching* (pp. 597–603). London: Routledge.

Long, M., & Robinson, P. (1998). Focus on form: Theory, research, and practice. In C. Doughty & J. Williams (Eds.), *Focus on form in classroom second language acquisition* (pp. 15–41). New York: Cambridge University Press.

Lyster, R. (2004). Differential effects of prompts and recasts in form-focused instruction. *Studies in Second Language Acquisition, 26*, 399–432.

Macaro, E. (2003). *Teaching and learning a second language. A guide to recent research and its applications.* London/New York: Continuum.

Meyer, D., & Kieras, D. (1997). A computational theory of executive cognitive processes and multiple-task performance: Part 1. Basic mechanisms. *Psychological Review, 104*, 3–65.

Newell, A. (1990). *Unified theories of cognition.* Cambridge, MA: Harvard University Press.

Newell, A., & Rosenbloom, P. (1981). Mechanisms of skill acquisition and the law of practice. In J. R. Anderson (Ed.). *Cognitive skills and their acquisition* (pp. 1–55). Hillsdale, NJ: Lawrence Erlbaum Associates.

Norris, J. M., & Ortega, L. (2000). Effectiveness of L2 instruction: A research synthesis and quantitative meta-analysis. *Language Learning, 50*, 417–528.

O'Malley, J., & Chamot, A. (1990). *Learning strategies in second language acquisition.* New York: Cambridge University Press.

Qin, Y., Anderson, J. R., Silk, E., Stenger, V., & Carter, C. (2004). The change of the brain activation patterns along with the children's practice in algebra equation solving. *Proceedings of the National Academy of Sciences, 100*, 5686–5691.

Raichle, M., Fiez, J., Videen, T., MacLeod, A.-M., Pardo, J. V., Fox, P., & Petersen, S. E. (1994). Practice-related changes in human brain functional anatomy during nonmotor learning. *Cerebral Cortex, 4*, 8–26.

Ranta, L., & Lyster, R. (2006). A cognitive approach to improving immersion students' oral production abilities: The awareness, practice, and feedback sequence. In R. DeKeyser (Ed.), *Practicing in a second language: Perspectives from applied linguistics and cognitive psychology.* New York: Cambridge University Press.

Robinson, P. (1997). Generalizability and automaticity of second language learning under implicit, incidental, enhanced, and instructed conditions. *Studies in Second Language Acquisition, 19*, 223–247.

Singley, M., & Anderson, J. R. (1989). *The transfer of cognitive skill.* Cambridge, MA: Harvard University Press.

Tanaka, T. (2001). Comprehension and production practice in grammar instruction: Does their combined use facilitate second language acquisition? *JALT Journal, 23*, 6–30.

Towell, R., & Hawkins, R. (1994). *Approaches to second language acquisition.* Clevedon, UK: Multilingual Matters.

Towell, R., Hawkins, R., & Bazergui, N. (1996). The development of fluency in advanced learners of French. *Applied Linguistics 17,* 84–119.

VanPatten, B. (Ed.) (2004). *Processing instruction. Theory, research, and commentary.* Mahwah, NJ: Lawrence Erlbaum Associates.

7

Input Processing in Adult Second Language Acquisition

Bill VanPatten
The University of Illinois at Chicago

Imagine a speaker of Spanish learning English. In a conversation or discussion she hears someone say, "The police officer was killed by the robber." Although for the native speaker it is clear that it was the police officer who died, the learner of English may interpret this sentence as "The police officer killed the robber." Why does she make this misinterpretation? It cannot be due to L1 influence because Spanish has the exact same construction: *El policía fue matado por el ladrón.*

Imagine an English speaker learning Spanish in a formal setting. He studies the preterit (simple past) in Spanish. A month later he hears someone say *Juan estudió en Cuernavaca* ("John studied in Cuernavaca.") However, he interprets this sentence to mean that John is studying in Cuernavaca, even though he knows how the past tense is formed in Spanish and even though English clearly marks past from present. Why does he make this misinterpretation?

Input Processing (IP) is concerned with these situations because acquisition is, to a certain degree, a byproduct of comprehension. Although comprehension cannot guarantee acquisition, acquisition cannot happen if comprehension does not occur. Why? Because a good deal of acquisition is dependent upon learners making appropriate form–meaning connections during the act of comprehension. A good deal of acquisition is dependent upon learners correctly interpreting what a sentence means (White, 1987; Carroll, 2001).

In this chapter I deal with the fundamentals of IP and the research associated with it. It will become clear that IP is not a comprehensive theory or model of language acquisition. Instead, it aims to be a model of what happens during comprehension that may subsequently affect or interact with other processes. We will begin with a sketch of the theory and its constructs.

THE THEORY AND ITS CONSTRUCTS

Input Processing is concerned with three fundamental questions that involve the assumption that an integral part of language acquisition is making form–meaning connections:

- Under what conditions do learners make initial form–meaning connections?
- Why, at a given moment in time, do they make some and not other form–meaning connections?
- What internal strategies do learners use in comprehending sentences and how might this affect acquisition?

Let's take a concrete example based on the introduction of this chapter. In English as an L2, learners must, at some point, map the meaning of *pastness* onto the verb inflection /–t/ (or *–ed* in written form). How does this happen, and why don't learners do this from the first time they encounter this form in a context in which the speaker is clearly making reference to the past? Thus, IP is a model of moment-by-moment sentence processing during comprehension and how learners connect or don't connect particular forms with particular meanings. It is a model of how learners derive the initial data from input for creating a linguistic system, in other words, the data that are delivered to other processors and mechanisms that actually store and organize the data (e.g., Universal Grammar. See White, chapter 3 this volume). This can be sketched as in Figure 7–1.

The model makes a number of claims about what guides learners' processing of linguistic data in the input as they are engaged in comprehension. These claims can be summarized in the following way:

- Learners are driven to get meaning while comprehending.
- Comprehension for learners is initially quite effortful in terms of cognitive processing and working memory. This has consequences for what the input processing mechanisms will pay attention to.
- At the same time, learners are limited capacity processors and cannot process and store the same amount of information as native speakers can during moment-by-moment processing.
- Learners may make use of certain universals of input processing but may also make use of the L1 input processor (or parser, which we will define shortly).

The first claim has led to the principle in IP that learners will seek to grasp meaning by searching for lexical items, although the precise manner in which

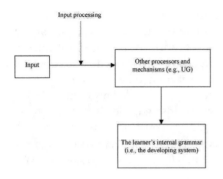

FIGURE 7–1. Where IP fits into an acquisition scheme.

this is done is still not clear.[1] In other words, learners enter the task of SLA knowing that languages have words. They are thus first driven to make form–meaning connections that are lexical in nature. For example, if they hear "The cat is sleeping" and this sentence is uttered in a context in which a cat is indeed sleeping, the learner will seek to isolate the lexical forms that encode the meanings of CAT and SLEEP, for instance, because the learner knows that those words must exist and must be somewhere there in the speech stream he or she is hearing. What is more, learners know that there are differences between content lexical items (e.g., *cat*, *sleep*) and noncontent lexical items (e.g., *the*, *is*) and will seek out content lexical items first. Thus, in "The cat is sleeping" the learner may initially only make the connections between cat–CAT and sleep–SLEEP. These claims are codified in the following IP principle:[2]

> *The Primacy of Content Words Principle: Learners process content words in the input before anything else.*

At this point, the learner most likely does not process the noncontent words or the inflections on nouns and verbs, *process* referring specifically to actually making connections between meaning and form (as opposed to mere "noticing"). If the learner does process noncontent words and/or inflections, it is likely that the (other) processors responsible for data storage and grammar building may not yet be able to make use of them and will dump them,

---

[1]It is not clear how learners of different languages actually come to know where word boundaries are in the language, but clearly they do. Issues of how learners process sounds and segment units of speech is part of another set of processes (see, for example, Carroll, this volume).

[2]Readers familiar with earlier work on IP will note that the principles examined here are not exactly the same as in, for example, VanPatten 1996 and 2004a. This is because the model continues to evolve.

preventing further processing. However, the model of IP also makes another claim regarding such things as inflections and grammatical markers, namely, that if the marker is redundant, it may not get processed because the learner is focused on getting content words first. Processing the content word obviates the need to process the grammatical marker if it encodes the same meaning. In this scenario, presented with a sentence such as "I called my mother yesterday," learners will not process tense markers. Instead, they will derive tense from their processing of adverbs of time (e.g., *yesterday, tomorrow* and so on). Thus, the first principle has consequences for what learners extract from the input when grammatical devices are present. This is codified in the following principle:[3]

> *The Lexical Preference Principle: Learners will process lexical items for meaning before grammatical forms when both encode the same semantic information.*

Learners will thus seek out lexical forms of semantic notions in the input before they seek out grammatical forms that encode the same semantic notions. There are two possible consequences of this particular principle. First, we might say that learners will begin to process redundant grammatical markers only when they have processed and incorporated corresponding lexical forms into their developing linguistic systems. Thus, past tense markers won't be processed and incorporated until learners have processed and incorporated lexical forms such as *yesterday, last night,* and so on.[4] If so, the Lexical Preference Principle might be revised to state the following:

> *(Revised) Lexical Preference Principle: If grammatical forms express a meaning that can also be encoded lexically (i.e., that grammatical marker is redundant), then learners will not initially process those grammatical forms until they have lexical forms to which they can match them.*

The other possible consequence is that learners may begin to rely exclusively on lexical forms for all information and never process grammatical markers in the input at all. In this scenario, the processing of lexical items overrides any need to process grammatical markers when redundancy is involved (i.e., the lexical form and the grammatical form express the same meaning as in PASTNESS /–ed, FUTURE /will, THIRD-PERSON SINGULAR /–s, and so

---

[3]Technically this principle is a corollary of the previous principle and, in the original model of IP, was listed as such. However for present purposes it is listed with its own name here.

[4]Clearly a learner need not process and incorporate all possible lexical items for a given grammatical marker. It is enough that the learner process one or two, for example.

on).[5] In either scenario, one of the predictions of the IP model is that as long as comprehension remains effortful, learners will continue to focus on the processing of lexical items to the detriment of grammatical markers, given that lexical items maximize the extraction of meaning, at least from the learner's point of view. Grammatical markers will be processed later, if at all.

Not all grammatical markers are redundant. In English, –ing is exclusively the sole marker of the semantic notion of an event in progress as in "The cat is sleeping [IN PROGRESS]." There is no lexical indication of IN PROGRESS in the sentence with –ing. This contrasts with something like "The cat sleeps ten hours everyday," in which the meaning of –s of "sleeps" [THIRD PERSON, SINGULAR, ITERATIVE] is encoded lexically in "the cat [THIRD-PERSON, SINGULAR]" and "everyday [ITERATIVE]." Because learners always search for ways in which meaning is encoded, if it is not encoded lexically, only then will they turn to grammatical markers to see if a semantic notion is expressed there. Thus, if learners are confronted with something like –ing on verb forms, they will be forced to make this form–meaning connection sooner than, say, third-person –s because the latter is redundant and the former is not. This leads to another principle of IP:

> The Preference for Nonredundancy Principle: Learners are more likely to process nonredundant meaningful grammatical markers before they process redundant meaningful markers.[6]

Until now, we have considered only grammatical markers that carry meanings such as –s on the end of a noun means "more than one" and –ing means "in progress." But there are some grammatical markers, albeit not many, that do not carry meaning. Consider that in the sentence John thinks that Mary is smart. What real word semantic information does that encode? It's not a tense marker. It's not an indication of whether the event is in progress or iterative. It's not a plurality marker or any other such semantically linked grammatical device. As a word, there is nothing in the world you can point to or describe

---

[5]Although the term third-person singular sounds like a grammatical concept and not a semantic concept, it actually is semantic and means "someone other than you or me." In English, it also carries the feature ITERATIVE (habitual) as opposed to IN PROGRESS (at one particular point in time).

[6]Learners do not enter the task of processing input already knowing what things are redundant and what things are not. They do, however, enter the task unconsciously knowing that redundancy exists in language more generally. The point here is that if a learner knows that the context is referring to an action in progress, he or she will look to see how that is encoded lexically first. If it is not, as in the case of English, then he or she will subsequently begin looking for grammatical markers that mark this nonredundant meaning.

and say *that's a that* as you might with *that's a cow* and *that's love*. It has a grammatical function, to be sure, to link two sentences (i.e., introduce an embedded clause) but it doesn't encode any semantic information. In Spanish, adjective agreement is similar. In the case of *el libro blanco* ("the white book") and *la casa blanca* ("the white house"), there is no semantic reason why in one case *blanco* must be used and in another *blanca* must be used.[7] Spanish just makes adjectives agree with nouns. The model of IP says that such formal features of language will be processed in the input later than those for which true form–meaning connections can be made. The principle says:

> *The Meaning before Nonmeaning Principle. Learners are more likely to process meaningful grammatical markers before nonmeaningful grammatical markers.*

However, input processing is more than making form–meaning connections. When a person hears a sentence, whether in the L1 or the L2, that person also does a microsecond-by-microsecond computation of the syntactic structure of that sentence. This is called *parsing*. For example, in English when a person hears "The cat . . ." the parsing mechanism (called a *parser*) does the following: the cat = NP (noun phrase) = subject. This is a called a *projection* because the parser projects a syntactic structure (i.e., the parser is making the best guess at what the grammatical relationships will be among words). If a verb follows, the parser may continue in this path. For example: "The cat chased . . . ," the cat = NP = subject, chased = verb [so far, so good for the syntactic projection]. If a phrase like "the mouse" comes next, the parser may continue: the cat = NP = subject, chased = verb, the mouse = NP = object; parsing completed, syntactic projection successful, sentence computed and understood. But if instead of "the mouse" what follows is "by the boy," the parser must reproject on the spot: the cat = NP = subject, chased = verb, by the boy = oops, not an object, therefore "the cat chased by the boy" = NP = subject. If a verb follows, such as "howled," the parser continues: the cat chased by the boy = NP = subject, howled = verb, parsing completed and successful.

The previous description of parsing is greatly simplified to be sure,[8] but for the present discussion it allows us to ask the following question: How do

---

[7]It is unfortunate that ancient grammarians adopted the semantic term *gender* to apply to nouns when inanimate nouns such as *house, shoe, moon, pie,* and *lamp* do not have gender. So when we talk about gender agreement in a language like Spanish, we are not talking about adjective agreement due to the biological sex of anything. We are talking about a purely grammatical phenomenon.

[8]For some work on parsing, see Pritchett (1992), Carreiras, García-Albea & Sebastián-Gallés (1996) and Clifton, Frazier & Rayner (1994).

learners parse sentences in the L2 when they do not have a fully developed parser as they do for L1 sentence processing?[9] There are two avenues we can pursue here and each needs additional research for support or disconfirmation. The first avenue is that learners possess universal parsing strategies (or procedures) and apply these as they begin interacting with the L2 input. The other avenue is that learners transfer or attempt to transfer their L1 parsing strategies (or procedures) when interacting with the L2 input. These two positions are clear when we examine sentences such as the following in English and Spanish:

(1) a. Mary hates John.
     b. María detesta a Juan.
     c. A Juan María lo detesta.
(2) a. Mary hates him.
     b. María lo detesta.
     c. Lo detesta María.
(3) a. She hates him.
     b. Lo detesta.

In English, only subject-verb-object (SVO) order is possible, regardless of whether an object is a full noun (*John*) or a pronoun (*him*) as in (1a), (2a) and (3a) above. This is true whether the sentence is a simple declarative or whether it is yes/no question. In Spanish, however, although SVO is certainly prototypical, SOV (with pronouns as in 2b above), OVS (with full nouns and pronouns as in 1c and 2c), and OV (when the subject is null, that is, not expressed as in 3b) are all possible.[10] In Spanish, OV and OVS are fairly standard for yes/no questions, are not infrequent in simple declaratives, and are the prototypical orders for sentences containing certain verbs. So what happens when a language learner, say of English L1 background, first encounters (and continues to encounter) OVS and OV type sentences? Research has shown that such learners misinterpret such sentences and reverse "who does what to

---

[9]Again, we are ignoring how learners come to perceive and process word boundaries in an L2.

[10]Spanish is what is called a null subject language because subject pronouns are not required in simple declarative sentences and in some cases, pronouns are prohibited. For example, in most discourse situations, subject pronouns are not used as in *¿Qué haces?* ("What are you doing?") In this sentence, there is no overt *you* expressed in Spanish. What is more, in English "It's raining" can never be "*Is raining." In Spanish, "it" cannot be expressed under any circumstances as a subject of weather expressions or time expressions and the sentence is simply *llueve* (or *está lloviendo*—progressive) with no overt subject noun or pronoun equal to "it."

whom." In the case of *A Juan lo detesta María*, learners misinterpret this as "John hates Mary" rather than "Mary hates John." In the case of *Lo detesta María*, they misinterpret this sentence as "He hates Mary" rather than "Mary hates him." This results in incorrect form–meaning connections (e.g., *lo* = he[subject] rather than *lo* = him[object]) and wrong data about sentence structure provided to the internal processors responsible for storage and organization of language; in this case, these processors receive incorrect information that Spanish is rigid SVO, and the pronoun system becomes a mess.

The question is this: Is this parsing problem due to some universal strategy or to the English parser interacting with Spanish input data?[11] In previous research, I have taken the position that this is a universal strategy and posed the following principle:

> *The First Noun Principle: Learners tend to process the first noun or pronoun they encounter in a sentence as the subject.*

Under this universal position, any learner, whether from an SVO language or a language with flexible word order or rigid OVS order, would initially process the first noun as the subject. Under the alternative position, when the L1 parser is transferred into L2 input processing, the principle would look different and would have different consequences. The principle might look like this:

> *The L1 Transfer Principle: Learners begin acquisition with L1 parsing procedures.*

In this case, problems would be language specific in terms of transfer. So the Italian speaker learning Spanish would not have difficulty with OV and OVS structures in Spanish because these exist in Italian and the L1 parser has computing mechanisms for dealing with them. The English speaker, on the other hand, would have difficulty due to the rigid word order of English with no parsing mechanism to handle non-SVO structures (except cleft sentences such as "Him, I hate").

As stated before, both positions—the universal strategy position and the transfer position—are tenable, and research needs to be conducted to determine which is correct. For example, is it the case that learners of Italian do not make the same misinterpretations as English speakers when they first encounter OVS structures in Spanish? If they don't, then the transfer position would seem to be correct. If they do make the same misinterpretation

---

[11]Universal strategy should not be construed as being part of Universal Grammar (see White, chapter 3 this volume). It is not clear that the two are related.

errors as English speakers, such results would support the universal strategy position.[12]

Other factors may influence how learners parse and thus interpret sentences. Consider the verb *scold*. Which is more likely, for a parent to scold a child or a child to scold a parent? In the real world, the first situation is more likely. So what happens if a learner hears "The child scolded the mother"? In such cases, it is possible (though not necessary) that the probability of real-life scenarios might override the First Noun Principle (or the alternative L1 Transfer Principle). The learner might incorrectly reparse the sentence to mean "the parent scolded the child" and send information to the internal processors that the language has OVS structures (when it may not). This is what would happen during parsing under this scenario: the child = NP = subject, scolded = verb, the parent = NP = object—but wait, children don't scold parents, parents scold children, so the sentence must mean that the parent scolded the child. Reanalyze the parse: the child = NP = object, scolded = verb, the parent = NP = subject. The influence of these event probabilities is captured in the following principle:

> The Event Probability Principle: Learners may rely on event probabilities, where possible, instead of the First Noun Principle to interpret sentences.

Similarly, learners also come to the task of parsing knowing that certain verbs require certain situations. For example, the verb "kick" requires an animate being with legs for the action to occur. Thus, people, horses, frogs, and even dogs can kick, but snakes, rocks, and germs cannot kick. When confronted with the sentence "The cow was kicked by the horse" the First Noun Principle (or L1 Transfer Principle) may cause a misinterpretation: the cow did the kicking. However, when confronted with the sentence "The fence was kicked by the horse," a faulty interpretation is unlikely (how can a fence kick anything?), and the sentence may actually cause the parser to reanalyze what it just computed (assuming there is time to do so). This situation involves what is called *lexical semantics*. Lexical semantics refers to the requirements that the meanings of verbs place on nouns for an action or event to occur. Does the event expressed by the verb require an animate being to bring the event about? Does the event require particular properties of a being or entity

---

[12]A combination of positions is certainly possible, namely that everyone starts with universal procedures for parsing but that the L1 parser is somehow "triggered" at some point and either assists or inhibits correct interpretation. Under this scenario, Italian and English speakers learning Spanish may both begin with the First Noun Principle but something would trigger the Italian parsers so that they would begin correctly processing OVS sentences sooner than speakers of English.

for the event to come about? Note that lexical semantics is different from event probabilities in a fundamentally different way. With event probabilities, either noun may be capable of the action but one is more likely; with lexical semantics, it could be that only one noun is capable of the action. Thus, both a child and a parent can scold, but one is more likely to scold the other (event probabilities). However, only a horse can kick something else; a fence cannot kick something else (lexical semantics). The use of lexical semantics during parsing can be expressed by the following principle:

> The Lexical Semantics Principle: Learners may rely on lexical semantics, where possible, instead of the First Noun Principle (or an L1 parsing procedure) to interpret sentences.

Research on L2 input processing has also demonstrated that context may affect how learners parse sentences. Consider the following two sentences:

(4a)   John is in the hospital because Mary attacked him.

(4b)   John told his friends that Mary attacked him.

In Spanish, the embedded clause can either be SOV (*María lo atacó*) or OVS (*lo atacó María*). If the First Noun Principle or its L1 alternative were active (for English speakers, say), the OVS structure could be misinterpreted as "he attacked Mary." But note that if the preceding context is "John is in the hospital" a misinterpretation is less likely. Why would John be in the hospital if he attacked Mary? He'd be in jail, if anything. No, it's most reasonable that he's in the hospital as the result of an injury, so Mary must have attacked him. If the preceding context is a neutral as in "John told his friends" there is nothing to constrain interpretation of the clause that follows it: John could equally tell his friends that he attacked Mary or that Mary attacked him. The effects of context, then, result in another principle:

> The Contextual Constraint Principle: Learners may rely less on the First Noun Principle (or L1 transfer) if preceding context constrains the possible interpretation of a clause or sentence.

So far we have dealt with processing issues that have centered on the connection between form and meaning and on parsing. There is another area of processing that enters the picture: where elements are more likely to appear in a sentence. Imagine you hear the following set of numbers:

11 32 51 4 8 42 71 39 7 22 60 15 96 12 85 44

If you are typical, you will remember the numbers at the beginning (say 11, 32) before you would remember numbers at the end (say 44, 85) and in turn would remember both before you would remember any numbers in the middle (say 39, 7, or 60). This ability to process and best remember best things at the beginning, followed by things at the end, followed by things in the middle is true of a good deal of human information processing, and language is no different. There is ample research to support the idea that learner processing is affected by this phenomenon, and we can couch it in the following principle:

> *The Sentence Location Principle: Learners tend to process items in sentence initial position before those in final position and those in medial position.*

To be sure, the principles just outlined (and any others that might affect input processing) do not act in isolation.[13] One can envision, for example, that even though object pronouns in Spanish can and do appear in the initial position does not mean that learners will process them correctly. The First Noun principle would most likely interact so that learners may indeed process the object pronoun because it is in initial position (as opposed to when it might normally appear in the medial position in the sentence) but they would process it incorrectly.

To review, the following constructs are important aspects of input processing:

form–meaning connection: The form–meaning connection explains how a real world referent or semantic notion is encoded in a grammatical form (e.g., *–ed* means PASTNESS, *–ing* means IN PROGRESS, *him* means MALE, NOT THE SUBJECT OR AGENT OF THE VERB, *cat* means SOME TYPE OF FELINE).

processing: Learners map meaning and function onto formal properties of language (as opposed to merely "noticing" them).

parsing: Learners assign syntactic structure to input sentences (the relationships of nouns to verbs, for example, and determining the subject of a sentence).

effortful comprehension: Unlike L1 native speakers, L2 learners must develop the ability to comprehend, and comprehension for some time may tax the computational resources as learners engage in the millisecond-by-millisecond analysis of a sentence.

---

[13]There are other possible factors that remain to be investigated but for which we have reason to believe may be important, such as acoustic stress. Syllables with stress may be processed before syllables with weak stress, for example. Frequency of occurrence of a form in the input is another factor.

WHAT COUNTS AS EVIDENCE?

It is probably clear that only data gathered during comprehension-oriented research is appropriate to make inferences about input processing. Typical research designs include sentence interpretation and eye tracking experimentation.

Sentence Interpretation Tasks

In this kind of experimentation, participants hear sentences and indicate what they understand. For example, in the case of word order, participants might hear "The cow was kicked by the horse." They are then asked to choose between two pictures that could represent what they heard. In one picture, the cow is kicking the horse. In the other, the horse is kicking the cow. If the participant chooses the first picture, we can infer that the first noun principle is guiding sentence processing. If the participant selects the second picture, then the first noun principle is not guiding sentence processing (see, e.g., VanPatten, 1984).

With form–meaning connections, a variation on this type of task may occur. Participants might hear sentences such as *Mi mamá me llamó por teléfono* ("My mother called me on the phone") and *Mi amigo me ayuda con la casa* ("My friend is helping me with the house.") Note that there are no adverbials of time in the sentences. At the same time, the subject may hear similar sentences but an adverbial of time is present, as in *Mi mamá me llamó anoche por teléfono* ("My mother called me on the phone last night.") Learners are then asked to indicate whether the action occurred in the past, is happening now or happens everyday, or is going to/will happen in the future. If learners fail to correctly make such indications when the adverbs are not present in sentences but correctly do so when they are, this tells us they are relying on lexical items to get semantic information and not verbal inflections.

Eye Tracking

Eye tracking research involves having participants read sentences or text on a computer screen while tiny cameras track eye pupil movements via a very small infrared light directed at their eyes. As people read, they unconsciously skip words and parts of words, regress to some words, and so on, on a millisecond-by-millisecond basis. Eye tracking can reveal, for instance, whether learners attend to verbal inflections during input processing and whether they regress like native speakers do when encountering something that does not seem right. For example, given the sentence "Last night my mother calls me on the phone," native speakers eye tracking reveals fixations on the verb *calls* often with regression to the phrase *last night*. We do not see the same eye movement from beginning and intermediate learners. However, when asked to press a button to indicate past, present, or future for the action, both native speakers and non-natives always press "past." These combined results suggest that learners do indeed rely on lexical cues for meaning as they process sentences and skip over grammatical markers that encode the same meaning.

COMMON MISUNDERSTANDINGS

There are several common misunderstandings about both input processing and the specific model of input processing described here.

Misunderstanding 1: IP is a model of acquisition. People who claim this believe that IP attempts to account for acquisition more generally. It does not. As stated, IP is only concerned with how learners come to make form–meaning connections or parse sentences. Acquisition involves other processes as well, including accommodation of data (how the data are incorporated into the developing linguistic system and why they might not be), the action of Universal Grammar on the data, restructuring (how incorporated data affect the system, such as when regular forms cause irregular forms to become regularized), how learners make output, how interaction affects acquisition, and others. In short, IP is only concerned with initial data gathering. Consider the following analogy of honey making. Bees have to make honey. To do so, they have to gather nectar. They go to some flowers but not others. They have to find their way to flowers and then back to the hive. They then do something to the nectar so that honey is created. They build combs to store the honey, and so on. All of these endeavors are part of honey making. But we can isolate our research to ask the following questions: How do bees gather nectar? Why do they select some flowers and not others? This is similar to the concerns of IP. How do learners make form–meaning connections? Why, at a given period in time, do they make some connections and not others? IP isolates one part of acquisition; it is concerned with the "nectar-gathering aspect" of acquisition and leaves other models and theories to account for what happens to the nectar when it gets to the hive.

Misunderstanding 2: Input processing discounts a role for output, social factors, and other matters. Under this scenario, the person believes that because there is a focus on one aspect of acquisition, therefore the researcher or scholar does not believe anything else plays a role in acquisition. We thus hear of such things as "the input versus output debate" or "comprehension versus production" in SLA. Again, if we go back to the honey analogy, clearly someone who examines how bees collect nectar and why they do it they way they do it understands quite well that gathering nectar is not the same as making honey. And someone who researches what happens in the hive once the nectar arrives clearly understands that without nectar there is no honey making. That a researcher focuses on one particular part of the acquisition puzzle does not mean he or she discounts the rest. It means that the researcher is merely staking out a piece of the puzzle to examine in detail. In the case of IP, such things as social factors, the role of output, and interaction are not deemed unimportant in acquisition; they simply do not figure into the specifics of the research questions that guide IP.

Misunderstanding 3: Input processing is a meaning-based approach to studying acquisition and ignores what we know about syntactic processes. People who say this are focused on aspects of the model in which lexical primacy and the quest to get meaning from the input drives sentence interpretation. Their conclusion is understandable, but it is not correct. As we have seen with the issue of the First Noun principle and with parsing, the model is concerned with syntactic aspects of parsing and how these affect sentence interpretation and processing (which in turn affects acquisition). What is more, sometimes the people who believe that IP ignores syntactic processes are thinking of what we know about adult native-speaking models of sentence interpretation, which are largely syntactic in nature. If this is what native-speaking processing models entail, shouldn't L2 models do the same? The answer is maybe. The position taken by those of us in IP research is that learners must develop processing mechanisms in the L2; they don't start with them. And what they start with may not be processing mechanisms that can make full use of syntactic processes in sentence interpretation the way native speakers can. For example, in one experiment researchers have shown that native speakers and non-natives process "gap" sentences differently. Gap sentences are those in which a *wh–* element (e.g., *who*) has been moved out of one part of the sentence into another: "The nurse who the doctor argued that the rude patient had angered is refusing to work late." In this kind of sentence, *who* (the relative clause marker) is actually linked to the verb *angered* (i.e., is the object of the verb *angered*). What the researchers noticed is that even though both natives and non-natives can equally determine who was rude to whom, their millisecond-by-millisecond processing reveals substantial differences in how they make use of syntactic processing, with the non-natives relying much more on lexical–semantic and other non-syntactic cues (Marinis, Roberts, Felser & Clahsen, 2005).

Misunderstanding 4: Input processing is about pedagogy. Some people believe that the model of IP as described here is a pedagogical model. This is because there is a pedagogical intervention called *processing instruction* that is derived from insights about IP. Processing instruction is directed at the following question: If we know what learners are doing wrong at the level of input processing, can we create pedagogical intervention that is comprehension based to push them away from non-optimal processing? IP, however, is not about pedagogy, nor is it concerned with what learners in classrooms do. As a model of processing, it is meant to apply to all learners of all languages in all contexts (in and out of classrooms). Thus, the First Noun principle could be researched with learners of English as immigrants in the United States, learners of English in a classroom in Canada, learners of English in a classroom in Saudia Arabia, and so on. The model attempts to describe what learners do on their own, the same way research on Universal Grammar describes what learners do on their own regardless of instruction.

AN EXEMPLARY STUDY: VANPATTEN AND HOUSTON (1998)

In this study, VanPatten and Houston set out to study the following question: Can context override the strong effects of the first noun principle? It is well established that for a considerable period of time (even with instruction on object pronouns), English-speaking learners of Spanish will incorrectly process OVS structures in the form of *Lo insultó Susana en la reunión* ("Susan insulted him at the meeting") as "He insulted Susan at the meeting." To test the effects of context, VanPatten and Houston manipulated a set of experimental sentences so that OVS structures were embedded in a clause and were preceded by main clauses that were either neutral in context or that ought to constrain context:

No context: *Ricardo me dice que lo insultó Susana en la reunión.*
"Richard tells me that Susan insulted him at the meeting."

Context: *Ricardo está enojado porque lo insultó Susana en la reunión.*
"Richard is ticked off because Susan insulted him at the meeting."

Based on research on the role of context in L1 sentence ambiguity resolution (e.g., Murray & Liversedge, 1994), VanPatten and Houston hypothesized that the internal context of the sentences of the context-type would push learners away from an incorrect processing of *lo insultó Susana* because it makes more sense for Richard to be angry if Susan insulted him rather than he insulting her (i.e., her insult caused his anger).

The participants were 46 English L1 learners of Spanish L2 who were in their third semester of college study of Spanish. They heard a series of 20 sentences (10 Context and 10 No Context) that were randomized among 40 distracter sentences (total = 60 sentences). The participants heard each sentence and then were asked to indicate on an answer sheet who did what to whom by filling in the blanks around a verb. For example, if they heard *Ricardo me dice que lo insultó Susana en la reunión*, the answer sheet contained the following: _____ insulted _____. For the distracters, subjects heard sentences with tense variation and were told to circle PAST PRESENT FUTURE depending on when they believed the action occurred. The target sentences contained the following verbs: *attacked, insulted, rejected, greeted,* and *kissed,* each with two context and two no-context conditions (e.g., Richard says that Gloria kissed him in a very public place [no context]; Richard turned red when Gloria kissed him in a very public place [context]. Jane told her friends that Robert kissed her in front of her parents [no context]; Jane was embarrassed because Robert kissed her in front of her parents [context]). Sentences were roughly equal length.

The results yielded a significant main effect for context, proving that context made a difference. The participants misinterpreted the embedded OVS structures as SVO sentences as much as three times more often in the no-context condition compared with the context condition.[14] VanPatten and Houston also found, however, that not all subjects made use of context. Only eight subjects consistently demonstrated consistent use of context overriding the First Noun Principle. On the other hand, another eight subjects never used context and seemed to be guided only by the First Noun Principle. The majority used context about 60% or less of the time. VanPatten and Houston concluded that although context may be available in the sentence, if learners are at a low level of processing ability (i.e., comprehension is effortful), they may not be able to keep prior context in working memory long enough for it to interact with the incoming information from the embedded clause. Thus, context may be of use only for learners who are able to process information with little cost to attentional efforts.

EXPLANATION OF OBSERVED FINDINGS IN SLA

Observation # 1. Exposure to input is necessary for SLA, and Observation # 2. A good deal of SLA happens incidentally. It goes without saying that IP incorporates the important role of input. What is more, however, is that the model of IP would suggest that most of acquisition is incidental. As we noted earlier, IP is dependent on comprehension (learners actively engaged in getting meaning from what they hear or read). In a certain sense, ac-

---

[14]There was some variation by verb. For example, with the insulted sentences, participants misinterpreted OVS as SVO three times more often in the no-context condition, whereas with the attacked sentences the misinterpretation was about twice as often.

quisition is a byproduct of learners' actively attempting to comprehend input. Their primary focus is on meaning and the connection of form–meaning and the parsing of sentences is a result of the learners' communicative endeavors.

Observation # 4: Learners follow predictable paths. . . .   Although it is not the goal of IP to explain all of SLA, there are certain observed phenomena for which it can help to account. SLA asks the question "Why do learners make some form–meaning connections and not others?" and thus can speak to orders of acquisition. When taken together, the various principles of IP account for why the verbal inflection system in English, for example, emerges the way it does. Learners will first process (and subsequently acquire) *–ing* due to the Meaning before Nonmeaning Principle and due to the Lexical Preference Principle (no lexical items carry the meaning of *–ing*). Third-person *–s* would be acquired last because of the Preference for Nonredundancy Principle (third-person *–s* is always redundant whereas the other verbal inflections in English are not).

Observation # 7. There are limits on the effects of frequency on SLA and Observation # 8. There are limits on the effect of a learner's first language on SLA.   Because IP is concerned with initial processing and the factors that affect it, frequency does not play a major role. For example, adjective agreement is frequent in Spanish, but the principle regarding redundancy mitigates initial processing of agreement. Other less frequent things, if they are not redundant, will get processed sooner. The problem with frequency is that sometimes it goes hand-in-hand with redundancy/nonredundancy. For example, *–ing* may be more frequent in English than simple past tense, *–ed*. But *–ing* is also never redundant whereas *–ed* often is (see above). The question then becomes whether frequency causes *–ing* to be processed before *–ed* or whether the redundancy principle outlined earlier in this chapter is the cause. Such questions can only be answered by continued research on a variety of languages.

IP also accounts for limits of the effects of both frequency and the L1. The various principles that deal with Lexical Preference, Nonredundancy, Meaning before Nonmeaning, and so on would mitigate the sheer effects of frequency as well as against the L1. Just because a form is highly frequent does not mean it will be processed if (1) it is redundant and/or (2) if it carries no meaning, for example. At the same time, if parsing strategies turn out to be at least partially universal rather than L1 based (see the discussion on the First Noun Principle), then the model of IP would account even more for the limited effects of the L1.

Observation # 9. There are limits on the effects of instruction on SLA. The present model of IP also helps to account for the limited effects of instruction. A good deal of instruction is centered on product rather than process.

That is, instruction is most often concerned with rules and with learner output. Our model of IP suggests that part of the learning problem is in processing. Thus, if instruction fails to account for how things get processed in the input, it may not be as useful as we think. Work on IP has lead to an instructional intervention called *processing instruction*, which speaks to this very issue. In processing instruction, instruction actually seeks to intervene during input processing, thus altering learners' processing behaviors and leading to more grammatically rich intake.

Observation #10. There are limits on the effects of output (learner production) on language acquisition. Although IP does not speak directly to issues of output, the model would suggest that the effects of learner output would be constrained if output does not help to alter learners' processing behaviors. For example, an English-speaking learner of Spanish can produce all the sentences he or she wants in a variety of contexts. But if the interaction does not lead the learner to realize that he or she has misinterpreted an OVS sentence, then little will change in terms of acquisition. That learner will continue to process Spanish first (pro)nouns as subjects. Under this scenario, output would be useful if it leads learners to register and then correct their misinterpretations of others' meanings.

CONCLUSION

Input processing as a phenomenon should be viewed as one part of a complex set of processes that we call acquisition. As such, any model or theory of IP should not be expected to be a model or theory of acquisition more generally. Ideally one would like to see various models that account for different processes in acquisition, and when viewed this way a better picture of acquisition ought to emerge.

Models and theories undergo change and evolution, and this is no less true for a model of L2 input processing. As is the case with almost every theory and model in SLA, challenges have been leveled against IP resulting in lively debate in the professional literature (see, for example, DeKeyser, Salaberry, Robinson & Harrington, 2002, and VanPatten 2002, as well as Harrington, 2004, Carroll, 2004, and VanPatten 2004b). However, these challenges are leveled at the specifics of the model and not at the underlying questions that drive the model, namely, "Why some form–meaning connections and not others? Under what conditions?" Some kind of model of input processing will need to co-exist alongside models that deal with how linguistic data are incorporated into the developing system as well as how learners access the system to make output, and so on. The current model of IP is our first pass at considering how learners process input during real time comprehension.

DISCUSSION QUESTIONS

1. IP theory claims that processing input is effortful for L2 learners and implies that learners cannot pay attention to everything at once. One consequence is that lexical items are privileged in input processing. Do you think lexical items are privileged in acquisition more generally? What about learner attempts to produce language? What about learner strategies in terms of overt attempts to learn a language (e.g., conscious strategies to try and comprehend what someone else is saying)?

2. VanPatten offers that L2 parsing may involve universal procedures or it may be L1-based initially (i.e., the L1 parser is "transferred"). Or, some combination may be at play. Which do you think is more likely? Can you think of additional experimentation and data that would help to determine which position is more likely?

3. The theory of IP in this chapter claims that learners' initial orientation toward input is to process it for meaning; that is, they do what they can to extract basic meanings from sentences. Can you think of any circumstances under which learners would approach processing sentences for form/structure first? Do you think this leads to acquisition?

4. Take the language you teach or are most familiar with and try to apply either the Lexical Preference Principle or the First Noun Principle to input processing for that language. Can you make any predications about processing problems? For example, under the Lexical Preference Principle, what formal features of the language tend to co-occur with lexical items or phrases that express the same concept? What is your prediction about processing?

5. One of the most well-known outcomes of the model of IP is VanPatten's *processing instruction*. Read one of the research chapters in VanPatten 2004 and present the results to your class.

SUGGESTED FURTHER READING

VanPatten, B. (Ed.). (2004). *Processing instruction: Theory, research, and commentary*. Mahwah, NJ: Lawrence Erlbaum Associates.

This book is essentially an update on VanPatten's 1996 book, *Input processing and grammar instruction: Theory and research*. The 2004 volume contains two important expository essays, one on input processing and one on processing instruction. Also included are 10 previously unpublished research papers. What makes the book interesting is the inclusion of commentary and criticism by six other scholars, offering a balance for the reader.

VanPatten, B., Williams, J., & Rott, S. (2004). Form–meaning connections in second language acquisition. In B. VanPatten, J. Williams, S. Rott & M. Overstreet (Eds.), *Form–meaning connections in second language acquisition* (pp.1–26). Mawah, NJ: Lawrence Erlbaum Associates.

This first chapter in the VanPatten, Williams, Rott, and Overstreet book offers an overview of the many factors that contribute to how form–meaning connections are made and strengthened. As such, it extends beyond the scope of IP theory, demonstrating how IP fits into a larger picture of acquisition.

REFERENCES

Carreiras, M., García-Albea, J., & Sebastián-Gallés, N. (Eds.) (1996). *Language processing in Spanish*. Mahwah, NJ: Lawrence Erlbaum Associates.

Carroll, S. (2001). *Input and evidence: The raw material of second language acquisition.* Amsterdam: Benjamins.

Carroll, S. (2004). Commentary: Some general and specific comments on input processing and processing instruction. In B. VanPatten (Ed.), *Processing instruction: Theory, research, and commentary* (pp. 293–309). Mahwah, NJ: Lawrence Erlbaum Associates.

Clifton, C., Frazier, L., & Rayner, K. (1994). *Perspectives on sentence processing*. Hillsdale, NJ: Lawrence Erlbaum Associates.

DeKeyser, R., Salaberry, R. Robinson, P., & Harrington, M. (2002). What gets processed in processing instruction? A commentary on Bill VanPatten's 'Processing Instruction: An Update.' *Language Learning, 52*, 805–823.

Harrington, M. (2004). IP as a theory of processing input. In B. VanPatten (Ed.), *Processing instruction: Theory, research, and commentary* (pp. 79–92). Mahwah, NJ: Lawrence Erlbaum Associates.

Marinis, T., Roberts, L., Felser, C., & Clahsen, H. (2005). Gaps in second language sentence processing. *Studies in Second Language Acquisition, 27*: 53–78.

Murray, W., & Liversedge, S. P. (1994). Referential context effects on syntactic processing. In C. Clifton, Jr., L. Frazier, & K. Rayner (Eds.), *Perspectives on sentence processing* (pp. 359–388). Hillsdale, NJ: Lawrence Erlbaum Associates.

Pritchett, B. L. (1992). *Grammatical competence and parsing performance*. Chicago: University of Chicago Press.

VanPatten, B. (1984). Learner comprehension of clitic object pronouns in Spanish. *Hispanic Linguistics, 1*, 56–66.

———. (1996). *Input processing and grammar instruction: Theory and research*. Norwood, NJ: Ablex.

————. (2002). Processing the content of input processing and processing instruction research: A response to DeKeyser, Salaberry, Robinson, and Harrington. *Language Learning, 52*, 825–831.

————. (2004a). Input processing in second language acquisition. In B. VanPatten (Ed.), *Processing instruction: Theory, research, and commentary* (pp. 5–31). Mahwah, NJ: Lawrence Erlbaum Associates.

————. (2004b). Several reflections on why there is good reason to continue researching the effects of processing instruction. In B. VanPatten (Ed.), *Processing instruction: Theory, research, and commentary* (pp. 325–335). Mahwah, NJ: Lawrence Erlbaum Associates.

VanPatten, B., & Houston, T. (1998). Contextual effects in processing L2 input sentences. *Spanish Applied Linguistics, 1*(2), 53–70.

White, L. (1987). Against comprehensible input: The input hypothesis and the development of L2 competence. *Applied Linguistics, 8*, 95–110.

8

Processability Theory

Manfred Pienemann
University of Paderborn and University of Newcastle upon Tyne

THE THEORY AND ITS CONSTRUCTS

Processability Theory (Pienemann, 1998, and elsewhere) is a theory of second language development. The logic underlying Processability Theory (PT) is the following: At any stage of development, the learner can produce and comprehend only those second language (L2) linguistic forms that the current state of the language processor can handle. It is therefore crucial to understand the architecture of the language processor and the way in which it handles an L2. This enables one to predict the course of development of L2 linguistic forms in language production and comprehension across languages.

The architecture of the language processor accounts for language processing in real time and within human psychological constraints, such as word access and working memory. The incorporation of the language processor in the study of L2 acquisition therefore brings to bear a set of human psychological constraints that are crucial for the processing of languages. The view on language production followed in PT is largely that described by Levelt (1989), which overlaps to some extent with the computational model of Kempen and Hoenkamp (1987) and Merrill Garrett's work (e.g. Garrett, 1976, 1980, 1982). The basic premises of the view of language processing in PT are the following:

- Processing components operate largely automatically and are generally not consciously controlled.
- Processing is incremental.
- The output of the processor is linear although it may not be mapped onto the underlying meaning in a linear way.
- Grammatical processing has access to a temporary memory store that can hold grammatical information (see Pienemann, 1998, for details).

137

The core of PT is formed by a universal processability hierarchy that is based on Levelt's (1989) approach to language production. PT is formally modeled using Lexical–Functional Grammar (Bresnan, 2001). PT is a universal framework that has the capacity to predict developmental trajectories for any L2. The notion *developmental trajectory* implies a developmental dimension known as staged development and a variational dimension accounting for individual differences between developmental trajectories.

In this paradigm, each stage represents a set of grammatical rules that share certain processing routines, and each interlanguage variety represents a specific variant of the grammatical rules. For instance, in ESL question formation the following developmental sequence has been found (e.g., Pienemann, 1998):

Stage	Structure	Example
Stage 1	SVO question	He live here?
Stage 2	*wh*– + SVO	Where he is?
Stage 3	Copula inversion	Where is he?
Stage 4	Aux-second	Where has he been?

Learners attempting to produce Aux-second at stage 3 (i.e., before they are ready for this structure) have been found to produce the following interlanguage variants:

A. Where he been?
B. Where has been?
C. Where he has been?
D. He has been where?

Variants A to D have in common that they get around placing the auxiliary in second position after an initial *wh*–word. In other words, they constitute different solutions to the same learning problem. In the course of L2 development, learners accumulate grammatical rules and their variants, allowing them to develop individual developmental trajectories while adhering to the overall developmental schedule. In this way, PT accounts for both universal stages of development and individual variation within stages.

There are two separate problems that are crucial to address in understanding L2 acquisition. The original version of PT focused solely on what is known as the "developmental problem" (i.e., why learners follow universal stages of acquisition). The extended version of PT (Pienemann, Di Biase, & Kawaguchi, 2005) also begins to address the so-called logical problem (i.e., how do learners come to know what they know if their knowledge is not represented in the input? see White, chapter 3 this volume). The developmental and the logical problems are the key issues of any theory of language acquisition, and PT addresses these issues in a modular fashion. One module deals with the developmental problem; a separate, but connected module deals with the logical problem. Both modules are based on Lexical–Functional Grammar (LFG) because LFG is designed to account for linguistic knowledge in a way that is compatible with the architecture of the language processor, and both these components are needed for PT to address the developmental and the logical problems. The developmental problem is addressed by describing the constraints the language processor places on development, and the logical problem is addressed using specific components of LFG that are summarized later in this chapter.

The basic claim of the original version of PT is that language development is constrained by processability. This affects first language (L1) and L2 development (albeit in different ways). It also affects interlanguage variation and L1 transfer. The extended version of PT adds to this the claim that the initial form of grammar in L2 acquisition is determined by the default relationship between what is known as argument structure—that is, the ideas expressed in a sentence—and the way they are expressed by the grammatical forms of the target language. We turn our attention now to the major constructs of the theory.

Processability Hierarchy

In Pienemann (1998) the processability hierarchy is based on the notion of transfer of grammatical information within and between the phrases of a sentence. For instance, in the sentence "Little Peter goes home" the grammatical information "third person singular" is present in the phrase *Little Peter* and in *goes*. This is commonly referred to as subject-verb agreement. In LFG and in Levelt's model of language generation it is assumed that the language processor checks if the two parts of the sentence, *Little Peter* and *goes*, contain the same grammatical information. To be able to carry out this matching operation, the procedures that build phrases in language generation need to have developed in the L2 processing system. In our example learners need to have developed a procedure for building noun phrases such as *Little Peter* and verb phrases such as *goes home*. They also need to have developed a procedure for putting these two phrases together to form a sentence. In Levelt's model of language generation it is assumed that the grammatical information "third person singular" needs to be stored in the procedures that build the phrases in which this information is used, and that the two sets of information are compared within the procedure that puts the two phrases together to form a sentence. The learner of a language needs to develop procedures that can handle the job of storing and comparing grammatical information. This way speakers can learn to decide which sentences are grammatically acceptable and which one are not. For instance, in the sentence "*Little Peter go home" the phrase *Little Peter* is marked for third person singular, but the verb is not. This would be detected by a competent speaker when the noun phrase and the verb phrase are assembled to form a sentence. However, if the learner has not yet developed a fully functioning sentence procedure, the mismatch will not be detected.

The same principle applies to grammatical information contained within phrases. For instance, in the noun phrase *two kids*, the grammatical information "plural" is contained in the numeral *two* and in the noun *kids*. In language generation these two bits of information are compared when the noun phrase is assembled by the noun phrase-procedure. In the case of *two* and *kids* the two bits of grammatical information match.

We can now see that in both examples grammatical information has to be matched between parts of the sentence. In LFG this process is called *feature unification*. In non-technical language we might describe this process as information matching. LFG uses formal means to account for such processes. The fact that LFG has this capacity is one of the key reasons why PT uses LFG to model these psycholinguistic processes.

The two examples we used also serve to illustrate the processability hierarchy. It is easy to see that in the *Little Peter* example, grammatical information has to be matched between a noun phrase and the verb phrase and that this occurs when the two pieces are assembled to form the sentence. In contrast, in the second example (i.e., *two kids*) the information matching occurs in the noun phrase procedure—*before* the sentence is assembled. In other words, there is a time sequence involved in the matching of grammatical information, which forms the basis of the original processability hierarchy. Noun phrases are assembled before verb phrases, which are assembled before sentences. In addition, individual words belong to categories such as "noun" and "verb," and category procedures are the memory stores that hold grammatical information such as "singular" or "past." Therefore category procedures appear before noun phrase procedures.

The following is an overview of the original processability hierarchy, following Pienemann (1998):

1. No procedure (e.g., producing a simple word such as *yes*).
2. Category procedure (e.g., adding a past-tense morpheme to a verb).
3. Noun phrase procedure (e.g., matching plurality as in "two kids").
4. Verb phrase procedure (e.g., moving an adverb out of the verb phrase to the front of a sentence "I went yesterday/yesterday I went.").
5. Sentence procedure (e.g., subject-verb agreement).
6. Subordinate clause procedure (e.g., use of subjunctive in subordinate clauses triggeed by information in a main clause).

The basic hypothesis underlying PT is that learners develop their gram-matical inventory following this hierarchy for two reasons: (a) the hierarchy is implicationally ordered, that is, every procedure is a necessary prerequisite for the next procedure; and (b) the hierarchy mirrors the time-course in language generation. Therefore the learner has no choice other than to develop along this hierarchy. Phrases cannot be assembled without words being assigned to categories such as "noun" and "verb," and sentences cannot be assembled without the phrases they contain and so forth. The fact that learners have no choice in the path they take in the development of processing procedures fol-lows from the time-course of language generation and the design of processing procedures. This is how the architecture of language generation constrains language development. So observed stages of development are a direct result of the stage of processing in which learners find themselves. For example, if learners are in stage 3 of processing (they can only exchange information in a phrase), they will produce *wh*–questions that do not exhibit processing abili-ties beyond stage 3 (e.g., they will not be able to use auxiliaries correctly as in "Where has he gone?") because such questions involve processing that relies on the exchange of information outside phrases.

As mentioned above, the original version of the processability hierarchy focuses on information transfer within phrase structure. In the extended ver-sion of PT (Pienemann et al. 2005) the processability hierarchy is extended to include further aspects of language generation, in particular the relationship between what is known as argument structure and grammatical structure. Argument structure refers to the basic ideas conveyed in a sentence: Who does what to whom? The extended version of PT also includes the relation-ship between what is intended to be said and the way this is expressed using L2 grammatical forms. This extension is also modeled using LFG. Details will be summarized later on.

Hypothesis Space

The processability hierarchy has been described as the sequence in which the fundamental design of the language processor develops in L2 acquisition, and it has been added that the learner is constrained to follow this sequence. At the same time, the processing procedures developed at every stage of the hier-archy do allow for some degree of leeway for the shape of the L2 grammar. Hy-pothesis Space is created by the interplay between the processability hierarchy and the leeway it generates at every level.

An example may illustrate the constraining effect of the processability hierarchy. At stage 3 (noun phrase procedure) grammatical information can be exchanged only within noun phrases, not beyond the phrasal boundary. Therefore grammatical structures requiring information exchange beyond the phrase boundary, such as subject verb-agreement, cannot be processed at this stage. At the same time, these constraints leave sufficient leeway for learners to find different solutions to structural learning problems. I illustrated this earlier with the example of the position of auxiliaries in English *wh*–questions. This position requires processing procedures from a much later stage in the hierarchy. L2 learners nevertheless must produce *wh*–questions. When they attempt to do this, they have four structural options that avoid the placement of the auxiliary in second position. The reader will recall the examples given previously. Note how the learner can remain in stage 3 or processing (i.e., only processing information in noun phrases) when confronted with target structures that require higher processing procedures. In each example below, you will see how learners delete something or use a nonstandard or unexpected word order to avoid moving elements across phrases.

A.   Where he been?
B.   Where has been?
C.   Where he has been?
D.   He has been where?

Transfer of Grammatical Information and Feature Unification

As mentioned earlier, the original version of PT focused on phrase structure (which is called *constituent structure* in LFG) and the transfer of grammatical information within it. This information transfer process is modeled using feature unification. Every entry in the learner's mental lexicon needs to be annotated for the specific features of the target language. For instance, the entry *Peter* needs to be assigned to the lexical class "noun." It needs to be annotated as a proper noun, and the feature NUMBER needs to have the value "singular." The lexical entry *sees* needs to be assigned to the lexical class "verb," and the features NUMBER, PERSON, TENSE, and ASPECT need to have the following values:

NUMBER = singular
PERSON   = 3
TENSE   = present
ASPECT   = noncontinuous

To achieve subject verb-agreement in the sentence "Peter sees a dog," the value of the features NUMBER and PERSON have to be matched (or unified). The features NUMBER and PERSON have the values "third" and "singular," and these values reside in the lexical entries of the noun *Peter* and the verb *sees*. This grammatical information is passed on to the noun phrase procedure (NP) and verb phrase procedure (VP), respectively. From there the two sets of information are passed on to the sentence procedure (S) where they are matched.

In the design of PT, the point of unification is related to the hierarchy of processability that reflects the time-course of real time processing. The hierarchy that results from a comparison of the points of feature unification can be ordered as follows:

1. No exchange of grammatical information (= no unification of features).
2. Exchange of grammatical information within the phrase.
3. Exchange of grammatical information within the sentence.

Once one applies this hierarchy to ESL morphology, the following developmental trajectory can be predicted:

1. Past *–ed*   will appear before,
2. Plural *–s*   which in turn will appear before
3. Third person *–s*.

In order to appreciate the universal nature of PT, it is crucial to consider that the processability hierarchy is not language specific and that, in principle, it applies to the transfer of grammatical information in any language. In contrast, the examples that were given for ESL morphology utilize this hierarchy and apply it to one specific target language.

What the above discussion suggests is that learners develop a lexically driven grammar; that is, the lexicon stores grammatical information. For instance, the lexical entry for *walked* is marked for past tense and it lists the core argument of the verb as *agent*. This lexical information is required in the assembly of the sentence and thus grammatical information and features must be matched or unified.

Lexical Mapping

Lexical Mapping Theory is a component of Lexical–Functional Grammar (e.g., Bresnan, 2001). LFG has three independent and parallel levels of representation, as shown in Figure 8–1: *argument structure*, *functional structure*, and *constituent structure*. Argument structure describes who does what to whom in a sentence. It is based on a universal hierarchy of argument roles that includes roles such as *agent, experiencer, locative,* or *patient*. The core argument roles for each verb are listed in the lexical entry of the verb. For instance, the argument

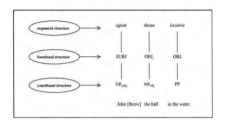

FIGURE 8–1. Sample of three levels of
structure in LFG.

roles of the English verbs throw are *agent, theme,* and *locative* (optional) and
see are *experiencer* and *theme.*

> John (agent) threw the ball (theme).
>
> John (agent) threw the ball (theme) in the water (locative).
>
> Peter (experiencer) sees ghosts (theme).

As mentioned above, constituent structure is basically another name for
phrase structure and describes the structure of the parts of sentences. This
component consists of universal units (such as "verb,'" "noun phrase," etc.),
but these are arranged in a way that is specific for every language. For instance, in some languages adjectives precede the noun, in other languages
they follow the noun. Functional structure consists of universal units (such as
SUBJECT or OBJECT) which are related to constituent structure in a language-specific way. Functional structure serves to connect argument structure
and constituent structure. These three levels are illustrated in Figure 8–1.

This design of LFG as a theory of language ensures that universal argument roles can be expressed using a whole range of different grammatical
forms. For instance, in English the argument role "agent" can be expressed as
a grammatical subject as can "experiencer" in the examples we saw above with
throw and see. But note that in English, other arguments can be expressed as
subjects in sentences such as passives: "The ball was thrown by John." In this
example, the theme is now the subject. In other words, the relationship between argument structure and the other two levels of structure is variable in a
specific language, and it also varies between languages. This variable relationship between what is intended to be said (argument structure) and the way it
is expressed using grammatical forms creates expressiveness in language, but it
also creates what Levelt (1981) calls "the linearisation problem." As mentioned previously, the output of the processor is linear while it may not be
mapped onto the underlying meaning in a linear way. This non-linear relationship can be seen, for instance, in subject-verb agreement where the information PERSON = 3 and NUMBER = singular is present in two places in
the output of the processor, and the two sets of information have to be assembled and coordinated by the speaker. In fact, this assembly can only be carried
out if the learner has developed the necessary processing procedures.

The linearisation problem also applies to the relationship between argument structure and functional structure. As demonstrated with the active–passive alternation above, the relationship between the underlying meaning and the way it is expressed can be variable. Therefore, the type of expression that deviates from a simple match between underlying meaning and grammatical form (as in the passive) introduces a degree of nonlinearity.

Unmarked Alignment

Lexical Mapping Theory accounts for the mapping of argument structure onto functional structure. In PT the default mapping principle is unmarked alignment, which is based on the one-to-one mapping of argument roles onto grammatical functions. In English, for instance, agent = SUBJECT is the prototypical or default association between argument structure and functional structure. But as we saw with passives, languages allow for a much wider range of relationships between argument structure and functional structure, and the ability to map these relationships develops step-wise in L2 acquisition. Principles of lexical mapping can account for these developmental processes. For L2 acquisition, unmarked alignment is the initial state of development and results in canonical word order. (i.e., the most typical word order for that language). For ESL this is SVO. Unmarked alignment simplifies language processing for the learner who, at this stage, will analyze the first noun phrase as the agent. This way, canonical word order avoids any kind of transfer of grammatical information during language processing.

PT implies that L2 acquisition starts with an unmarked functional structure and that changes of the relationship between arguments and functional structure will require additional processing procedures that will be acquired later. Hence the unmarked alignment hypothesis implies a developmental prediction for L2 structures that affect the relationship between argument structure and functional structure. Let's return to the passive we saw earlier. In the passive, the relationship between argument roles and syntactic functions may be altered as illustrated in examples (1) through (4).

(1) John threw the ball.
(2) *throw*   [*agent,*   *theme*]
                     | |
              SUBJ   OBJ
(3) The ball was thrown by John.
(4) *thrown*   [*agent,*   *theme*]
                     | |
                     Ø   SUBJ   (ADJ)

Sentences (1) and (3) describe the same event involving two participants. The difference between the two is that in (3) the constituent *the ball* that is OBJECT in (1) is realized as SUBJECT, and the constituent *John* that is SUBJECT in (1) is realized as PRESPOSITIONAL PHRASE.

These alterations of the relationship between argument roles and syntactic functions constitute a deviation from unmarked alignment. In order for this type of marked alignment to be possible, the function of a noun phrase (SUBJECT, OBJECT, or PREPOSITIONAL PHRASE, among others) can be established only by assembling information about the constituents in the sentence procedure, and this construction requires a procedure in the processability hierarchy higher than the category procedure. Therefore PT predicts that in English the passive is acquired later than active SVO sentences.

The TOPIC Hypothesis

As mentioned earlier, Lexical Mapping Theory specifies the relationship between argument structure and functional structure, and PT derives developmental predictions from the language-specific relationship between argument structure and functional structure using Lexical Mapping Theory. Similar predictions can also be derived from the relationship between functional structure and constituent structure. One set of such predictions is entailed in the TOPIC Hypothesis. To account for developmental dynamics in the relationship between functional structure and constituent structure, Pienemann et al. (2005) propose the TOPIC hypothesis, which predicts that learners will not initially differentiate between SUBJECT and other grammatical functions in sentence-initial position (e.g., TOPIC). In this context it is important to note that in LFG, TOPIC is a grammatical function. For instance in the sentence "Ann, he likes" Ann has two functions, OBJECT and TOPIC. The TOPIC function is assigned to a constituent in sentence-initial position other than the SUBJECT that introduces new information to the discourse (for instance, *Ann* in the above example) This process is referred to as topicalization. When the learner is able to add a constituent before the subject position, this will trigger the differentiation of the grammatical functions TOPIC and SUBJECT.

The TOPIC hypothesis predicts that TOPIC will first be assigned to so-called noncore functions, which do not relate to arguments listed in the lexical entries of verbs. Noncore functions are those other than SUBJECT and OBJECT. Later they will also be assigned to core functions such as OBJECTS. The reason for this is that that the assignment of TOPIC to core functions alters the unmarked alignment between arguments and functions. In other words, the TOPIC hypothesis predicts three overall stages in the mapping of functional structure onto constituent structure:

1. TOPIC and SUBJECT are not differentiated.

    (Peter saw Mary.)   He liked the girl.
                                  | |
                                 SUBJ   OBJ

2. The initial constituent is an ADJUNCT or a question-word. TOPIC is differentiated from SUBJECT.

    Yesterday everyone smiled
       | |
      ADJ   SUBJ

3. The TOPIC function is assigned to a core argument other than SUBJ.

    Ann, I think, he likes.
      | |
     OBJ . . . .   SUBJ

WHAT COUNTS AS EVIDENCE?

Given the focus of PT on developmental dynamics, the most suitable research design is a longitudinal or cross-sectional study with a large set of data relevant for the phenomena under scrutiny. In such studies the researcher collects naturalistic or elicited speech data that form the corpus on which the study is based. Relevant data does not equal a large data set. The data need to be relevant to the point to be studied. For instance, the study of subject-verb agreement marking requires a large set of contexts for subject-verb agreement marking. This will allow the researcher to decide if the verbal marker is supplied. If no context appears, no conclusion can be drawn. However, even the presence of a number of morphological markers is no guarantee that these are based on productive interlanguage rules. In order to exclude the use of formulae and chunks, the researcher needs to check lexical and morphological variation (i.e., same morpheme on different words and same word with different morphemes).

Apart from corpus data, reaction time experiments also constitute a valid basis of a test of PT. As an example, a learner might be tested on subject-verb agreement. The learner reads two sentences on a computer screen and must judge if the two sentences are identical by pressing particular computer keys for yes or no. Some pairs of sentences are grammatical and some are not. The trick is that the sentences only appear briefly, say, for 300 milliseconds. The time it takes the learner to make the judgment is measured. The predication is that ungrammatical sentences take longer to process because the learner is "checking for feature agreement."

COMMON MISUNDERSTANDINGS

A major misunderstanding regarding PT is that it can be applied to any language without first considering how particular features of a target language are processed, that is, how to describe the feature using LFG as the linguistic framework. For example, some scholars who have tried to apply PT to a new target language have based their application on the developmental trajectories found for English and German, the two key target languages in previous research. These researchers looked for such things as agreement or word order phenomena that appeared similar to the developmental stages found in English and German. But the grammars of individual languages may vary considerably—as may the processes involved in producing specific structures. For example, English requires subjects, especially in third-person constructions such as *Is he coming?* versus **Is coming?*, *It is raining* versus **Is raining.* Thus, for English there is a clear and fairly constant exchange of information between subject and verb, which we previously identified as involving sentence-level processing procedures. But now consider a language like Spanish. In Spanish, subjects are optional in many instances, and subjects are prohibited in expressions related to weather and time and in impersonal expression ("It's two o'clock," "It's important," "It's nice that you're here"). Thus, whereas English requires a pronoun in *It is raining*, Spanish prohibits one and the sentence is realized as *Está lloviendo.* Conversely, there are sentences in which overt subjects appear in Spanish, especially when beginning a new topic: *Mi amigo se casa* ("My friend is getting married.") But all verbs in Spanish must agree with a subject such that either *Está lloviendo* or *Mi amigo se casa* would be wrong if the verbs were, say, *están* or *se casan* (both third person plural). What is more, in Spanish, with nonthird person, subject pronouns may be rarely used. It is typical for someone to say *¿Cómo estás?* and not *¿Cómo estás tú?* whereas in English one would have to say *How are you?* and never *How are?* The question becomes, how is subject-verb agreement treated by LFG in Spanish when sometimes grammatical information needs to be exchanged between subjects and verbs, and when sometimes there is no subject for the verb to exchange information with—and Spanish may not even allow a subject in that particular kind of construction? Clearly, there is something different about how such information is processed in Spanish during speech, and thus the rules for English and German cannot be applied wholesale to Spanish, nor can the stages of development that lead up to subject-verb agreement.

Note how the exemplary study presented in this chapter does not fall into this misunderstanding. As we shall see in the study below on Japanese SLA, the processability hierarchy needs to be applied to a new target language on the basis of the fundamental principles of PT, not on the basis of developmental trajectories found in specific target languages. Utilizing fundamental principles of PT includes a detailed analysis of the information transfer required for the production of specific structures. This is best done on the basis of an LFG analysis of the structures in question.

AN EXEMPLARY STUDY: KAWAGUCHI (2005)

Given that PT has been designed as a universal theory of L2 development, it is important to demonstrate that it can be applied to typologically distant languages and that the predictions for developmental trajectories derived from this application are borne out by empirical studies. Kawaguchi's (2005) study exemplifies the applicability of PT to the acquisition of Japanese by deriving a developmental trajectory for Japanese as a Second Language (JSL), which is supported by longitudinal data.

In order to appreciate Kawaguchi's application of PT to JSL it is crucial to consider some of the key features of Japanese grammar that the predicted developmental trajectory is based on: Japanese is an SOV language, and the verb is always in final position. However, syntactic relations (such as SUBJECT, OBJECT, etc.) are not marked by word order (unlike in English). Instead, syntactic relations are marked by nominal particles that follow the noun to be marked. Kawaguchi gives the following example:

(5) Piano-o   Tamiko-ga   hiita
    Piano-ACC   Tamiko-NOM   play-PAST
    'Tamiko played the piano'

In this example the marker –o marks the word *piano* for accusative, and the particle –ga marks *Tamiko* for nominative. These markers allow the correct interpretation of the sentence with Tamiko as the agent and *piano* as the theme. As Kawaguchi points out, Japanese word order is relatively free. Therefore the two noun phrases in (5) may be scrambled without affecting the meaning of the sentence.

Kawaguchi derives a specific and testable developmental trajectory from PT and Lexical Mapping Theory for Japanese as a second language. For the purpose of this chapter, I will summarize only the four example structures that follow from the hypotheses discussed above:

Level	Information transfer	Structure
1. Lexical procedure	category	$-TOP_{SUBJ}$ (O)V
2. Phrasal procedure	phrase	−Topic + S(O)V
3. Sentence procedure	sentence	−Passive
		−OBJECT Topicalization

The unmarked alignment hypothesis predicts that SLA learners will not initially differentiate between TOPIC and SUBJECT. This is reflected in the structure $\underline{TOP_{SUBJ}\ (O)V}$ where $\underline{TOP_{SUBJ}}$ is simultaneously TOPIC and SUBJECT. Note that this initial structure also follows the canonical word order that applies to Japanese (SOV). At the phrasal level TOPIC and SUBJECT can be two different phrases ($\underline{Topic + S(O)V}$), and at the sentence level objects can be in initial—that is, topic—position. The latter two steps are also predicted by the TOPIC hypothesis, which states that the TOPIC function will first be applied to noncore arguments (for instance, adjuncts) and only then to core arguments (that is, to OBJECTS in Kawaguchi's study). The position of the passive in the processability hierarchy follows from alterations in the relationship between argument structure and functional structure. Kawaguchi demonstrates that these structures are related to the general levels of the processability hierarchy as shown earlier. It is this systematic linkage of the specific JSL structures with the processability hierarchy that yields the crucial prediction of a JSL developmental trajectory.

Kawaguchi conducted two longitudinal studies spanning two and three years, respectively. The informants were Australian native speakers of English who started learning Japanese in a formal setting. The informants also had regular contact with Japanese exchange students using Japanese. The informants received six hours of linguistic input per week for 24 weeks per year. Data were collected in natural conversation and using communicative tasks. Data collection started four weeks after commencement of the course. Each session lasted between 20 and 30 minutes. Samples were collected every month. The data were transcribed and further transliterated using a romanization system that permits a computer-based analysis of the data. To test the hypotheses derived from PT, Kawaguchi carried out a distributional analysis of the data. For this analysis the structures that are included in the hypothesized developmental trajectory are searched in the learner data. The absence or presence of these structures is counted for every sample.

The data analysis revealed that in Kawaguchi's corpus, all structures included in her hypotheses follow the predicted sequence: The verb appeared in the last position in every sentence and for every session right from the start. The structure $TOP_{SUBJ} (O)V$ appeared in a clearly distinguishable next step, and this was followed by structures in which TOPIC and SUBJECT are differentiated. Thus, the results support the predications made by PT involving how processing constrains language development.

EXPLANATION OF OBSERVED FINDINGS IN SLA

Processability Theory can account for several of the observed phenomena in SLA outlined in chapter 1.

Observation #4. Learner's output often follows paths with predictable stages in the acquisition of a given structure.   Explaining this observation is one of the key points of Processability Theory. PT has the capacity to predict stages of acquisition in typologically diverse languages by locating grammatical structures of the L2 within the processability hierarchy. These predictions can be universally applied because they are specified within LFG.

Observation # 5. Second language learning is variable in its outcome. Interlanguage variability is generated by the leeway defined by Hypothesis Space at every stage of development. I demonstrated earlier that every learning problem (i.e., every developmental structure) can be solved in a limited number of different ways and that the range of solutions is defined by Hypothesis Space. In the course of development the learner thus accumulates different variants of developmental structures. The accumulated choices made by the learner determine the shape of the interlanguage variety of the learner. One class of choices made by learners implies that the specific interlanguage rule cannot develop further. When learners accumulate many of these choices the interlanguage stabilizes. Different degrees of "bad choices" made by the learner determine the point in development at which the interlanguage system stabilizes.

Observation # 7. There are limits on the effects of frequency on second language acquisition.   Given the hierarchical nature of the processability hierarchy none of the processing procedure constraints in the hierarchy can be skipped because every lower procedure constitutes a prerequisite for the next higher one. Therefore frequency cannot override the constraints of the hierarchy.

Observation # 8. There are limits on the effect of a learner's first language on second language acquisition. The key assumption of PT is that L2 learners can produce only those linguistic forms for which they have acquired the necessary processing procedures. Under this scenario, L1 features and structures can only be transferred when the learner begins to process L2 features and structures that are relevant to the L1. For example, learners cannot transfer knowledge or abilities regarding L1 subject-verb agreement until they get to the stage where they can process this kind of grammatical information in the L2. This claim is referred to as the "developmentally moderated transfer hypothesis" (Pienemann, Di Biase, Kawaguchi, & Håkansson, 2005).

Observation # 9. There are limits on the effects of instruction on second language acquisition. Given that every processing procedure in that hierarchy forms a key prerequisite for the next higher stage, none of the stages/prerequisites can be skipped. Therefore stages of acquisition cannot be skipped through formal instruction. In other words, the effect of teaching is constrained by processability. This was formerly referred to as the Teachability Hypothesis (Pienemann, 1984) and has been subsumed under PT.

Observation #10. There are limits on the effects of output (learner production) on language acquisition. Because output is constrained by processability, learners cannot produce structures that are beyond their level of processing. Thus, practice does not make perfect in language learning, and interaction in which learners may become aware of structures may not lead to their being produced. Production of new features and structures reflects a change in processing and is not the cause of it.

DISCUSSION QUESTIONS

1. How does Processability Theory explain staged development in SLA?
2. In what ways is Processability Theory different from (or similar to) generative or cognitive theories used in SLA research?
3. For the language you are involved in, select two different structures. What would you predict about their relative-order emergence based on PT? What processing procedures seem to be involved?
4. What instructional implications, if any, do you see in Pienemann's work?
5. Why does PT require "naturalistic" or "spontaneous" production data as evidence?

SUGGESTED FURTHER READING

Readings on processability tend to be difficult to follow for beginning students of SLA. Here we include just three, which are useful for advancement of understanding the theory.

Pienemann, M. (1998). *Language processing and second language development. Processability Theory*. Benjamins: New York.

This is the first book published on PT and is essential reading. The first and second chapters are particularly useful for grasping the basic tenets of the theory.

———(Ed.) 2005. *Cross-linguistic aspects of Processability Theory*. Benjamins: New York.

This volume contains a good overview of PT in the first chapter. Other chapters include empirical research on the predictions made by PT to languages such as Arabic, Chinese, and Japanese—although these readings may be challenging for the novice SLA student.

REFERENCES

Bresnan, J. (2001). *Lexical-functional syntax*. Malden, MA: Blackwell.

Garrett, M. F. (1976). Syntactic process in sentence production. In R. Wales & E. Walker (Eds.), *New approaches to language mechanisms* (pp. 231–256). Amsterdam: North Holland.

———. (1980). Levels of processing in sentence production. In B. Butterworth (Ed.), *Language production: Vol. 1. Speech and Talk* (pp. 177–220). London: Academic Press.

———. (1982). Production of speech: Observations from normal and pathological language use. In A. W. Ellis (Ed.), *Normality and pathology in cognitive functions* (pp. 19–76). London: Academic Press.

Kawaguchi, S. (2005). Argument structure and syntactic development in Japanese as a second language. In M. Pienemann (Ed.), *Cross-linguistic aspects of Processability Theory* (pp.253–298) New York: Benjamins.

Kempen, G., & Hoenkamp, E. (1987). An incremental procedural grammar for sentence formulation. *Cognitive Science, 11*, 201–258.

Levelt, W. J. M. (1981). The speaker's linearisation problem. *Philosophical Transactions. Royal Society London.* B295, 305–315.

———. (1989). *Speaking. From intention to articulation.* Cambridge, MA: M.I.T. Press.

Pienemann, M. (1984). Psychological constraints on the teachability of languages. *Studies in Second Language Acquisition, 6*, 186–214.

———. *Language processing and second language development: Processability Theory.* Amsterdam: Benjamins.

Pienemann, M., Di Biase, B., & Kawaguchi, S. (2005). Extending Processability Theory. In
    M. Pienemann (Ed.), *Cross-linguistic aspects of Processability Theory* (pp.199–252).
    New York: Benjamins.
Pienemann, M., Di Biase, B., Kawaguchi, S., & Håkansson, G. (2005). Processing con-
    straints on L1 transfer. In J. F. Kroll & A. M. B. DeGroot (Eds.), *Handbook of bilin-
    gualism: Psycholinguistic approaches.* New York: Oxford University Press.
Vigliocco, G., Butterworth, B., & Garrett, M. F. (1996). Subject-verb agreement in Spanish
    and English: Differences in the role of conceptual constraints. *Cognition, 61,* 261–298.

9

Autonomous Induction Theory

Susanne E. Carroll
The University of Calgary

The Autonomous Induction Theory (AIT) is a theory of SLA that shares some properties with most of the theories described elsewhere in this book but is also unique in some ways. Like research seeking evidence for Universal Grammar (UG) in interlanguage, AIT is concerned with explaining a learner's linguistic competence and draws from current formal linguistic research to do so. It too conceptualizes changes in linguistic competence as changes in mental grammar and hypothesizes that these changes come about through the activities of a psychological mechanism: the Language Acquisition Device (LAD). AIT also attributes an important role to UG to explain how learners possess knowledge of essential properties of grammars despite impoverished input. However, the view of UG taken by AIT is that it is manifested implicitly in the operations of LAD, which is in turn constrained by the modular processing systems with which it interacts. There is no component of the mind consisting of representations with UG principles as their content, and hence, it makes no sense to talk of "accessing" UG (see White, chapter 3 this volume).

AIT is designed to trace the course of development and characterize the processes that LAD uses to restructure grammars. It hypothesizes that LAD can do basically two things: It can (re)combine features to create categories or structures through a process called *feature unification*, or it can equate a category of one type (say, a phonological representation of a word) with a category of a quite different type (say, a morphosyntactic representation of a word). Unification and categorical correspondence are mental operations that occur unconsciously and outside of a learner's control. This is why I say that LAD rather than the learner restructures grammars. AIT is quite different from the interactionist paradigm in how it views attention, noticing, and intention as explanatory mechanisms in acquisition (e.g., Gass & Mackey, chapter 10 this volume).

THE THEORY AND ITS CONSTRUCTS

1. *Knowledge of language is encoded in* mental representations *that crucially exhibit structure (often unique to language)*.

AIT views grammatical knowledge in terms of formal features, which combine (unify) to form formal categories, which combine (unify), in turn, to form hierarchical structures. For example, all languages have a syntactic category that can refer to the concepts PERSON, THING, or PLACE. This syntactic category is referred to in traditional grammars as a *noun*, but contemporary linguists hypothesize that all referential categories are phrasal. Thus, the category that fits the traditional definition is a Noun Phrase, or NP, rather than a word (in some theories, the referential category is DetP for Determiner Phrase). The referential expression contains a morpheme that is its *head*. The head of an NP is thus an N. This label N, however, is understood to be an abbreviation of a set of morphosyntactic features, such as ANIMACY, and GENDER, among others. These features are made available to the LAD as part of its universal stock of primitives ("provided by UG"). (For discussion of features associated with nouns, see Harley & Ritter, 2002.)

Languages differ in the features that must be instantiated in nouns, so not all features appear in every noun or pronoun or, indeed, in every language. English, for example, has no gender distinction at all in its nouns, while French and German do. This means that French and German nouns must bear some gender feature specification but English nouns cannot. This difference will be important in discussing the L2 acquisition of gender later in this chapter. Dutch and Swedish, like French and German, have gender systems, but these four systems are not identical. Dutch and Swedish distinguish only between animate and inanimate (called common and neuter nouns) while French and German distinguish both masculine and feminine nouns. Thus, Dutch and Swedish nouns need bear only a specification for inanimate; animate nouns will receive a default specification. In French, there is no inanimate specification at all, and nouns must be specified when feminine. Masculine appears to function as a default gender marking. German has not only a masculine–feminine contrast but also a neuter subclass.

Lest there be some confusion about these observations, let me point out that we must distinguish between *grammatical gender* (a grammatical property of nouns) and *biological sex* classes (a semantic attribute of the referent of a noun). While there is a distinction between *he* and *she*, *him* and *her*, *his* and *her* in the animate personal pronoun system of English (nonliving things being referred to by *it* and *its*) this distinction is semantic and not morphosyntactic. It is not encoded in the grammatical representation of the pronoun but rather in the semantic representation of the sentences in which pronouns occur. It is this distinction which makes it possible to refer to my dog Daisy with a feminine pronoun in English, where German requires a masculine: *My dog Daisy likes to sleep in #his/her basket* versus *Mein Hund Daisy schläft gerne in seinem(his)/ *ihrem(her) Körbchen.* (Here "#" indicates semantic oddity while "*" indicates ungrammaticality.) I shall simplify the manner of talking about this distinction by saying that English does not have *grammatical gender* while French and German do.

To sum up this point, in languages with gender, each noun must have features that characterize its gender subclass. The word for a certain kind of chair in French is *chaise*, and it has a feature specification indicating that it belongs to the subclass of feminine nouns. In German, the word is *Stuhl* and it has a feature specification indicating that it belongs to the subclass of masculine nouns. Gender class is "cued" by variation in the form of agreeing modifiers: for example, *Der* (masc.) *Stuhl ist rot* ("The chair is red") but not **Die* (fem.) *Stuhl ist rot* ("The chair is red).

To say that languages differ in the features of their nouns is to say that the actual feature composition of nouns must be acquired by learners. Learners of French, German, Dutch, or Swedish must unconsciously come to know that these languages have gender systems. Because not all gender systems are alike, learners must learn from primary linguistic evidence which features must be selected. UG simplifies LAD's discovery process, of course, in that LAD functions so that a feature like MASCULINE can only occur if the target system also shows appropriate feature distinctions. Once the specific structure of the target language system has been discovered by LAD, these feature specifications define what it means to be a noun in that language and are present in linguistic memory as the lexical representation of that noun.

Returning to more general matters of grammatical patterning, in addition to the structural nature of words and phrases, there are also relationships between constituents in sentences and across sentences. Agreement relationships are just such a relationship. Not only must a determiner agree in gender with its head noun in French or German, but also adjectives which modify a given noun must also agree in gender: *J'ai vu la belle* (fem.) *chaise/*J'ai vu la beau* (masc.) *chaise* ("I saw the handsome chair"); *La chaise que tu veux acheter est belle/*La chaise que tu veux acheter est beau* ("The chair that you want to buy is handsome"). These relationships are subject to severe constraints and provide some of the strongest evidence for the Poverty of the Stimulus Hypothesis (e.g., White, chapter 3 this volume).

AIT invokes a theory of grammar in which the sound system, the morphosyntax, and the semantic system are described in parallel. Syntax does not precede phonology or semantics in any sense whatsoever. There are features, categories, and structures in the phonology (*prosodic structures*) which are unique not only in the fact that they pick out properties of sound systems but also in the fact that they do not align in a one-to-one fashion with *morphosyntactic structures* (e.g., gender and animacy in nouns). There are yet other features, *conceptual structures*, that are the representations for encoding meanings. These three kinds of mental representations are constrained by distinct principles (provided by UG) and are linked by *correspondence rules*. We will see below that correspondences can play a key role in explaining developmental paths.

> 2. *To characterize language acquisition, it is necessary to describe the acquisition processes that create novel structural distinctions in each of the three types of structural representations (prosodic structures, morphosyntactic structures, and conceptual structures); it is also necessary to describe the acquisition processes that create novel correspondences across levels of representation.*

Much of the generative SLA literature has been directed toward explaining structural distinctions within a given level of representation and has not concerned itself with explaining how the learner might come to represent such distinctions. *Cue-based theories*, in contrast, are concerned with how the contents of one kind of structural representation might cue the contents of another kind. Cues play an important role in AIT's vision of language acquisition and UG.

Functional approaches appear to take for granted that conceptual structures are the sole or the primary source of cues about the internal organization of morphosyntactic structures and have had virtually nothing to say about how the learner arrives at correct Prosodic Structures. AIT asserts that both prosodic structures and conceptual structures can provide cues to morphosyntactic structure via correspondence rules.

Although much of the psychological literature refers to acquisition in terms of skills and habits, AIT asserts that the learner has acquired linguistic knowledge when some learning process creates a novel structure or establishes a novel correspondence across levels of representation. Acquisition is just the creation of a novel mental representation.

> 3. *Language acquisition must be defined from analysis of input and is not equivalent to control of linguistic distinctions in speech production.*

There may be a significant time lag between the moment when the learner constructs a mental representation encoding a given distinction (or establishes a novel correspondence across levels of representation) and the point in time when the learner can reliably activate this mental representation in long-term memory for speech production purposes. A learner may be able to perceive and comprehend a sentence like *Eine Katze frißt eine Maus* ("A cat eats/is eating a mouse" or ("A mouse eats/is eating a cat") long before the same learner can actively recall the words for the concepts *cat* or *mouse* or that *eine* is used not only to refer to some nonspecific *cat* or *mouse* but also to indicate that both *Katze* and *Maus* belong to the subset of feminine nouns. Indeed, it is a well-attested fact that English-speaking learners of German do indeed understand sentences with gender-marked determiners long before they can accurately reproduce gender-agreement in their own speech and writing. (See Pienemann, chapter 8 this volume, for a theory on speech production.)

    4. LAD is sensitive to structural distinctions when it changes mental representations.

LAD builds structures; it changes them. Language acquisition is, therefore, not merely a question of strengthening associations between forms and meanings. It may nonetheless make sense to talk of the strength of an encoding when talking about memory and recall. Of necessity, we are observing not only learners' grammars but also their memory systems. It will normally not be enough for learners to merely encode a distinction for us to know that they have acquired it; for learners to be able to actually perceive, parse, and comprehend speech reliably, they must be able to reliably activate grammatical distinctions in memory. This will be a matter of "practice makes perfect." AIT has little to say about how memory for linguistic encoding improves over time but acknowledges the critical role played by performance systems in investigating SLA (see DeKeyser, chapter 6 this volume).

    5. Structure-building operations occur in the sound system (phonology), in the morphosyntax, and in the meaning system. Each system is both autonomous *and* modular.

AIT postulates that there are distinct components of the mental grammar in which prosodic structures, morphosyntactic structures, and conceptual structures are created. Saying that the representations are autonomous is just saying that distinctions encoded in a phonetic representation (adverting to constructs like vocal fold vibration, bursts of noise, wave duration, or wave amplitude) are quite different from the distinctions encoded in a conceptual structure (adverting to constructs like Agent or Action, primitive functions like CAUSE, DO, or GO, quantificational notions like ALL or SOME, and so on).

AIT also hypothesizes that the language faculty consists of *modules*. A module is a processing component which operates on a very limited form of representation (that processor's own *input*) and outputs a very limited form of representation. The functional architecture of the language processing system (and ultimately of LAD) is derived from work by Jackendoff (2002).

Jackendoff's functional architecture hypothesizes two categories of processors. There are *integrative processors* that integrate primitives of some level of representation into complex structures. These are the processors that build structural representations. Input to an integrative processor will be any set of symbols that the processor can process. So, for example, the phonetic processor takes the speech signal as input and creates some sort of prelexical phonetic representation, encoding sequences of pitch, rhythm, and duration. The phonological processor takes such phonetic representations and other aspects of the segmented signal as input and creates a structured prosodic representation as output (= a *sound form* or *prosodic word*). This representation activates a lexical entry of the word in the mental lexicon. This activation process makes available the word's morphosyntactic features and its transitivity and argument structure, as well as its semantic features. The morphosyntactic processor takes the morphosyntactic information contained in the activated lexical entry and uses it to integrate that word into a morphosyntactic structure of the sentence. A distinct semantic processor will take the semantic information in the activated lexical entry and attempt to build a conceptual structure containing the relevant meaning of the word.

AIT also postulates *correspondence processors* because the distinct autonomous representations must nonetheless be linked. The correspondence processors have as their input a complex representation at one level of representation (say, the phonology), and their output is a representation at a different level of representation (say, the morphosyntax). The operation of these processors has *not* been extensively studied, and figuring out how correspondences work from the extant literature is not easy. Correspondence processors are, however, essential for explaining how information can pass "bottom-up"—from the signal to the conceptual system—or "top-down"—from the conceptual system to the phonology.

> 6. *LAD cannot perform the exact same structural operations as a speech processor or language parser.*

By definition, language acquisition is about changes to the learner's grammar, and parsing is about analysing speech given the contents of the language user's grammar. Parsing presupposes linguistic competence; acquisition presupposes the absence of it. By definition, then, LAD is quite distinct from the speech processors and sentence parser.

> 7. *AIT distinguishes three types of input:* primary linguistic data *or stimuli*, input-to-processing-mechanisms, *and* input-to-the-LAD.

Only primary linguistic data provide objective properties that can be measured in the environment. Input-to-processing-mechanisms and input-to-the-LAD are themselves contained in mental representations. Thus, input to the morphosyntactic parser becomes available when a lexical entry is activated (say, when *Katze* becomes available). The contents of this entry might inform the parser that *Katze* has features such as ANIMATE and FEMININE.

Of course, if the learner has not learned the fact that German nouns belong to gender classes, then lexical activation might only make available the features available in the L1, for example, this is a count noun, it is third person, and it is singular. If LAD is to restructure this representation so that it contains the additional feature, some additional bit of information, some input-to-the-LAD, must become available from somewhere and trigger the restructuring process.

  8. *Acquisition is error driven.*

AIT integrates language processing and language acquisition. It does so by hypothesizing that language acquisition is "error driven" in that LAD is triggered when the parsing system fails. Breakdowns—or an inability to parse an input-to-a-parser—can occur in each processor. A failure in the phonetic processor will result in an inability to hear the signal as recognizable speech sounds. A failure in the accurate construction of a prosodic representation will result in an underspecified or an inaccurate representation of a sound form in long-term memory. If learners have not accurately encoded the phonological properties of a sound form, they should not be able to recognize it when they hear it nor be able to use a prosodic representation to speak. The same goes for the representation of the prosodic properties of larger stretches of speech over which tonal and rhythmic properties of the L2 phonology are organized.

  9. *Transfer operates through the language-specific processing procedures of the L1.*

AIT hypothesizes that as children learn their L1, they develop processing procedures that are "tuned" not only to the specific grammatical properties of the L1 but also to the frequency with which particular structures occur. As a result of this tuning, language users reveal preferences for parsing sentences in particular ways even when other analyses are grammatically possible. AIT hypothesizes that such preferences transfer; thus the initial sensitivities of L2 learners to some linguistic distinction will directly reflect grammatical distinctions encoded in the L1 processing system as well as the frequencies with which such distinctions occur in the L1. On first exposure to the L2, in the absence of any knowledge of its grammar, vocabulary, and sound system, perceptual and parsing procedures of the L1 are the only means initially available to analyze the L2 speech signal. Learners automatically and unconsciously transfer these procedures to the task of hearing and comprehending speech. These transferred procedures will normally lead to perceptual or processing failure, triggering LAD. Thus, the processing system of the L1 functions as a kind of filter of the actual primary linguistic data. This is called the *Filter Hypothesis* and also serves to explain why L2 learning can fossilize: If the L1 parser continually filters out relevant data, then LAD is not triggered.

AIT also hypothesizes that learners will rely on L1-specific processing preferences even at later stages of acquisition, once they have achieved a certain level of proficiency in parsing sentences. Processing procedures will apply in phases as the learner's increasing knowledge makes it possible to process stimuli of greater complexity. AIT hypothesizes that when a transferred parsing procedure can do the job, it will—and no acquisition will take place. If L1 procedures can lead the learner from the signal to an interpretation, there will be no need for LAD to function. The learner does not have to learn.

To summarize, parsers process the speech signal using extant grammatical distinctions encoded in processing procedures when they can. Initially, this means they apply the procedures and categories of the L1. When such transferred procedures are not adequate for analyzing the L2 speech signal, various kinds of breakdowns may be observed: failure to hear the signal as "sounds"; failure to recognize the sounds as a given word (e.g., as the sounds of *Maus*); failure to understand the meaning of a word (e.g., the meaning of *fressen*, which is a manner of eating); failure to construct the intended syntactic phrases of a sentence (e.g., [[[[the] [mouse]] [[is] [[eating] [[the] [[cat]]]]]]]). Where processors fail, LAD must go into action if the learner's system is to be restructured. Processors merely process speech given existing grammatical distinctions; only LAD can change the contents of the learner's mental representations. If LAD fails to create new representations, it will fail to provide the parsing system with the distinctions required to analyze the same kind of input correctly the next time around. When LAD leads to grammatical restructuring, however, the parsing system (using what has been acquired) *will* be able to deal with the sounds, words, or structures the next time around. This, put crudely, is how AIT envisions SLA.

WHAT COUNTS AS EVIDENCE?

Given that AIT is a complex theory, evidence for the theory must consist of evidence for the different components of the theory. There will be distinct kinds of evidence supporting the claims of autonomous representations and modular processing, of the error-driven nature of acquisition, and for the constrained interactions of LAD and the processors. There will be yet other kinds of evidence testing the particular kinds of grammatical representations that AIT favours. Relevant evidence must, however, be *type-appropriate* to the claims in question.

Longitudinal or Cross-sectional Studies

Studies of this sort (corpus-based analyses, elicited production, or comprehension studies) will provide evidence pertaining to developmental paths (what is acquired first, what later, what not at all). This evidence might, however, reveal competence differences or performance differences. Only appropriate experimentation can tease apart competence and performance.

Perceptual or Processing Experiments

Evidence pertaining to processing preferences must come from processing experiments. The researcher must show that despite possessing knowledge of a given structure, category, or representation, learners prefer to process them in a given way. Such experiments typically measure reaction time or processing speed.

Tasks that Tap Perception, Processing, and Production

Experimental tasks that compare what learners can perceive and parse versus what they can produce under either elicited conditions or spontaneously are needed to provide evidence that learners can cognize distinctions in perception and comprehension *before* they can manipulate the same distinctions in speech production. Such evidence would show that processing speech leads to acquisition (in the sense used here)—not to production.

Learning Experiments and Input Studies

Learning experiments that expose learners to the same kinds of stimuli and that show they arrive at different analyses are evidence for the complex interactions of L1 processing procedures and the nondeterministic kinds of solutions that LAD produces (see Housen, 2002, for illustration of the variability of learner solutions, and see below).

Given that AIT is concerned with questions of input, learning experiments could provide evidence that learners are sensitive to particular linguistic distinctions in performing a given task. This would mean that their processing systems could make use of those distinctions. By hypothesis, any distinction that the processors can make use of is a distinction that has already been acquired. Conversely, evidence that learners are impervious to a particular linguistic distinction (when performing a particular task) is evidence that it has yet to be acquired.

COMMON MISUNDERSTANDINGS ABOUT AIT

While Carroll (2001) has been widely read and reviewed, it has not yet been subjected to heated criticism nor applied to research interests other than my own. It would be premature to claim that there are misunderstandings about the theory—common or uncommon. I would nonetheless like to insist that AIT is not merely a repackaging of Jackendoff's functional architecture of mind for SLA researchers. The theory is a synthesis of proposals from various sources, including results from much of my own research, covering topics in syntax, semantics/pragmatics, and phonetics/phonology, as well as studies of how learners learn from positive and negative evidence, feedback, and correction. There has been some discussion of my take on the Noticing Hypothesis (e.g., Schmidt, 1990), so it merits some clarification.

I view "noticing" as a result of processing, not an objective input to it. I follow Jackendoff in assuming that "noticing" (conscious awareness) is a by-product of the processing of phonological representations. Given the modular nature of the processing system, this means that the contents of phonetic, morphosyntactic, and semantic systems will be inaccessible to "noticing" and attention. Thus, we cannot consciously attend to the internal contents of a morphosyntactic representation, and as a result we cannot attend to the details of representations, such as those that encode agreement. Similarly, we cannot attend to the internal contents of conceptual structures or phonetic structures. It follows that attention is a prerequisite for learning only in the trivial sense that unconscious detection of distinctions is a basic component of the Noticing Hypothesis.

AN EXEMPLARY STUDY: SABOURIN (2003)

Unfortunately for the purposes of the present volume, there is no single study that tests AIT or its hypotheses in any way similar to studies presented in other chapters. However, there are a number of studies on gender acquisition that illustrate how the results are predicted by AIT. In this section, I will review one. But first we need to review several facts about gender.

In languages where the cues to gender are not found in affixes of the noun but rather on agreement markers (on determiners or adjectives, and so on), the learner will have to be exposed to words in sentences to cognize that the language has gender and to learn the gender representation of nouns because only sentences present the appropriate linguistic context. Western European languages tend to fall into this class of gender system. So in French, determiners (le tour, "the circuit", la tour, "the tower"), adjectives (les tours cour[t = 0]s = "the short circuits", les tours cour[t]es = "the short towers") and participles (les *tours que Lance a pri*[*s* = *0*] = "the circuits that Lance took", *les tours que le roi a pri*[*z*]*es* = "the towers that the king captured") can serve as cues to gender class. Because learning that these words are gender cues cannot, in principle, be acquired just by learning the noun from a list of other nouns, we predict that acquiring French gender cannot occur by learning vocabulary lists.

In English, neither determiners nor adjectives agree with nouns, and there are no syntactic domains within which gender marking is required. I pointed out the fact that English personal pronouns vary depending upon the meaning of the sentence, and claimed that this is not gender agreement but rather a reflection of semantic–syntactic correspondences that reflect reference and intentions to refer. Research on monolingual learners of French, German, and Hebrew provide overwhelming evidence that they select *form-related* cues to gender attribution. Studies of infants learning French and another language simultaneously produce similar results; infant learners are extremely sensitive to variability in the form of the determiners and possessives which co-occur with nouns, e.g., *un tour*, "a circuit," but *une tour*, "a tower;" *mein Hund*, "my dog" (general class) versus *meine Hundin*, "my bitch." The gender system is acquired fairly quickly and once in place, learners make few errors. They seem to quickly identify that the variation in the modifiers of nouns are cues to gender subclasses.

Sabourin (2003) shows important results on the learning of Dutch gender. Her participants were adult learners from various L1 backgrounds (German, Romance, and English). Sabourin investigated knowledge of gender in the L2 via three nonproduction tasks. The first was an acceptability judgment task taken as a paper and pencil test. Participants were asked to judge whether a particular sentence was acceptable in the L2. Saborin mixed grammatical and ungrammatical sentences in which gender agreement between the head noun and various modifiers was the target structure. The second task was an on-line version of the paper and pencil task. In the on-line version, participants read sentences word by word on a computer screen and pressed one of two computer keys (after presentation of the complete sentence) to indicate if the sentence was acceptable or not. At the same time, while participants read the sentences on-line (Task 2), neural electroencephalographic (EEG) activity was recorded by means of electrodes placed at 18 different sites on the participant's scalp.

Sabourin found that performance varied with the tasks used, in particular, that the L2 subjects performed much better when they were not time-pressured (i.e., on the off-line task). Native speakers' performance was not dramatically different on off-line and on-line versions of the task. In addition, performance on the tasks did not correlate with length of time that the subjects had been exposed to Dutch, but it did depend on the nature of the L1. These data clearly show that the ability to put one's knowledge of gender to use is dependent on the task to be performed, something predicted by AIT.

Sabourin's study also suggests competence differences among the participants. She chose her L1s to obtain certain contrasts among the learners. Thus,
German has a gender system that is marked in similar ways as Dutch (choice
of determiner and adjective form); this ought to facilitate transfer. To be proficient at Dutch gender, however, German learners cannot simply map the
gender feature of a German word onto the corresponding Dutch cognate or
translation equivalent. German learners have to map a three-gender system
(masculine, feminine, neuter) onto a two-gender system (common, neuter).
Deterministic transfer would lead to numerous errors.

Romance languages, like Dutch, manifest a binary classification of nouns.
In Romance languages, however, the relevant subclasses are masculine or feminine. There is no neuter class as there is in Dutch. This is theoretically important given claims that feature systems can be reduced to a lexical specification of *one* of the classes, the other being filled in by a default rule. If this
analysis is correct, the distinction between Dutch and the Romance languages
appears to be less great than the distinction between Dutch and German. By
this analysis, Dutch words would be marked in the lexicon if they are neuter,
with the common nouns getting a default specification. In continental varieties of French, feminine words would be lexically specified and the masculine
words would be marked by default rule. In German, it is much less obvious
which genders must be lexically specified and which might be assigned by a
default rule. English nouns, as we saw, are not subdivided into gender classes.

What Sabourin found was that all subjects displayed a response bias, tend-
ing to respond "yes" on the acceptability tasks. This means that their performance was quite good on the grammatical items and much worse on the ungrammatical items. Sabourin showed that, this response bias notwithstanding,
the Germans performed best on all tasks. On the grammatical items on several
tasks (using determiners), their performance was very close to that of the native speakers. On a task measuring adjective agreement, they performed very
well on the grammatical items (97.7%) but much less well (78.7%) on the ungrammatical items. They did very well in correctly identifying relative pronouns
matched to antecedents for gender (96.7%) and less well (81.1%) in rejecting
ungrammatical relative pronouns. On the whole, however, the Germans performed rather well. The Germans performed much better on frequent Dutch
words, even when these differed from the German translation equivalents.
From this observation, Sabourin concludes that the German learners were
able to learn L2-specific gender marking, given exposure to appropriate cues.
On the less frequent items, the German learners displayed a default strategy
favoring the common gender.

The Romance-language learners did much less well than the German L2
learners when identifying the definite determiners which co-occur with high
frequency nouns (89.3% Romance learners versus 95.6% German learners). If

these learners were simply transferring their lexical representations, they would make more errors. They did better on the neuter nouns although there is no neuter gender in French to transfer. This might be, however, what one would expect if they were lexically marking neuter words and using a default strategy to mark the common nouns. On the grammatical stimuli involving grammatical agreement, they did extremely well (95.2% accuracy on the adjective agreement items versus 96.6% on the relative pronouns) but did much worse (70.3% versus 71.1%) when required to reject ungrammatical stimuli. Once more, these results indicate that the learners have indeed learned the gender features of individual words, given exposure to primary linguistic data, but that they have not abstracted the correct system permitting them to reject ungrammatical forms (which are *not* part of the primary linguistic data they would have heard), and that basing their judgments on the contents of the L1 lexical entries does not help for the task they have to perform.

As for the English speakers, they performed almost as well as the Germans and the Romance speakers on the grammatical items, somewhat less well but still very well in identifying the correct determiner to go with a noun (82.9%) but were scoring at chance on the ungrammatical items involving adjective and relative pronoun agreement (45.4% and 50.5% respectively). This reflects the fact that there is no lexical information to transfer from English, no sensitivity to the morphosyntactic cues to gender, hence no abstraction of the underlying system.

To summarize, learners were clearly acquiring knowledge of the right determiners to use with Dutch nouns given primary linguistic data. Given exposure to Dutch nouns, learners could learn which determiners should be used. Thus, determiners were clearly better cues to gender than all other cues. Learners were doing different things, depending on the properties of gender in the L1, with the German learners finding the greatest correspondence between the contents of their L1 translation equivalents of Dutch stimuli, and the Anglophones finding the least. According to Sabourin, transfer is playing an important role in characterizing the learner data, just what one would predict on the assumption that lexical items form a type of cross-level correspondence rule and that correspondences transfer from the L1 to the L2.

AIT is well suited to account for some of the other observations reported in the L2 gender literature. First of all, because it does not see linguistic competence as a monolithic "box-in-the-mind" but rather as the grammatical distinctions encoded in various kinds of processing procedures, it can readily account for variability in learner performance based on task. Moreover, this explanation does not merely rely on the claim that certain tasks interfere with attention or strain working memory. Such approaches to task variability cannot, in principle, explain why the English speakers are persistently poor performers when they have to classify the gender of unfamiliar words. In my view, the problems of the Anglophones are problems of mental representation, not merely of processing speed, reflecting the absence of the appropriate features in their feature structures for nouns.

Secondly, AIT also predicts transfer of processing strategies and lexical content. That adults transfer the content of lexical representations is clearly shown; the more the L1 system matched that of the L2, the easier it was for the learner to perform correctly on the assigned tasks.

Thirdly, because AIT says that learners learn from input, it can explain the discrepancy between knowledge of grammatical cases and ungrammatical cases. Learners will analyze determiner + N sequences they hear or read. Learners can learn to associate a particular determiner with a particular noun. They cannot analyze ungrammatical sequences.

Why do older Anglophone learners have such difficulties learning the gender of French or German? AIT hypotheses that when English speakers learn French or German, they segment the speech stream with transferred segmentation procedures. This will have the effect of sectioning off the determiner that precedes the noun: *J'ai*[*lu/e*][*livre*], "I have [read the] [book]." In addition, they manifest a preference to map L2 formatives onto existing L1 lexical entries, where possible. These two tendencies will work together to ensure that the primary cue to a noun's gender in French or German will be stripped off by the learner's segmentation and correspondence strategies. This ensures that these expressions will be encoded as separate words, not as gender cues. Indeed, studies of English speakers learning French reveal the ease with which older children and adults come to recognize and represent the functions of *un/une* as markers of indefinite reference and *le/la* as markers of definite reference. It is not, therefore, that Anglophone learners of French or Dutch do not analyze determiners in linguistic stimuli; they clearly do. They can analyze the formatives as functional categories and they can assign them some of their determiner meanings. However, they fail to analyze them as cues to gender subclasses and appear not to be able to restructure their lexical entries to encode a gender feature as a defining categorical feature. From the perspective of AIT, the route to segmentation (bottom-up versus top-down) explains the differences in the mental representations of gender in these two groups of learners.

EXPLANATION OF OBSERVED FINDINGS IN SLA

Observation # 1. Exposure to input is necessary for SLA. It seems almost trivial to suggest that input is necessary for SLA, but as AIT predicts, acquisition proceeds from processing cues in the primary linguistic data and not from language production. Because the theory relies on modularity and views language processing as separate from other kinds of processing, input data are necessary for acquisition to proceed (when it does).

Observation # 2. A good deal of SLA happens incidentally. AIT would predict that most if not all acquisition, as defined by the creation of a grammar in the learner's head, is incidental in that it happens as a byproduct of learners interacting with language in some kind of setting. Because of the nature of language processing, conscious processing of grammar is simply not a viable means by which to develop any kind of mental representation of language including all of its underlying abstract categories and features. These come about without the learner knowing, so in this sense they are incidentally learned.

Observation # 3. Learners come to know more than what they have been exposed to in the input. Because AIT incorporates a role for UG in acquisition, learners must by the very nature of language come to know more than what they have been exposed to—assuming advanced levels of knowledge. As the various processors interact with each other to create new linguistic representations in the learner's mind, they draw upon UG for information about constraints and possibilities for those representations.

Observation # 4. Learner's output (speech) often follows predictable paths with predictable stages in the acquisition of a given structure. Although AIT is concerned with how mental representation changes over time and not speech production, it follows from the various tenets and constructs within AIT that mental representation will change incrementally and structurally rather than monolithically (i.e., acquisition of a particular feature or formative may not happen in one fell swoop). To the extent that output *may* be a reflection of mental representation (though this is certainly not always the case, and as I have argued, mental representation will precede the ability to use that representation productively), as the mental representation changes, so will learners' performance that taps that representation. AIT does not explain the particulars of the production stages or predictable paths in production of any given structure (e.g., negation in English); instead, it explains more generally why there are stages and predictable paths.

Observation # 5. Second language learning is variable in its outcome. AIT predicts variability in a number of ways. Because L1 transfer forms part of the processing procedures, AIT allows for differential outcomes based on the learner's L1 as in the case of the Sabourin study. AIT also predicts variability on tasks. Because it separates representation from performance, different kinds of tasks may not lead to the same outcomes with the same learner or group of learners. AIT, however, does not speak to individual differences in acquisition and individual outcomes (e.g., two learners under the same conditions of exposure having different mental representations), though there is nothing in the theory antithetical to such a notion.

Observation # 6. Second language learning is variable across linguistic subsystems. AIT would predict some kind of variability in outcome, especially, say, phonological distinctions versus syntactic constraints. The processors that analyze speech streams for prosodic and phonological cues, for example, could miss various allophonic variations in the input and yet still deliver data to other processors (say, morphosyntactic and conceptual systems) that allow for the development of native-like mental representations in these areas. Thus, the phonological processors may miss the distinction between catS and dogZ, but features of plurality and how they interface with syntax may still be processed.

Observation # 9. There are limits on the effects of instruction on SLA. As per observations 1 and 2 above, AIT predicts that explicit instruction and practice will not lead to changes in the learner's mental representation unless the instruction itself causes changes in processing of primary linguistic data. Even then it is not the explicit instruction per se that has an effect; what has an effect is the manipulation of input by external means (as in VanPatten's processing instruction—e.g., VanPatten, 2004) that leads to failure in processing (parsing). Recall that in AIT, LAD is triggered only when there is a parsing/ processing failure, and this can only happen during the act of comprehension.

Observation #10. There are limits on the effects of output (learner production) on language acquisition. Again, as per observations 1, 2, and 9, AIT predicts that acquisition (i.e., changes in mental representation) happen only one way: when there is a parsing/processing problem that leads to failure. Output processing involves a distinct set of procedures as suggested by Pienemann (chapter 8 this volume and elsewhere) that engage mental representation for use but do not create it.

ADDITIONAL COMMENTS AND CONCLUSION

Empirical investigation of SLA from the perspective of AIT is in its infancy. Consequently, there is much work to be done teasing out the logical properties of any learning problem (as seen from the perspective of linguistic theory) and then testing the initial sensitivity of learners from a given population to the

presence of stimuli of a given sort in the linguistic environment. There is ample support for the Filter Hypothesis in SLA, but this cannot be a permanent
hindrance to learning most aspects of an L2 grammar; after all, people are ultimately successful in achieving high, sometimes near-native-like, degrees of
proficiency in an L2. We must now conduct *micro-analyses* of the acquisition of
various phenomena, looking at a variety of populations and examining both
the linguistic competences of the learners and the ways in which they process
speech. I believe that AIT has the right sorts of properties to explain the rapid
and constrained acquisition of certain phenomena and the incremental, sometimes deviant paths taken in acquiring others. It has the right sorts of properties to explain why transfer can occur in some parts of the system (segmentation strategies, lexical correspondences) but not in others (unification of
categories into larger structures). I have framed the discussion to emphasize
what AIT has to say about input, but it should be clear that AIT is actually a
theory of grammatical restructuring, embedded in an interesting processing architecture and embodying a serious set of constraints on acquisition processes.

DISCUSSION QUESTIONS

1.   Describe what Carroll means by "three distinct types of input."
2.   A key feature of AIT is that acquisition is failure driven. Give an exam-
     ple of what is meant by this claim.
3.   What is the Filter Hypothesis? Can you think of instances in which
     acquisition may not be triggered because of filtering?
4.   AIT includes phonological segmentation as part of the processing pro-
     cedures with input. Thus some grammatical features of language may
     prove to be problematic for acquisition because of the way learners
     process the phonological structure. What evidence is there for this? Can
     you apply this idea to a potential problem in the language you are inter-
     ested in?
5.   How would you compare AIT with other theories you have read in this
     book? Select one and describe to what extent AIT is compatible with it
     or different from it.

SUGGESTED FURTHER READINGS

Carroll, S. E. (2001). *Input and evidence: The raw material of second language
     acquisition.* Amsterdam: Benjamins.
     This volume provides much more detail about the theoretical under-
     pinnings of AIT and empirical motivation for it. It does, however, require

some background in linguistics, and in SLA more generally, on the part of the reader.

Jackendoff, R. (2002). *Foundations of language: Brain, meaning, grammar, evolution*. Oxford: Oxford University Press.

This volume provides a detailed discussion of the functional architecture of mind which underpins AIT and on which it draws heavily. It also provides additional references to Jackendoff's work in semantics and cognition, which serve as a necessary foundation for AIT.

Language Specific Processing

Carreiras, M., Garcia-Albea, J. E., & Sebastian-Gallés, N. (Eds.) (1996). *Language processing in Spanish*. Mahwah, NJ: Lawrence Erlbaum Associates.

Fernández, E. M. (2003). *Bilingual sentence processing: Relative clause attachment in English and Spanish*. Amsterdam: Benjamins.

Mazuka, R., & Nagai, N. (Eds.) (1995). *Japanese sentence processing*. Hillsdale, NJ: Lawrence Erlbaum Associates.

These volumes are largely concerned with language-specific and language-independent aspects of syntactic parsing, (e.g., language-specific preferences for early versus late attachment of relative clauses).

Speech Perception

Strange, W. (Ed.) (1995). *Speech perception and linguistic experience: Issues in cross-linguistic research*. Baltimore, MD: York Press.

This volume presents a series of chapters surveying issues in the L1 and L2 acquisition of phonetic and phonemic categories in perception. Taken together, the various chapters provide considerable evidence for early "tuning" of our processing systems to the properties of the input relevant for the L1, and the transfer of the L1 system of categorization to the perception of the L2. This book requires some familiarity with the vocabulary of phonetic and phonological description.

REFERENCES

Harley, H., & Ritter. E. (2002). Person and number in pronouns: A feature-geometric analysis. *Language, 78*, 482–52.

Housen, A. (2002). A corpus-based study of the L2 acquisition of the English verb-system. In S. Granger, J. Hung, & S. Petch-Tyson (Eds.), *Computer learner corpora, second language acquisition and foreign language teaching* (pp. 77–116). Amsterdam: Benjamins.

Sabourin, L. (2003). *Grammatical gender and second language processing: An ERP study.* Doctoral dissertation, Rijksuniversiteit Groningen. Groningen Dissertations in Linguistics 42.

Schmidt, R. (1990). The role of consciousness in second language learning. *Applied Linguistics, 11,* 17–46.

VanPatten, B. (Ed.) (2004). *Processing instruction: Theory, research, and commentary.* Mahwah, NJ: Lawrence Elrbaum Associates.

10

Input, Interaction, and Output in Second Language Acquisition

Susan M. Gass
Michigan State University

Alison Mackey
Georgetown University

THE THEORY AND ITS CONSTRUCTS

As VanPatten and Williams note in chapter 1, a distinction needs to be made between models and theories. Notably, they distinguish between the *how* and the *why*. They also describe hypotheses, which differ from theories in that a hypothesis "does not unify various phenomena; it is usually an idea about a single phenomenon" (p. 5). This chapter deals with input, interaction, feedback, and output in second language acquisition (SLA). These constructs have been integrated and referred to as the *Interaction Hypothesis*.

In its current form, the Interaction Hypothesis subsumes some aspects of the *Input Hypothesis* (e.g., Krashen, 1982, 1985) together with the *Output Hypothesis* (Swain, 1985, 1995, 2005). It has also been referred to as the *input, interaction, and output model* (Block, 2003) and *Interaction Theory* (Carroll, 1999). As Mackey (in press) notes, "It is important to point out that the Interaction Hypothesis was not intended or claimed to be a complete theory of SLA, despite the fact that it is occasionally characterized this way in the literature . . . as Pica points out, 'as a perspective on language learning, [the Interaction Hypothesis] holds none of the predictive weight of an individual theory. Instead, it lends its weight to any number of theories.'" (Pica, 1998, p. 10)

If we follow the distinction provided by VanPatten and Williams, it becomes clear that the Interaction Hypothesis of SLA includes elements of a hypothesis (an idea that needs to be tested about a single phenomenon), elements of a model (a description of processes or a set of processes of a phenomenon) as well as elements of a theory (a set of statements about natural phenomena that explains why these phenomena occur the way they do). These changes reflect the nature and development of the Interaction Hypothesis from its inception over the past two and a half decades. In fact, Jordan (2005) suggests that the Interaction Hypothesis shows signs of progression towards a theory, using it as an example of how "an originally well-formulated hypothesis is upgraded in the light of criticism and developments in the field" (p. 220). At this stage of SLA research, various aspects of the Interaction Hypothesis have been tested and links between interaction and learning have been clearly demonstrated, thereby suggesting that it may be time for a change in the term *hypothesis*. Its inclusion in this volume on current theories of SLA and references to it as the "model that dominates current SLA research" (Ramírez, 2005, p. 293) and "the dominant interactionist paradigm" (Byrnes, 2005, p. 296) support this view, together with the appearance of book-length critiques of it (Block, 2003) that collectively suggest that researchers are now moving toward thinking about the Interaction Hypothesis in terms of a model of SLA. Using the framework of this book, for example, the Interaction Hypothesis is a model in the sense that it describes the processes involved when learners encounter input, are involved in interaction, and receive feedback and produce output. However, it is moving toward the status of a theory in the sense that it also attempts to explain why interaction and learning can be linked, using cognitive concepts derived from psychology, such as noticing, working memory, and attention. In this chapter we refer to it as the *interaction approach*.

Since the early 1980s and since Long's update in 1996, the interaction approach has witnessed a growth in empirical research. It is now commonly accepted within the SLA literature that there is a robust connection between interaction and learning. This chapter provides an update in which we present a description of the constructs of the interaction approach as well as a discussion of the theoretical underpinnings that account for the link between interaction and learning.

The interaction approach attempts to account for learning through the learner's exposure to language, production of language, and feedback on that production. As Gass (2003) notes, interaction research "takes as its starting point the assumption that language learning is stimulated by communicative pressure and examines the relationship between communication and acquisition and the mechanisms (e.g., noticing, attention) that mediate between them" (p. 224). In the following sections, we turn to an examination of the major components of this approach.

Input

Input is the *sine qua non* of acquisition. Quite simply it refers to the language that a learner is exposed to (i.e., from reading or listening, or, in the case of sign language from visual language). In all approaches to second language acquisition, input is an essential component for learning in that it provides the crucial evidence from which learners can form linguistic hypotheses.

Because input serves as the basis for hypotheses about the language being learned, researchers within the interaction approach have sought, over the years, to characterize the input that is addressed to learners, and like UG researchers (see White, chapter 3 this volume), interaction researchers also see input as providing positive evidence, that is, information about what is possible within a language. Early interaction researchers have shown that the language addressed to learners differs in interesting ways from the language addressed to native speakers and fluent second-language speakers (for overviews, see Gass & Selinker, 2001; Hatch, 1983; Wagner-Gough & Hatch, 1975). The language that is addressed to learners has been referred to as modified input or, in the earlier literature, as foreigner talk.

One proposal concerning the function of modified input is that modifying input makes the language more comprehensible. If learners cannot understand the language that is being addressed to them, then that language is not useful to them as they construct their second language grammars. An example of how individuals modify their speech and the resultant comprehensibility follows (from Kleifgen, 1985). In this example, a teacher of kindergarteners, including native (NS) and nonnative speakers (NNS) of English at varying levels of proficiency, is providing instructions to the class and to individuals.

(1) Instructions to a kindergarten class
    a. Instructions to English NSs in a kindergarten class
        These are babysitters taking care of babies. Draw a line from Q to q.
        From S to s and then trace.
    b. To a single NS of English
        Now, Johnny, you have to make a great big pointed hat.
    c. To an intermediate level native speaker of Urdu.
        No her hat is big. Pointed.
    d. To a low intermediate level native speaker of Arabic.
        See hat? Hat is big. Big and tall.
    e. To a beginning level native speaker of Japanese.
        Big, big, big hat.

As shown in the example, when addressing a learner of a language, speakers often make adjustments that are likely to render the language comprehensible, which in turn eases the burden for the learner. It is important to note that simplifications are not the only form of adjustments, which can also include elaborations, thereby providing the learner with a greater amount of semantic detail. An example of elaboration is seen in (2). In this example, when the NNS indicates a possible lack of understanding (*Pardon me?*), the NS replies by elaborating on her original comment about nitrites, adding an example and restating that she does not eat them.

(2) Elaboration
    NNS: There has been a lot of talk lately about additives and preservatives in food. In what ways has this changed your eating habits?
    NS: I try to stay away from nitrites.
    NNS: Pardon me?
    NS: Uh, from nitrites in, uh like, lunch meats and that sort of thing. I don't eat those.
                                                                    (Gass & Varonis, 1985)

Input, along with negative evidence obtained through interaction (to which we turn next) is believed to be crucial for acquisition to occur, not only in the interaction approach but also in other approaches as well (e.g., input processing—see VanPatten, chapter 7 this volume).

Interaction

Interaction, simply put, refers to the conversations that learners participate in. Interactions are important because it is in this context that learners receive information about the correctness and, more important, about the incorrectness of their utterances. Within the interaction approach, negative evidence—as in the UG literature (see White, chapter 3 this volume)—refers to the information that learners receive concerning the incorrectness of their own utterances. For our purposes, learners receive negative evidence through interactional feedback that occurs following problematic utterances and provides learners with information about the linguistic and communicative success or failure of their production. Gass (1997) presents the model in Figure 10–1 to characterize the role negative evidence plays in the interaction–learning process.

Interpreting this figure, negative evidence, which can come *inter alia* through overt correction or negotiation, is one way of alerting a learner to the possibility of an error in his or her speech. Assuming that the error is noticed,

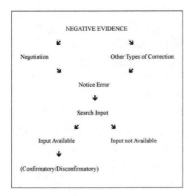

FIGURE 10–1.   The function of negative evidence.

the learner has to determine what the problem is and how to modify existing linguistic knowledge. The learner then comes up with a hypothesis as to what the correct form should be (e.g., *he wented home* versus *he went* home). Obtaining further input (e.g., listening, reading) is a way of determining that in English one says *he went home* but one never says *he wented home*. Thus, listening for further input is a way to confirm or disprove a hypothesis that she or he may have come up with regarding the nature of the target language. The learner may also use output to test these hypotheses, which we address next.

Output

Swain's (1985, 1993, 1995, 1998, 2005) observations about the importance of output emerged from her research that took place in the context of immersion programs in Canada. Based on this research, she formulated the Output Hypothesis. Swain observed that children who had spent years in immersion programs still had a level of competence in the L2 that fell significantly short of native-like abilities. She hypothesized that what was lacking was sufficient opportunities for language use. She claimed that language production forces learners to move from comprehension (semantic use of language) to syntactic use of language. As Swain stated:

> Output may stimulate learners to move from the semantic, open-ended nondeterministic, strategic processing prevalent in comprehension to the complete grammatical processing needed for accurate production. Output, thus, would seem to have a potentially significant role in the development of syntax and morphology. (1995, p. 128)

For example, after producing an initially problematic utterance ("what happen for the boat?") and receiving feedback about its lack of comprehensibility in the form of a clarification request ("what?"), the NNS in (3) appears to realize that his utterance was not understood. Pushed to reformulate his initial utterance in order to facilitate NS understanding, he modifies his linguistic output by reformulating the utterance in a more target-like way.

(3) Modified output
    Learner: what happen for the boat?
    NS: what?
    Learner: what's wrong with the boat?

                             (McDonough, 2005)

In addition to pushing learners to produce more target-like output, another function of production is that it can be used to test hypotheses about the target language. An example of hypothesis testing is provided in example (4). This example comes from a study in which learners were involved in interactions (videotaped) and then interviewed immediately following, using the video as a prompt. The retrospective comments (in particular, "I'll say it and see") demonstrate that the learner was using the conversation as a forum through which she could test the accuracy of her knowledge.

(4) (INT = interviewer)
    NNS: *poi un bicchiere*
           then a glass
    INT: *un che, come?*
           a what, what?
    NNS: *bicchiere*
           glass

NNS Recall Comments: "I was drawing a blank. Then I thought of a vase but then I thought that since there was no flowers, maybe it was just a big glass. So, then I thought I'll say it and see."

                (Mackey, Gass, & McDonough, 2000)

Another function of output is to promote automaticity, which refers to the routinization of language use. Little effort is expended when dealing with automatic processes (e.g., driving from home to work is automatic and does not require much thought as to the route to take). Automatic processes come about as a result of "consistent mapping of the same input to the same pattern of activation over many trials" (McLaughlin, 1987, p. 134; see DeKeyser, chapter 6 this volume). We can consider the role of production as playing an integral role in automaticity. To return to the example of driving, the automaticity of the route from home to work occurs following multiple trips along that route. The first time may require more effort and more concentration. With regard to language learning, continued use of language moves learners to more fluent automatic production.

How Interaction Brings about Learning

The relationship among these three components can be summed up by Long's (1996) frequently cited explanation that:

> . . . *negotiation for meaning*, and especially negotiation work that triggers *interactional* adjustments by the NS or more competent interlocutor, facilitates acquisition because it connects input, internal learner capacities, particularly selective attention, and output in productive ways (pp. 451–452).
>
> . . . it is proposed that environmental contributions to acquisition are mediated by selective attention and the learner's developing L2 processing capacity, and that these resources are brought together most usefully, although not exclusively, during *negotiation for meaning*. Negative feedback obtained during negotiation work or elsewhere may be facilitative of L2 development, at least for vocabulary, morphology, and language-specific syntax, and essential for learning certain specifiable L1–L2 contrasts (p. 414).

In this view, through interaction a learner's attentional resources (selective attention) are directed to problematic aspects of knowledge or production. First, the learner may notice that what she says differs from what a native speaker says. This is often referred to as *noticing the gap* (Schmidt & Frota, 1986). In addition, learners may notice that since they can't express what they want to express, they have a hole in their interlanguage (Swain, 1998). The interaction itself may also direct learner's attention to something new, such as a new lexical item or grammatical construction, thus promoting the development of the L2.

Feedback

There are two broad types of feedback: explicit and implicit. Explicit feedback includes corrections and metalinguistic explanations. Of concern to us here are implicit forms of feedback, which include negotiation strategies such as:

- Confirmation checks (expressions that are designed to elicit confirmation that an utterance has been correctly heard or understood, for example, *Is this what you mean*).

- Clarification requests (expression designed to elicit clarification of the interlocutor's preceding utterances, for example, *What did you say?*).
- Comprehension checks (expressions that are used to verify that an interlocutor has understood, for example, *Did you understand?*).
- Recasts (a rephrasing of an incorrect utterance using a correct form while maintaining the original meaning).

Feedback may help to make problematic aspects of learners' interlanguage salient and may give them additional opportunities to focus on their production or comprehension, thus promoting L2 development. For instance, in example (5) below, the NS's provision of implicit feedback in the form of confirmation checks (lines 2 and 4) gives the learner the opportunity to infer (from her interlocutor's lack of comprehension) that there was a problem with her pronunciation.

(5) Implicit feedback

    1 NNS: There's a basen of flowers on the bookshelf

    2 NS: a basin?

    3 NNS: base

    4 NS: a base?

    5 NNS: a base

    6 NS: oh, a vase

    7 NNS: vase

                                   (Mackey, Gass & McDonough, 2000)

Feedback often occurs during *negotiation for meaning*. Long (1996) defines negotiation as

> the process in which, in an effort to communicate, learners and competent speakers provide and interpret signals of their own and their interlocutor's perceived comprehension, thus provoking adjustments to linguistic form, conversational structure, message content, or all three, until an acceptable level of understanding is achieved (p. 418).

Negotiation for meaning has traditionally been viewed and coded in terms of the "three Cs": confirmation checks, clarification requests, and comprehension checks, each of which we defined above. A confirmation check was seen in example (5) above. Examples (6) and (7) exemplify clarification requests. In example (6) the clarification request and rephrasings result in input that the learner finally seems to understand.

(6) Clarification request and rephrasing

NS: A curve slightly to the left here and then straight ahead the road goes.

NNS: A Er er straight?

NS: No, it goes on a curve left first, then it goes straight ahead.

NNS: No, because dry cleaner is the way is here? Curve? It means how?

NS: Exactly so go a little bit to the left, curve slightly left, then go straight ahead with it.

NNS: Oh a little bit left around then straight ahead goes first curve.

NS: Right, like that, exactly, right, curve, go straight ahead, no, no, no, I mean left right curve left [laughs].

NNS: [laughs] curve

(Mackey, 2000)

Example (7) illustrates a clarification request, in which Learner 2 needs more information in order to understand Learner 1's question about what is important to the character in the task.

(7) Clarification request

   Learner 1: ¿Qué es importante a ella?
                  What is important to her?

→ **Learner 2:** ¿Cómo?
                  What?

   Learner 1: ¿Qué es importante a la amiga? ¿Es solamente el costo?
                  What is important to the friend? Is it just the cost?

(Gass, Mackey, & Ross-Feldman, 2005)

A comprehension check is an attempt to anticipate and prevent a breakdown in communication. In example (8) Learner 1 asks if Learner 2 needs him to repeat what he has just said, basically checking to see if Learner 2 has understood the previous utterance.

(8) Comprehension check

   Learner 1: La avenida siete va en una dirección hacia el norte desde la calle siete hasta la calle ocho. ¿Quieres que repita?
                  Avenue Seven goes in one direction towards the north from Street Seven to Street Eight. **Do you want me to repeat?**

Learner 2: Por favor.
Please.

Learner 1: La avenida seven, uh siete, va en una dirección hacia el norte desde la calle siete hasta la calle ocho.
Avenue Seven, uh Seven, goes in one direction towards the north from Street Seven to Street Eight.?:

(Gass, Mackey, & Ross-Feldman, 2005)

Through negotiation, input can be uniquely tailored to individual learners' particular strengths, weaknesses, and communicative needs, providing language that is in line with learners' developmental levels. Pica (1994, 1996) describes how negotiation contributes to the language learning process, suggesting that negotiation facilitates comprehension of L2 input and serves to draw learners' attention to form-meaning relationships through processes of repetition, segmentation, and rewording. Gass (1997) similarly claims that negotiation can draw learners' attention to linguistic problems and proposes that initial steps in interlanguage development occur when learners notice mismatches between the input and their own organization of the target language.

Recent interaction research, with its focus on the cognitive processes that drive learning, has augmented and in some cases replaced the three C's with other constructs, such as *recasts*. Recasts, a form of implicit feedback, have received a great deal of attention in recent research. Nicholas, Lightbown, and Spada (2001) define recasts as "utterances that repeat a learner's incorrect utterance, making only the changes necessary to produce a correct utterance, without changing the meaning" (p. 733). In other words, recasts are interactional moves through which learners are provided with more linguistically target-like reformulations of what they have just said. A recast does not necessarily involve the repetition of a learner's entire utterance, and may include additional elaborations not present in the original propositional content, but it is semantically contingent upon the learner's utterance and often temporally juxtaposed to it. For instance, in example (9), a NS recasts a NNS's utterance.

(9) Recast
Student: Why did you fell down?
Teacher: Why did you fall down?
Student: Fall down, yes.

(Oliver & Mackey, 2003)

Recasts have been associated with L2 learning in a number of studies (e.g., Ayoun, 2001; Braidi, 2002; Han, 2002; Iwashita, 2003; Leeman, 2003;

Mackey & Philp, 1998; Philp, 2003; Storch, 2002). Current research has also indicated that recasts and negotiation may work to impact learning in different ways. For example, recasts are complex discourse structures that have been said to contain positive evidence (a model of the correct form), and negative feedback (since the correct form is juxtaposed with the non-targetlike form) in an environment where the positive evidence is enhanced (because of the juxtaposition). If learners do not selectively attend to and recognize the negative feedback contained in recasts, then the documented contribution of recasts to learning might be attributed to the positive evidence they contain, or to the enhanced salience of the positive evidence, as suggested by Leeman (2003). While negotiation for meaning always requires learner involvement, as shown in example (5) above, recasts do not consistently make such participatory demands, as shown by the learner's simple "yes" in response to the recast in example (9).

As a number of researchers (e.g., Lyster, 1998a, 1998b) have pointed out, reformulations sometimes occur after grammatical utterances as well, and a recast may be perceived as responding to the *content* rather than the *form* of an utterance, or as an optional and alternative way of saying the same thing. Thus, learners may not repeat or rephrase their original utterances following recasts, and they may not even perceive recasts as feedback at all (Mackey, Gass, & McDonough, 2000). It also must be kept in mind that even when learners *do* understand the corrective nature of recasts, they may have trouble understanding and addressing the source of the problem (as discussed by several researchers, including Carroll, 2001). However, it is possible that neither a response nor a recognition of the corrective intent of the recast is crucial for learning (Mackey & Philp, 1998), and a substantial body of research using increasingly innovative methods has linked recasts with L2 learning of different forms, in different languages, and for a range of learners in both classroom and laboratory contexts (see Mackey & Gass, 2006, for review).

Language-Related Episodes

Another construct, language-related episodes (LREs), is also studied within the context of interaction. Briefly defined, LREs refer to instances where learners consciously reflect on their own language use or, more specifically, "instances in which learners may (a) question the meaning of a linguistic item; (b) question the correctness of the spelling/pronunciation of a word; (c) question the correctness of a grammatical form; or (d) implicitly or explicitly correct their own or another's usage of a word, form or structure" (Leeser, 2004, p. 56; see also Swain & Lapkin, 1998; Williams, 1999). LREs, as Williams (1999) notes, encompass a wide range of discourse moves, such as requests for assistance, negotiation sequences, and explicit and implicit feedback, and are generally taken as signs that learners have noticed a gap between their inter-languages (or their partners' interlanguages) and the system of the target lan-guage. Example (10) illustrates a language-related episode where students dis-cuss the gender of the word for *map*.

(10) Language-related episode
      Learner 1: Los nombres en el mapa. ¿Es el mapa o la mapa?
                      The names on the map. Is it the (m.) map or the (f.) map?
      Learner 2: El mapa
                      The (m.) map
                                          (Gass, Mackey & Ross-Feldman, 2005)

Based on this example, it might be possible to conclude that Learner 1 recognized a gap in her knowledge of Spanish gender, and thus produced an LRE (an explicit request for assistance). A number of studies investigating L2 learners' use of LREs have found that LREs not only represent language learn-ing in process (Donato, 1994; Swain & Lapkin, 1998) but are also positively correlated with L2 development (e.g., Basturkmen, Loewen & Ellis, 2002; Leeser, 2004; Williams, 2001).

Attention

While input such as that provided in recasts may be regarded as a catalyst for learning, and while LREs may be regarded as evidence that learning processes are being engaged, attention is believed to be one of the mechanisms that me-diates between input and learning (or intake, as the input–learning process is sometimes called). It is widely agreed that second language learners are ex-posed to more input than they can process, and that some mechanism is needed to help learners "sort through" the massive amounts of input they re-ceive. As Gass, Svetics, and Lemelin (2003) explain, "language processing is like other kinds of processing: Humans are constantly exposed to and often overwhelmed by various sorts of external stimuli and are able to, through at-tentional devices, 'tune in' some stimuli and 'tune out' others" (p. 498). Atten-tion, broadly conceptualized, may be regarded as the mechanism that allows learners to tune in to a portion of the input they receive.

Although generally held to be crucial for SLA, attention has nevertheless been the focus of much recent debate in the field. Schmidt (1990, 2001), for example, argues that learning cannot take place without awareness because the learner must be consciously aware of linguistic input in order for it to be-come internalized; thus, awareness and learning cannot be dissociated. Simi-larly, Robinson (1995, 2001, 2002) claims that attention to input is a consequence of encoding in working memory, and only input encoded in working memory may be subsequently transferred to long-term memory. Thus, in Robinson's model, as in Schmidt's, attention is crucial for learning, and in both models no learning can take place without attention and some level of awareness. An alternative and distinct perspective, emerging from work in cognitive psychology (Posner, 1988, 1992; Posner & Peterson, 1990), is presented by Tomlin and Villa (1994), who advocate a disassociation between learning and awareness. As can be seen from this brief overview, not all researchers use the same terminology when discussing attention, and in fact, there have been proposals that have divided attention into different components. What is important for the current chapter is that interaction researchers assume that the cognitive constructs of attention and awareness and the related construct of noticing are part of the interaction-L2 learning process.

WHAT COUNTS AS EVIDENCE?

As Mackey and Gass (2005) point out, the goal of much interaction-based research involves manipulating the kinds of interactions that learners are involved in, the kind of feedback they receive during interaction, and the kind of output they produce in order to determine the relationship between the various components of interaction and second language learning. Thus, longitudinal designs, cross-sectional designs (sampling learners at different proficiency levels), and case studies are all appropriate methods. However, the most common way of gathering data is to involve learners in a range of carefully planned tasks.

Tasks

Various ways of categorizing task types have been discussed (see Ellis, 2003; Pica, Kanagy, & Falodun, 1993, for discussions of task categorization). For example, a common distinction is to classify tasks as one-way and two-way. In a one-way task, the information flows from one person to the other, as when a learner describes a picture to her partner. In other words, the information that is being conveyed is held by one person. In a two-way task, there is an information exchange whereby both parties (or however many participants there are in a task) hold information that is vital to the resolution of the task. For example, in a story completion task, each learner may hold a portion of the information and must convey it to the other learner(s) before the task can be successfully completed. Each type of task may produce different kinds of interaction, with different opportunities for feedback and output.

Interaction researchers are usually interested in eliciting specific grammatical structures in order to test whether particular kinds of interactive feedback on non-targetlike forms are associated with learning. Learning is sometimes examined through immediate changes in the learners' output on the particular structures about which they have received interactional feedback, although short- and longer-term change on post-tests is generally considered to be the gold standard.

Obviously, tasks need to be carefully pilot-tested in order to ensure they produce the language intended. It is also possible, and becoming more common in interaction research, to try to examine learners' thought processes as they carry out a task or to interview learners on previous thought processes. For example, if a researcher employed a dictogloss task (a type of consensus task in which learners work together to reconstruct a text that has been read to them, Swain & Lapkin, 2002), that researcher could examine the text that learners produce (the output). Or, instead of examining the output in isolation, the researcher could also ask the learners to think aloud as they carry out the task (this is known as an introspective protocol or "think aloud"). Alternatively, the researcher could ask the learners to make retrospective comments as soon as they are finished with a task. This is often done by providing the learners with a video replay of the task to jog their memories (this is known as a retrospective protocol or "stimulated recall") (Gass & Mackey, 2000).

Difficulties in Determining Learning

It is often difficult to determine if learning has actually taken place. One difficulty, common in any approach to SLA, is in the operationalization of learning. If a learner utters a new form once and then does not do so again for two months, does that constitute knowledge? If a learner utters a new form two times, does that constitute knowledge? All of these (and many more) are questions that are often faced when conducting research on second language learning.

A second difficulty in determining learning occurs when considering actual interactions in the absence of post-tests or in the absence of some commentary, as in a stimulated recall or a language-related episode. If we consider the example presented in (5) above, for instance, it might appear on the surface that the NS and NNS have negotiated the difficulty to the point where the NS did understand that the NNS is referring to a *vase* rather than a *basin*. But when we focus on the NNS, we need to ask what learning has occurred. Is she simply repeating what the NS had said without true understanding, or did some type of learning take place? Or was some process engaged that might eventually lead to, or facilitate, later learning. Example (11), taken from Hawkins (1985) illustrates a similar concern:

(11)

	NS:	Number two, . . . is . . . the man . . . look for help
	NNS:	Uh-huh, ((yes)) for help.
	NS:	Help, you know. . . . "Aah! Help" (shouts softly)
	NNS:	Uh-huh. ((yes))
	NS:	No Up . . . HELP.
→	NNS:	Help
	NS:	Yeah . . . He asked, . . . he asked . . . a man . . . for . . . help.
→	NNS:	. . . for help
	NS:	Yeah. . . . he asked . . . the man . . . for telephone.

(Hawkins, 1985)

The question that must be addressed is what does *help* and *for help* mean. Is it a recognition that implies comprehension? Or can we assume that this learner has indicated comprehension and that this is indeed an initial part of the learning process? In fact, an interview with the participants showed that no comprehension had taken place and, hence, no learning. The response was only a means for keeping the social discourse from falling apart.

These examples help foreground the concern that whatever the data source, the important point is not to rely solely on the transcript of the interaction but also to investigate the link between interaction and learning by whatever means possible. For this reason, research designs that employ pretests and post-tests (and ideally, delayed post-tests and possibly tailor-made post-tests as well) and/or designs that include introspective or retrospective protocols are of value. As research designs progress, clearer answers to the questions about interaction and learning can be obtained.

COMMON MISUNDERSTANDINGS

Here we will consider two common areas of misunderstanding about input, interaction and SLA. These relate to the nature of the interaction approach and the relationship of the interaction approach to teaching methods.

The first misunderstanding concerns the scope of the interaction approach. Although occasionally criticized for not addressing all aspects of the learning process (such as how input is processed, or the sociocultural context of learning), the interaction approach, like all SLA approaches and theories, takes as its primary focus particular aspects of the second language learning process. Some theories focus on innateness, others on the sociolinguistic context, and still others purely on the cognitive mechanisms involved in learning a language. The interaction approach, for the time being, is focused primarily on the role of input, interaction, and output in learning. Future research will undoubtedly be enriched by exploring the connections between various approaches to SLA in greater depth, so as to arrive at a more comprehensive explanation of the second language acquisition process.

A second misunderstanding is that the interaction approach can be directly applied to classroom methodology. Work on task-based language teaching (see Bygate, Skehan, & Swain, 2001; Ellis, 2003) and focus on form (Long & Robinson, 1998) both draw heavily on the interaction hypothesis as part of their theoretical basis. Task-based language teaching and the research that supports its use, in the words of Ellis (2003), "has been informed primarily by the interaction hypothesis." (p. 100). Like most SLA researchers, however, Ellis is cautious about making direct connections between theory, research, and teaching practice, saying that "the case for including an introduction to the principles and techniques of task-based teaching in an initial teacher-training program is a strong one" and "if task-based teaching is to make the shift from theory to practice it will be necessary to go beyond the psycholinguistic rationale . . . to address the contextual factors that ultimately determine what materials and procedures teachers choose" (p. 337). The interaction approach, like most other accounts of second language acquisition, is primarily focused on how languages are *learned*. Thus, direct application to the classroom may be premature.

EXEMPLARY STUDY:
MACKEY, GASS, AND MCDONOUGH (2000)

The study carried out by Mackey, Gass, and McDonough (2000) illustrates many of the issues and constructs discussed in this chapter. Their research investigated how second and foreign language learners perceived the feedback they received in the course of interaction. The main research questions were: (1) Could learners accurately perceive feedback that was offered to them during task-based interaction? (2) Did learners perceive the feedback as feedback? (3) Did they recognize the linguistic target(s) of the feedback?

The participants were nonnative speakers in an ESL context and in an Italian as a Foreign Language (IFL) context. They were adult learners enrolled in language courses at a U.S. university. The ESL learners ($n = 10$) were from a variety of L1 backgrounds including Cantonese, French, Japanese, Korean, and Thai. The IFL learners ($n = 7$) had studied or were studying Italian at the same university. All participants were classified at the beginner or lower-intermediate level.

Each learner carried out a communicative task with a native (English) or near-native (Italian) interviewer. The tasks were two-way information exchange activities. All participants had a picture that was similar to their partners' picture. The tasks involved the learners and interviewers working together to identify the differences between their pictures. Each session lasted for approximately 15–20 minutes and was videotaped. During the interaction, the English and Italian interviewers provided interactional feedback when the participants produced a non-targetlike utterance. The interviewers were instructed to provide interactional feedback whenever it seemed appropriate and in whatever form seemed appropriate during the interaction. Thus, the feedback provided during the task-based interaction occurred in response to errors in morphosyntax, phonology, lexis, or semantics and occurred in the form of negotiation and recasts.

Introspective data were collected from the learners using stimulated recall methodology (Gass & Mackey, 2000). Immediately following completion of the task-based activities, the videotape was rewound and played for each learner by a second researcher who also gave the directions for this part of the research to the learner. While watching the videotape, the learners could pause the tape if they wished to describe their thoughts at any particular point in the interaction. The researcher also paused the tape after episodes in which interactional feedback was provided and asked learners to recall their thoughts at the time the original interaction was occurring. These recall sessions, which were audiotaped, were conducted in English (the L2 for the ESL participants and the L1 for the IFL participants). This recall procedure was aimed at eliciting learners' original perceptions about the feedback episodes—that is, their perceptions at the time they were taking part in the interaction.

The interactional feedback episodes and the stimulated-recall comments that were provided about the episodes were coded and analyzed. The number of feedback episodes in the ESL data in which the learners perceived the target of the feedback differed according to the feedback type. Whereas learners' reports indicated they often recognized the feedback for lexis and phonology (83% and 60%, respectively), they generally did not indicate that they recognized the target of morphosyntactic feedback (13%). In relation to morphosyntactic feedback, ESL learners were more likely to report that they were thinking about the semantic content of the morphosyntactic episodes (38%) or not about the content at all (21%). With such a small percentage of morphosyntactic feedback being recognized as being about morphosyntax, the window of opportunity for these learners to notice grammar in interaction may have been relatively small. Having said this, it is important to note that although the study did touch upon the learners' reports and therefore their internal processes, more focused research is necessary to examine the relationship between noticing and L2 development.

For the Italian learners, when the feedback provided to the learner during interaction was morphosyntactic in nature, learners recognized the nature of 24% of the feedback. Almost half of the time, they perceived morphosyntactic feedback as being about lexis. The amount of phonological feedback provided to the learners was quite low (18%), with less than a quarter being perceived as related to phonology. In contrast, lexical feedback episodes were perceived to be about lexis almost two-thirds of the time (66%).

In summary, this study of L2 learners' perceptions about feedback in conversational interaction showed that learners were most accurate in their perceptions about lexical and phonological feedback and were generally inaccurate in their perceptions about morphosyntactic feedback. Morphosyntactic feedback was often perceived as being about semantics for the ESL learners and about lexis for the IFL learners. Proponents of the interaction approach have suggested that interaction can result in feedback that focuses learners' attention on aspects of their language that deviate from the target language. If learners' reports about their perceptions can be equated with attention, then the findings in this study are consistent with the claims of the Interaction Hypothesis, at least with regard to the lexicon and phonology.

EXPLANATION OF OBSERVABLE PHENOMENA

As we noted in the first section of this chapter, the interactionist approach does not address all aspects of SLA and therefore does not account for all of the observable phenomena outlined in chapter 1 of this volume. In this section, therefore, we discuss the observable phenomena that are most relevant to the interactionist approach.

Observation #1: Exposure to input is necessary for SLA. The interactionist approach relies heavily on input to account for SLA and so is in agreement with observation #1. However, there is no assumption in the interactionist approach that input alone is sufficient. In fact, it is the way that a learner interacts with the input (through interaction) that is at the heart of this approach. If input were sufficient, we would not have so many learners who, despite years in a second language environment, are not highly proficient. For example, the French immersion students Swain makes reference to in her studies should have been able to acquire native-like proficiency in the L2 as they were consistently exposed to the L2.

Observation #2: A good deal of SLA happens incidentally. The interactionist approach does not deal specifically with incidental learning, but insofar as attention is seen a driving explanatory force behind the interactionist approach, incidental learning is not seen as major part of second language learning. Within the interactionist approach, learning takes place through an interactive context. For example, negotiation for meaning involves the learner in directing specific attention towards a linguistic problem.

Observation #5. Second language learning is variable in its outcome. To the extent that this observation is compatible with the idea that individuals vary in whether and how they negotiate and to the extent to which they focus attention on specific parts of language, it is in keeping with interactionist proposals. Keeping in mind the importance to interaction proposals of the individual learner and their cognitive capacity (as opposed to innate dispositions), this would suggest, then, that individuals will have different results in terms of their outcomes.

Observation #7. There are limits on the effects of frequency on SLA. A frequency-based explanation of SLA is compatible with some of the interactionist claims in that interactional modifications are claimed to impact development is through facilitating pattern identification and recognizing matches and mismatches. However, input frequency is not sufficient to account for learning in the absence of some other considerations. For example, in an interactionist approach, the native language might play some role when trying to understand which forms a learner might attend to following feedback, particularly implicit feedback. The impact of frequency is dependent on a learner's noticing the input. Other factors such as the native language may play a role in determining what is noticed and what is not.

Observation #10. There are limits on the effects of output (learner production) on language acquisition. At this point in SLA research, no approach or theory can account for all learning. The interactionist approach is no exception. The interactionist approach takes a particular perspective on output and highly values pushed or modified output, or output that involves a learner attempting to go beyond his/her current level of knowledge. In other words, the most important output is output that stretches the limited linguistic resources of a learner. Thus, while output that is pure practice may be important for automatization, it is less valuable for language development.

CONCLUSION

In this chapter the perspective offered by input and interaction has been presented. The central tenet of the hypothesis is that interaction facilitates the process of acquiring a second language as it provides learners with opportunities to receive modified input and to receive feedback, both explicitly and implicitly, which in turn may draw learners' attention to problematic aspects of their interlanguage and push them to produce modified output.

DISCUSSION QUESTIONS

1. Describe the role of negative evidence within Gass and Mackey's approach. Does this differ from other approaches you have read about in this volume?
2. Is the interaction approach compatible with, for example, the UG approach (White) and frequency-based approach (Ellis)?
3. The authors describe this approach as a model and not a theory. Do you agree? Why, or why not?
4. The concept of "negotiation of meaning" has gained wide acceptance in language teaching circles. Why do you think this is so? Is there a Western bias in the construct of negotiation of meaning?
5. One possible critique of the interaction approach is that it ignores the broader social context of language learning the variables that may come to play in people's interactions, for example, power relationships, social status, and gender, among others. Do you think this is a valid criticism? To what extent would a theory of SLA need to consider such social factors?

SUGGESTED FURTHER READING

Gass, S. M. (1997). *Input, interaction, and the second language learner*. Mahwah, NJ: Lawrence Erlbaum Associates.

    This book provides a thorough and accessible introduction to the main components of the interaction approach, including classroom applications and implications.

Gass, S. M. (2003). Input and interaction. In C. Doughty & M. H. Long (Eds.), *Handbook of second language acquisition* (pp. 224–255). Oxford: Blackwell.

    This chapter presents an overview of input and interaction in second language.

Long, M. H. (1996). The role of the linguistic environment in second language acquisition. In W. Ritchie & T. K. Bhatia (Eds.), *Handbook of language acquisition: Vol. 2. Second language acquisition* (pp. 413–468). San Diego, CA: Academic Press.

One of the most often cited articles in the field, Long's article discusses the theoretical underpinnings of the interaction approach, including positive evidence, comprehensible input, input and cognitive processing, and negotiating for meaning.

Mackey, A. (in press). Interaction and second language development: Perspectives from SLA research. In R. DeKeyser (Ed.), *Practice in second language learning: Perspectives from linguistics and psychology.* Cambridge: Cambridge University Press.

In this chapter, research on interaction in second language acquisition pointing to the importance of a range of interactional processes in the second language learning process is discussed. These processes include negotiation for meaning, the provision of feedback, and the production of modified output. Highlighted in this chapter is the importance of cognitive (learner-internal) factors such as attention, noticing, and memory for language.

Mackey, A., & Abbuhl, R. (2005). Input and interaction. In C. Sanz (Ed.), *Internal and external factors in adult second language acquisition.* Washington, DC: Georgetown University Press, pp. 207–233.

This chapter provides a detailed overview of the interaction approach, discussing both empirical work that has investigated the relationship between interaction and L2 development as well as implications for L2 pedagogy.

REFERENCES

Ayoun, D. (2001). The role of negative and positive feedback in the second language acquisition of the passé composé and imparfait. *Modern Language Journal, 85,* 226–243.
Basturkmen, H., Loewen, S., & Ellis, R. (2002). Metalanguage in focus on form in the communicative classroom. *Language Awareness, 11,* 1–13.
Block, D. (2003). *The social turn in second language acquisition.* Edinburgh: Edinburgh University Press.
Braidi, S. (2002). Reexamining the role of recasts in native-speaker/nonnative-speaker interactions. *Language Learning, 52,* 1–42.
Bygate, M., Skehan, P., & Swain, M. (2001). *Researching pedagogic tasks: Second language learning, teaching, and testing.* Harlow, England: Pearson.
Byrnes, H. (2005). Review of task-based language learning and teaching. *The Modern Language Journal, 89,* 297–298.
Carroll, S. (1999). Putting "input" in its proper place. *Second Language Research, 15,* 337–388.

———. (2001). *Input and evidence: The raw material of second language acquisition*. Amsterdam: Benjamins.

Donato, R. (1994). Collective scaffolding in second language learning. In J. Lantolf & G. Appel (Eds.), *Vygotskian approaches to second language research* (pp. 33–56). Norwood, NJ: Ablex.

Ellis, R. (2003). *Task-based language learning and teaching*. Oxford: Oxford University Press.

Gass, S. M. (1997). *Input, interaction, and the second language learner*. Mahwah, NJ: Lawrence Erlbaum Associates.

———. (2003). Input and interaction. In C. Doughty & M. H. Long (Eds.), *Handbook of second language acquisition* (pp. 224–255). Oxford: Blackwell.

Gass, S. M., & Mackey, A. (2000). *Stimulated recall methodology in second language research*. Mahwah, NJ: Lawrence Erlbaum Associates.

Gass, S. M., Mackey, A., & Ross-Feldman, L. (2005). Task-based interactions in classroom and laboratory setting. *Language Learning*.

Gass, S. M., Mackey, A., & Ross-Feldman, L. (2005). Task-based interaction in classroom and laboratory settings. *Language Learning, 55*, 575–611.

Gass, S. M., & Selinker, L. (2001). *Second language acquisition: An introductory course*. Mahwah, NJ: Erlbaum.

Gass, S. M., Svetics, I., & Lemelin, S. (2003). Differential effects of attention. *Language Learning, 53*, 497–545.

Gass, S. M., & Varonis, E. (1985). Variation in native speaker speech modification to nonnative speakers. *Studies in Second Language Acquisition, 7*, 37–57.

Han, Z. (2002). A study of the impact of recasts on tense consistency in L2 output. *TESOL Quarterly, 36*, 543–572.

Hatch, E. (1983). *Psycholinguistics: A second language perspective*. Rowley, MA: Newbury House.

Hawkins, B. (1985). Is an "appropriate response" always so appropriate? In S. M. Gass & C. Madden (Eds.), *Input in second language acquisition* (pp. 162–180). Rowley, MA: Newbury House.

Iwashita, N. (2003). Negative feedback and positive evidence in task-based interaction. *Studies in Second Language Acquisition, 25*, 1–36.

Jordan, G. (2005). *Theory construction in second language acquisition*. Amsterdam: Benjamins

Kleifgen, J. (1985). Skilled variation in a kindergarten teacher's use of foreigner talk. In S. M. Gass & C. Madden (Eds.), *Input in second language acquisition* (pp. 59–68). Rowley, MA: Newbury House.

Krashen, S. (1982). *Principles and practices in second language acquisition*. Oxford: Pergamon.

———. (1985). *The input hypothesis: Issues and complications*. London: Longman.

Leeman, J. (2003). Recasts and second language development: Beyond negative evidence. *Studies in Second Language Acquisition, 25*, 37–63.

Leeser, M. J. (2004). Learner proficiency and focus on form during collaborative dialogue. *Language Teaching Research, 8*, 55–81.

Long, M. H. (1996). The role of the linguistic environment in second language acquisition. In W. Ritchie & T. K. Bhatia (Eds.), *Handbook of language acquisition: Vol. 2. Second language acquisition* (pp. 413–468). San Diego, CA: Academic Press.

Long, M. H., & Robinson, P. (1998). Focus on form: Theory, research, and practice. In C. Doughty & J. Williams (Eds.), *Focus on form in classroom second language acquisition* (pp. 15–41). New York: Cambridge University Press.

Lyster, R. (1998a). Recasts, repetition, and ambiguity in L2 classroom discourse. *Studies in Second Language Acquisition, 20,* 51–81.

———. (1998b). Negotiation of form, recasts, and explicit correction in relation to error types and learner repair in immersion classrooms. *Language Learning, 48,* 183–218.

Mackey, A. (2000, October). *Feedback, noticing and second language development: An empirical study of L2 classroom interaction.* Paper presented at the Annual Meeting of the British Association for Applied Linguistics, Cambridge, UK.

Mackey, A. (in press). Introduction. In A. Mackey (Ed.). *Conversational interaction and second language acquisition: A series of empirical studies.* Oxford: Oxford University Press.

Mackey, A., & Abbuhl, R. (2005). Input and interaction. In C. Sanz (Ed.), *Internal and external factors in adult second language acquisition* (pp. 207–233). Washington, DC: Georgetown University Press.

Mackey, A., & Gass, S. M. (2006). *Second language research: Methodology and design* (pp. 169–178). Mahwah, NJ: Lawrence Erlbaum Associates.

———. (in press). Introduction: Methodological innovation in interaction research. *Studies in Second Language Acquisition, 28.*

Mackey, A., Gass, S., & McDonough, K. (2000). How do learners perceive interactional feedback? *Studies in Second Language Acquisition, 22,* 471–497.

Mackey, A., & Philp, J. (1998). Conversational interaction and second language development: Recasts, responses, and red herrings? *Modern Language Journal, 82,* 338–356.

McDonough, K. (2005). Identifying the impact of negative feedback and learners' responses on ESL question development. *Studies in Second Language Acquisition, 27,* 79–103.

McLaughlin, B. (1987). *Theories of second-language learning.* London: Arnold.

Nicholas, H., Lightbown, P., & Spada, N. (2001). Recasts as feedback to language learners. *Language Learning, 51,* 719–758.

Oliver, R., & Mackey, A. (2003). Interactional context and feedback in child ESL classrooms. *The Modern Language Journal, 87,* 519–533.

Philp, J. (2003). Constraints on "noticing the gap": Nonnative speakers' noticing of recasts in NS NNS interaction. *Studies in Second Language Acquisition, 25,* 99–126.

Pica, T. (1994). Research on negotiation: What does it reveal about second-language learning conditions, processes, and outcomes? *Language Learning, 44,* 493–527.

———. (1996). Second language learning through interaction: Multiple perspectives. *University of Pennsylvania Working Papers in Educational Linguistics, 12,* 1–22.

———. (1998). Second language learning through interaction: Multiple perspectives. In V. Regan (Ed.), *Contemporary approaches to second language acquisition* (pp. 1–31). Dublin: University of Dublin Press.

Pica, T., Kanagy, R., & Falodun, J. (1993). Choosing and using communication tasks for second language instruction and research. In G. Crookes & S. M. Gass (Eds.), *Tasks and language learning: Integrating theory and practice* (pp. 9–34). Clevedon, England: Multilingual Matters.

Posner, M. I. (1988). Structures and functions of selective attention. In T. Boll & B. Bryant (Eds.), *Clinical neuropsychology and brain function: Research, measurement, and practice* (pp. 173–201). Washington, DC: American Psychological Association.

———. (1992). Attention as a cognitive and neural system. *Current Directions in Psychological Science, 1,* 11–14.

Posner, M. I., & Peterson, S. (1990). The attention system of the human brain. *Annual Review of Neuroscience, 13,* 25–42.

Ramírez, A. G. (2005). Review of *The social turn in second language acquisition. The Modern Language Journal, 89,* 292–293.

Robinson, P. (1995). Review article: Attention, memory and the "noticing" hypothesis. *Language Learning, 45,* 283–331.

———. (Ed.) (2001). *Cognition and second language instruction.* Cambridge: Cambridge University Press.

———. (Ed.) (2002). *Individual differences and instructed language learning.* Amsterdam: Benjamins.

Schmidt, R. (1990). The role of consciousness in second language learning. *Applied Linguistics, 11,* 129–158.

———. (2001). Attention. In P. Robinson (Ed.), *Cognition and second language instruction* (pp. 3–32). Cambridge: Cambridge University Press.

Schmidt, R., & Frota, S. (1986). Developing basic conversational ability in a second language. A case study of an adult learner of Portuguese. In R. Day (Ed.), *Talking to learn: Conversation in second language acquisition* (pp. 237–326) Rowley, MA: Newbury House.

Storch, N. (2002). Patterns of interaction in ESL pair work. *Language Learning, 52,* 119–158.

Swain, M. (1985). Communicative competence: Some roles of comprehensible input and comprehensible output in its development. In S. Gass & C. Madden (Eds.), *Input in second language acquisition* (pp. 235–253). Rowley, MA: Newbury House.

———. (1993). The output hypothesis: Just speaking and writing aren't enough. *Canadian Modern Language Review, 50,* 158–164.

———. (1995). Three functions of output in second language learning. In G. Cook & B. Seidlhofer (Eds.), *Principle and practice in applied linguistics* (pp. 125–144). Oxford: Oxford University Press.

———. (1998). Focus on form through conscious reflection. In C. Doughty & J. Williams (Eds.), *Focus on form in classroom second language acquisition* (pp. 64–81). Cambridge: Cambridge University Press.

———. (2005). The output hypothesis: Theory and research. In E. Hinkel (Ed.), *Handbook on research in second language learning and teaching.* Mahwah, NJ: Lawrence Erlbaum Associates.

Swain, M., & Lapkin, S. (1998). Interaction and second language learning: Two adolescent French immersion students working together. *The Modern Language Journal, 82,* 320–337.

———. (2002). Talking it through: Two French immersion learners' response to reformulation. *International Journal of Educational Research, 37,* 285–304.

Tomlin, R., & Villa, V. (1994). Attention in cognitive science and second language acqui-
    sition. *Studies in Second Language Acquisition, 16*, 183–203.
Wagner-Gough, J., & Hatch, E. (1975). The importance of input data in second language
    acquisition studies. *Language Learning, 25*, 297–308.
Williams, J. (1999). Learner-generated attention to form. *Language Learning, 51*, 303–346.
———. (2001). The effectiveness of spontaneous attention to form. *System, 29*, 325–340.

11

Sociocultural Theory and Second Language Learning

James P. Lantolf and Steven L. Thorne
The Pennsylvania State University

The intent of this chapter is to familiarize readers with the principles and con-structs of an approach to learning and mental development known as *Socio-cultural Theory*.[1] Sociocultural Theory (SCT) has its origins in the writings of the Russian psychologist L. S. Vygotsky and his colleagues. SCT argues that human mental functioning is fundamentally a *mediated* process that is orga-nized by cultural artifacts, activities, and concepts (Ratner, 2002).[2] Within this framework, humans are understood to utilize existing cultural artifacts and to create new ones that allow them to regulate their biological and be-havioral activity. Language use, organization, and structure are the primary means of mediation. Practically speaking, developmental processes take place through participation in cultural, linguistic, and historically formed settings such as family life and peer group interaction, and in institutional contexts like schooling, organized sports activities, and work places, to name only a few. SCT argues that while human neurobiology is a necessary condition for higher order thinking, the most important forms of human cognitive activity develop

---

[1]Recently, some scholars working in this theory have begun to use the term Cultural-Historical Activity Theory, or CHAT. However, most research conducted on L2 learning within this general theoretical framework has used the term sociocultural, and for this rea-son we will use this term throughout the chapter. We also think it is important to point out that the term sociocultural has been used by researchers who do not work directly within the theoretical perspective we are addressing in this chapter. These researchers use the terms sociocultural to refer to the general social and cultural circumstances in which indi-viduals conduct the business of living.

[2]In this chapter, we restrict our discussion to symbolic artifacts, in particular language. For a full discussion of mediation see Lantolf and Thorne (2006).

through interaction within these social and material environments. This chapter describes the major theoretical principles and constructs associated with SCT and focuses specifically on second language acquisition (SLA). In the first section, we elaborate on mediation—the central construct of the theory. We then discuss and relate to SLA other aspects of SCT, namely internalization, regulation (closely connected to mediation and internalization), the zone of proximal development, and the genetic method.

THE THEORY AND ITS CONSTRUCTS

Mediation

SCT is associated with the work of Vygotsky, whose goal was to overcome what at the time (early 20th century) he characterized as a "crisis in psychology." This crisis arose because of the diversity of perspectives and objects of study, all of which were grouped under the general rubric of psychology. At that time, various approaches to the study of psychological processes were grouped into two broad categories: one followed a natural science approach to research (e.g., behaviorism) and sought out causes of psychological processes; the second followed the humanistic tradition and emphasized the description and understanding of mental activity (e.g., psychoanalysis). The causal natural science branch of psychology focused its research on the study of elementary, or biologically endowed, mental processes—that is, those processes that humans shared with other species, especially primates. These processes were largely automatic and included involuntary memory and attention, and reflex reactions to external stimuli. The descriptive branch focused its concern on what Vygotsky called higher (mental) processes such as problem-solving, voluntary memory and attention, rational thought, planning, and meaning-making activity.

Vygotsky developed a unified theory of human mental functioning, but he rejected earlier attempts that had tried to cobble together a little of the scientific approach and a little of the humanistic approach.[3] Instead he argued that to create a truly unified psychology required a completely new way of thinking about human mental development. Vygotsky acknowledged that the human mind was comprised of a lower-level neurobiological base, but the distinctive dimension of human consciousness was its capacity for voluntary control over biology through the use of higher-level cultural tools (i.e., language, literacy, numeracy, categorization, rationality, logic.). These higher-level cultural tools

---

[3]You can read more about the crisis and how Vygotsky proposed dealing with it in the following references: Kozulin (1990); van der Veer and Valsiner (1991); Wertsch (1985).

serve as a buffer between the person and the environment and act to mediate the relationship between the individual and the social–material world.

To better understand psychological mediation via conceptual and semiotic tools, we can consider the more obvious relationship between humans and the physical world that is mediated by concrete material tools. If we want to dig a hole in the ground in order to plant a tree, it is possible, following the behavior of other species, to simply use our hands. However, modern humans rarely engage in such nonmediated activity; instead we mediate the digging process through the use of a shovel, which allows us to make more efficient use of our physical energy and to dig a more precise hole. We can be even more efficient and expend less physical energy if we use a mechanical digging device such as a backhoe. Notice that the object of our activity remains the same whether we dig with our hands or with a tool, but the action of digging itself changes its appearance when we shift from hands to a shovel or a backhoe. Moreover, and this is going to be an important point when we return to our discussion of mental activity, in order to use a tool to dig a hole, we have to first inhibit any automatic digging response as we decide what kind of tool to use. As soon as it senses the bone, it begins an automatic digging response. Once humans select the appropriate tool, however, we are generally not completely free to use it in any way we like. The material form of a tool as well as the habitual patterns of its use affect the purposes to which it is put and methods we use when we employ it (see Thorne, 2003). Thus, a shovel requires one type of motion and a backhoe another. Physical tools, which are culturally constructed objects, imbue humans with a great deal more ability than natural endowments alone. Physical tools allow us to change the world in ways that simple use of our bodies does not. Moreover, by transforming our social and material environment, we also change ourselves and the way we live in the world.

Regulation. One form of mediation is *regulation*. When children learn language, words not only function to isolate specific objects and actions, they also serve to reshape biological perception into *cultural* perception and concepts. For children, thinking and actions at early stages of ontogenetic development are at first subordinated to the words of adults (Luria & Yudovich, 1972). According to Luria and Yudovich, subordination of the child's actions and thinking to adult speech lifts the child's mental and physical activity to a new, and qualitatively higher, stage of development. It signals the onset of a "long chain of formation of complex aspects of his [*sic*] conscious and voluntary activity" (p. 24). By subordinating their behavior to adult speech, children acquire the particular language used by the other members of a community (usually adults and older children) and eventually utilize this language to regulate their own behavior. In other words, children develop the capacity to regulate their own activity through linguistic means by participating in activities (mental and physical) in which their activity is initially subordinated, or regulated, by others. This process of developing self-regulation moves through three general stages.

In the first stage, children are often controlled by or use objects in their environment in order to think. This stage is known as object-regulation. For example, given the task by a parent of fetching a particular object such as a toy, a very young child is easily distracted by other objects (a more colorful, larger, or more proximate toy) and may thus fail to comply with the parent's request. This is a case of the child being regulated by objects. At a slightly later age, children learning mathematics may find it difficult or impossible to carry out simple addition inside of their heads and must rely on objects for external support (e.g., blocks). This is an example of using objects to regulate mental activity. The second stage, termed other-regulation, includes implicit and explicit mediation (involving varying levels of assistance, direction, and what is sometimes described as scaffolding) by parents, siblings, peers, coaches, teachers, and so on. In our discussion of the zone of proximal development we will illustrate how other-regulation functions in the case of second language (L2) learning.

Self-regulation, the final stage, refers to the ability to accomplish activities with minimal or no external support. Self-regulation is made possible through internalization—the process of making what was once external assistance a resource that is internally available to the individual (though still very much social in origin, quality, and function). Thus, at some point children no longer need blocks to add $2 + 5$. Some activities, however, are rarely if ever completely carried out inside of our heads (Wertsch, 1998). Thus, when asked to multiply multidigit numbers, most adults use paper and pencil to write down the numbers and carry out the necessary calculations in culturally specified ways. To be a proficient user of a language, first language (L1) or otherwise, is to be self-regulated; however, self-regulation is not a stable condition. Even the most proficient communicators, including native speakers, may need to re-access earlier stages of development (i.e., other- or object-regulation) when confronted with challenging communicative situations. Under stress, for example, adult native users of a language produce ungrammatical and incoherent utterances (see Frawley, 1997). In this instance, individuals may become regulated by the language as an object, and instead of controlling the language they falter and may require assistance from another person or from objects such as a thesaurus, dictionary, or genre-specific text. Each of the three stages discussed—object-regulation, other-regulation, and self-regulation—are "symmetrical and recoverable, an individual can traverse this sequence at will, given the demands of the task" (Frawley, 1997, p. 98).

Mediation by symbolic artifacts. Vygotsky reasoned that humans also have the capacity to use symbols as tools—not to control the physical environment but to mediate their own psychological activity. He proposed that while physical tools are outwardly directed, symbolic tools are inwardly or cognitively directed. Just as physical tools serve as auxiliary means to enhance the ability to control and change the physical world, symbolic tools serve as an auxiliary means to control and reorganize our biologically endowed psychological processes. This control is voluntary and intentional and allows humans, unlike other species, to inhibit and delay the functioning of automatic biological processes. Rather than reacting automatically and non-thoughtfully to stimuli, which could result in inappropriate and without thought, we are able to consider possible actions (i.e., plan) on an ideal plane before realizing them on the objective plane. Planning itself entails memory of previous actions, attention to relevant (and overlooking of irrelevant) aspects of the situation, rational thinking, and projected outcomes. All of this, according to Vygotsky, constitutes human consciousness. From an evolutionary perspective, this capacity imbues humans with a considerable advantage over other species because through the creation of auxiliary means of mediation we are able to assay a situation and consider alternative courses of action and possible outcomes on the ideal or mental plane *before* acting on the concrete objective plane (see Arievitch & van der Veer, 2004).

We can illustrate the above ideas with an example. A spider spins its web in precisely the same way each time, and it functions efficiently to catch and hold its prey. However, the spider clearly does not plan the web prior to constructing it, nor can it voluntary decide to change the shape and size of the web. It automatically follows its natural instinct. The human architect, on the one hand, plans a building on paper in the form of a blueprint before actually constructing it in objective physical space. The blueprint is the ideal form of the building, which of course no one can inhabit, but at the same time it must be sensitive to the physics that operate in the concrete world. The blueprint, then, is a culturally constructed symbolic artifact that represents the actual building and also serves to mediate the construction of the real building. It allows the architect to make changes ideally without ever having to act on the objective physical world.

Language is the most pervasive and powerful cultural artifact that humans possess to mediate their connection to the world, to each other, and to themselves.[4] It is this latter psychological function of language that is our primary concern in this chapter. Language imbues humans with the capacity to

---

[4] Humans also use other cultural artifacts to mediate their mental and social activity, including numbers, graphs, charts, art, music, and the like.

free themselves from the circumstances of their immediate environment and enables us to talk and think about entities and events that are displaced in both time and space, including those events and entities that do not yet exist in the real world (e.g., the building planned by the architect).

To summarize the discussion so far, Vygotsky's proposal for unifying psychology was that while biological factors formed the basis of human thinking, in and of themselves, they were insufficient to account for our ability to voluntarily and intentionally regulate our mental activity. We achieve this ability as a result of the internalization of culturally constructed mediating artifacts including, above all, language. We now turn our attention to the L2 as a tool for mediation.

Mediation Through a Second Language

We begin with the following question: To what extent are we able to use L2s to mediate our mental activity? The primary way in which we use language to regulate our mental functioning is through *private speech*. When we communicate socially, we appropriate the patterns and meanings of this speech and utilize it inwardly to mediate our mental activity, a phenomenon called private speech. Considerable research has been carried out on the development of private speech among children learning their first language (see Diaz & Berk, 1992; Wertsch, 1985). L2 researchers, beginning with the work of Frawley and Lantolf (1985), have also begun to investigate the cognitive function of private speech in the case of L2 users.

Among the features of private speech are its abbreviation and the meaning that it imparts. Vygotsky suggested that private speech, as is the case of social speech between people who have a great deal of shared knowledge, need not be fully syntactic in its form. Thus, close friends might produce a dialogue such as the following: A: "Eat yet?" B: "No, you?" where it isn't necessary to use the full version of the question and response: "Did you eat yet?" or "Have you eaten?" "No, have/did you?" In the case of private speech, it is assumed that the speaker already knows the topic addressed in the speech and is instead having problems figuring out what to do about it. Hence, in documented cases of private speech in children (e.g., Diaz & Berk, 1992; Wertsch, 1985), we find examples such as the following: The child is trying to solve a puzzle and says to himself or herself, "Now, the red one," or "Next?" Without full access to what it going on, it is difficult to know what the child is referring to in either case, but—and this is the point—the utterances are not intended to be interpreted by others. They are addressed by the child to himself or herself. Frawley (1997) argues that such utterances serve to focus the speaker's attention on what needs to be accomplished, how to accomplish it, and when something has been accomplished, and then allows the speaker evaluate what has been accomplished. He points out that different languages offer their speakers different linguistic options for carrying out such mental activities. Common expressions frequently encountered in the private speech of L1 English speakers include "Oh!" (often indicating that speakers have discovered what it is they are to do or that they have recovered a particular word from memory), "Next," "OK" (often used to direct the self to begin to do a task), "Let's see" (an indication that the speaker needs to take time to think about what the task or problem is), or "There" (indicating that a task has been completed). Importantly, as Frawley (1997) points out, all of these forms are derived from their use in social interaction.

Internalization

The process through which cultural artifacts, such as language, take on a psychological function is known as *internalization*. This process, along with mediation, is one of the core concepts of SCT. As Kozulin (1990, p. 116) puts it, "the essential element in the formation of higher mental functions is the process of internalization." Internalization is a negotiated process that reorganizes the relationship of the individual to her or his social environment and generally carries it into future performance (Winegar, 1997, p. 31). Internalization accounts for the organic connection between social communication and mental activity and is the mechanism through which we gain control over our brains, the biological organ of thinking (Yaroshevsky, 1989, p. 230). Vygotsky captured the interconnection established by internalization in his general law of genetic development: Every psychological function appears twice, first between people on the interpsychological plane and then within the individual on the intrapsychological plane (Vygotsky, 1987).

Imitation

Vygotsky proposed that the key to internalization resides in the uniquely human capacity to imitate the intentional activity of other humans. Imitation, however, is not understood as the mindless mimicking often associated with behaviorism in psychology and the audiolingual method in language pedagogy.[5] Instead it involves goal directed cognitive activity that can result in transformations of the original model. As Vygotsky states, "development based on collaboration and imitation is the source of all the specifically human

---

[5]Imitation is a process that is often associated with behaviorist theories of learning. However, the way Baldwin, Vygotsky and others including recent researchers such as Tomasello (1999) use it, it is not a process connected with behaviorism in any way.

characteristics of consciousness that develop in the child" (Vygotsky, 1987, p. 210) and as such imitation is "the source of instruction's influence on development" (p. 211).

Child language researchers have recently found that imitation plays an important role in language acquisition. Speidel and Nelson (1989), for instance, note that imitation is a complex mechanism involving motor and neurological processing. It is not a simple copy of what someone else says but is an intentional and self-selective behavior on the child's part, and one which is not driven by frequency of exemplars in the input (Tomasello, 2003). Indeed, imitation plays a central role in Tomasello's usage-based model of child language acquisition (see Lantolf & Thorne, 2006, for a discussion).

An especially important feature of imitation that is linked to internalization is that the imitative process need not occur immediately after a given pattern appears in the learner's linguistic environment. Rather imitation can occur with a delay of a day or more, even in children as young as nine months of age (Meltzoff, 2002, p. 21). Deferred imitation permits children to analyze language "off-line" (Meltzoff & Gopnik, 1989, p. 38) and, according to Speidel (1989, p. 163), points to a continuum between imitation and spontaneous language production, with deferred imitation serving as "essential building blocks for spontaneous speech." The research of Kuczaj (1983) and Weir (1962) recorded examples of delayed imitation among L1 children when they were alone in their cribs just before falling asleep.

Saville-Troike (1988) documents examples of both delayed and immediate imitation produced by L2 children as they engaged in various educational and play activities in their classroom. One five-year-old L1 Japanese child was recorded talking to herself in English: "I finished, I am finished, I have finished, I'm finished" (Saville-Troike, 1988, p. 584). While no direct evidence of this process is available from adult learners, Gillette (1994) and Lantolf and Genung (2002) found, using interview and diary study techniques, that some adults report practicing L2 patterns they heard in their classes when outside of the classroom and engaged in everyday activities such as walking a dog, jogging, or walking across campus.

Children in Saville-Troike's study also produced immediate imitative responses to the communicative utterances of their teacher and English-speaking classmates, as illustrated in (1) from a four-year-old Chinese L1 speaker:

(1)
      Teacher: You guys go brush your teeth. And wipe your hands on the towel.
      Child: Wipe your hand. Wipe your teeth.
                                          (Saville-Troike, 1988, p. 584)

This example is interesting because the child did not respond to the teacher with a communicative move but with a self-directed imitative pattern that exhibits the transformative possibilities of this process. The child did not repeat the teacher's utterance verbatim; instead she produced a reduced pattern which overgeneralized the collocate of "wipe" to include "teeth," which normally does not occur in English with the meaning intended by the teacher's original utterance.

Saville-Troike's research also documents instances where children imitated the speech of their classmates while eavesdropping on conversations between peers. Ohta (2001) attests similar patterns, or what she refers to as "vicarious response" in the case of adult foreign language learners of Japanese. Ohta found that learners frequently responded quietly to interactions between the instructor and other students. The students also practiced patterns in Japanese in what appeared to be delayed imitations that were similar to Saville-Troike's children. One of Ohta's students, for example, was observed to experiment with the Japanese stem *waru-* (bad) in which she first expands it to form the adverbial "*waruku*" and then changes it to the non-past adjective form "*warui*" (Ohta, 2001, p. 64).

Among the numerous examples of imitation documented in Centeno-Cortés' (2003) research is the case of a student who reports having encountered the Spanish word for postage stamp, *sello*, "on the street" in Spain. She was then recorded practicing the word in class and alternating between *sello* and *sella*. In a stimulated recall with the researcher, the student mentioned that her motivation for practicing the form was that she wasn't sure of its gender. At one point she is recorded saying to herself "*se . . . ello*" where the pause indicates her uncertainty. The student also comments that she finally figured out the correct form of the word through a combination of classroom and outside experience.

The examples considered above illustrate how learners use private speech in language classrooms as a means of internalizing the linguistic features available in their environment.[6] An important finding of this research, as attested in the studies by Ohta (2001), Centeno-Cortés (2003), and Lantolf and Yañez (2003), is that learners appear to have their own agendas for which aspects of the language they decide to focus on at any given time. This agenda does not

---

[6]While the research on private speech and internalization is more robust than we are able to present in our brief discussion here, it is nowhere near as rich as it should be. If SCT research is to make substantive claims about private speech and internalization with regard to second language learning, much more data is required. In particular, future research must focus on establishing a connection between internalization and externalization, or the use of the features in social speech. To date, only Centeno-Cortés's research (2003) has uncovered some evidence that addresses this important issue.

necessarily coincide with the intent of the instructor. As described in Lantolf and Yañez's 2003 study, a teacher may intend for the students to learn the difference between use of the copula *ser* (to be) in true passives (e.g., *La música fue compuesta por Mozart*, "The music was composed by Mozart") and the copula *estar* (to be) in adjective constructions with past participles (e.g., *La montaña estaba cubierta de nieve*, "The mountain was covered by/with snow") but a student may focus on the difference between the prepositions *por* and *de* used in these constructions. This is important information for teachers when deciding on appropriate pedagogical interventions that can maximally promote student learning, a topic that we take up in the following section that deals with the zone of proximal development.

The Zone of Proximal Development

The zone of proximal development (ZPD) has had a substantial impact in a variety of research areas, among them developmental psychology, education, and applied linguistics. The most frequently referenced definition of the ZPD is "the distance between the actual developmental level as determined by independent problem solving and the level of potential development as determined through problem solving under adult guidance or in collaboration with more capable peers" (Vygotsky, 1978, p. 86).

The ZPD has captivated educators and psychologists for a number of reasons. One is the notion of assisted performance, which, although not equivalent to the ZPD, has been the driving force behind much of the interest in Vygotsky's research. Another compelling attribute of the ZPD is that in contrast to traditional tests and measures that only indicate the level of development already attained, the ZPD is forward-looking through its assertion that what one can do today with assistance is indicative of what one will be able to do independently in the future. In this sense, ZPD-oriented assessment provides a nuanced determination of both development achieved and developmental potential.

The story of the ZPD concept begins with Vygotsky's genetic law of cultural development. Vygotsky's well-known formulation is that:

> Any function in the child's cultural development appears twice, or on two planes. First it appears on the social plane, and then on the psychological plane. First it appears between people as an interpsychological category, and then within the child as an intrapsychological category. This is equally true with regard to voluntary attention, logical memory, the formation of concepts, and the development of volition. . . . [I]t goes without saying that internalization transforms the process itself and changes its structure and functions. Social relations or relations among people genetically underlie all higher functions and their relationships. (Vygotsky, 1978, p. 57)

Two issues standout in the preceding characterization of the ZPD: that cognitive development results from social and interpersonal activity becoming the foundation for intrapersonal functioning, and that this process involves internalization (discussed earlier in the chapter).

With the ZPD, Vygotsky put into concise form his more general conviction that "human learning presupposes a specific social nature and a process by which children grow into the intellectual life of those around them" (1978, p. 88).[7] Vygotsky was particularly intrigued with the complex effects that schooling had on cognitive development. The activity of participation in schooling involved, at least in part, learning through participation in socioculturally and institutionally organized practices. One of Vygotsky's most important findings is that learning collaboratively with others, particularly in instructional settings, precedes and shapes development. The relationship between learning and development is not directly causal, but intentionally designed learning environments (e.g., instructed L2 settings) can stimulate qualitative developmental changes. In this sense, the ZPD is not only a model of the developmental process but also a conceptual tool that educators can use to understand aspects of students' emerging capacities that are in early stages of maturation. When used proactively, teachers using the ZPD as a diagnostic have the potential to create conditions for learning that may give rise to specific forms of development in the future.

WHAT COUNTS AS EVIDENCE?

As we explain in the section on research methodology, sociocultural research is grounded in the genetic method. Consequently, single snapshots of learner performance do not constitute appropriate evidence of learning and development within this theoretical framework. Evidence must have a historical, or genetic, perspective. This is not necessarily an argument for the exclusive use of long-term longitudinal studies that cover extensive time spans. While development may surely occur over the course of months, years, or even the entire lifetime of an individual or group, it may also occur over relatively short periods of time, as documented in the study by Aljaafreh and Lantolf (1994), when learning takes place during a single interaction between the tutor and the student. Moreover, development arises in the dialogic interaction that transpires among individuals (this includes the self-talk that people engage in

---

[7]In a related vein, elsewhere Vygotsky remarks that "social relations or relations among people genetically underlie all higher functions and their relationships" (1981, p. 163).

when they are trying to bootstrap themselves through difficult activities such as learning another language) as they collaborate in the ZPD. Evidence of development from this perspective is not limited to the actual linguistic performance of learners. On the face of it, this performance in itself might not change very much from one time to another. What may change, however, as Aljaafreh and Lantolf's study shows, is the frequency and quality of assistance needed by a particular learner in order to perform appropriately in the new language. On one occasion a learner may respond only to explicit mediation from a teacher or peer to produce a specific feature of the L2, and on a later occasion (later in the same interaction or in a future interaction) the individual may only need a subtle hint to be able to produce the feature. Thus, while nothing has ostensibly changed in the learner's actual performance, development has taken place because the quality of mediation needed to prompt the performance has changed.

Development within the ZPD is not just about performance per se; it is also about where the locus of control for that performance resides—in someone else or in learners themselves. As learners assume greater responsibility for appropriate performances of the L2, they can be said to have developed, even when they exhibit little in the way of improvement in their overt performance. This means that evidence of development can be observed at two distinct levels: at the level of overt independent performance and at the level where performance is mediated by someone else. This second type of evidence will go undetected unless we keep in mind that development in the ZPD is understood as the difference between what an individual can do independently and what he or she is able to do with mediation. As a corollary to this principle, it is necessary to observe if and how the mediation is modified over time. By the same token, two learners who appear to be at the same developmental level, assessed on the basis of their independent performance, may be at very different levels of development when we take account of the quantity and quality of mediation they each require to perform appropriately. Finally, because SCT construes language as a cultural tool used to carry out concrete goal directed activities, tasks such as traditional language tests designed to elicit displays of a learner's linguistic knowledge are insufficient evidence of development. Such evidence must be sought in tasks in which language is a means to some concrete end. These can be tasks that parallel activities in the everyday world, or they may be tasks that are typical of instructional programs in the classroom setting, such as in the case of project-based learning. In sum, evidence of development in a new language is taken to be changes in control over the new language as a means of regulating the behavior of the self and of others in carrying out goal-directed activity.

COMMON MISCONCEPTIONS ABOUT SCT

Within the field of second language research, two misconceptions about the nature of SCT have arisen. Both are related to the theoretical claim that mental functioning develops from external social interaction to internal psychological activity. The first, more general misconception claims that because the source of development in SCT is social interaction, the theory has difficulty accounting for the appearance of unattested L1 forms in L2 speaker performance, and therefore it is better seen as a sociolinguistic rather than a psycholinguistic theory (e.g., Ellis, 1997). To give a specific example, L2 speakers frequently regularize the past tense of English verbs such as *eat, take,* and *go* (*eated, *taked, *goed), but the regular forms do not occur in the speech of adult native speakers of English. They must therefore be created by the learners through an analogical process that uses regular past tense forms as a model (e.g., *talked, reached, pushed*). Given that the incorrect regular forms are not in the linguistic environment and are instead manufactured by the learners, social factors alone are not sufficient to explain the learning process. The problem is that the argument is grounded in the mistaken assumption that SCT proposes that learning is simply a copying process. As we showed in our discussion of internalization, specifically with regard to imitation, this is not what the theory proposes. Indeed, it argues that internalization through imitation is not a matter of copying but entails an active, and frequently creative, reasoning process.

The second misconception relates more directly to the ZPD, which is easily the most widely used and yet least understood of the central concepts of SCT (Chaiklin, 2003). There are two general misconceptions about the ZPD. The first is that the ZPD is the same thing as scaffolding or assisted performance, and the second is that it is similar to Krashen's notion of $i + 1$ (e.g., Krashen, 1982). Both assumptions are inaccurate. Scaffolding, a term coined by Jerome Bruner and his colleagues nearly three decades ago (see Wood, Bruner, & Ross, 1976), refers to any type of adult–child (expert–novice) assisted performance. This is not what the ZPD is about. For one thing, in such expert–novice interactions, the goal is to complete the task rather than to help the child develop, and therefore the task is usually carried out through other-regulation, whereby the adult controls the child's performance instead of searching for opportunities to relinquish control to the child. Scaffolding, unlike the ZPD, is thought of in terms of the amount of assistance provided by the expert to the novice rather than in terms of the quality, and changes in the quality, of assistance negotiated between expert and novice (Stetsenko, 1999).

With regard to misconceptions about the ZPD and Krashen's $i + 1$, the fundamental problem is that the ZPD focuses on the nature of the concrete dialogic relationship between expert and novice and its goal of moving the novice toward greater self-regulation through the new language, while Krashen's concept focuses on language and the language acquisition device, which is assumed to be the same for all learners, with very little room for differential development (e.g., Dunn & Lantolf, 1998; Thorne, 2000). Krashen's hypothesis claims that language develops as a result of learners comprehending input that contains features of the new language and that are "slightly" beyond their current developmental level. As researchers have pointed out, there is no way of determining precisely the $i + 1$ of any given learner in advance of development. It can only be assumed after the fact. In terms of the ZPD, development can be predicted in advance for any given learner on the basis of his or her responsiveness to mediation. This means that what an individual is capable of with assistance at one point in time, he or she will be able to do without assistance at a future point in time. Moreover, as we mentioned in our discussion of the ZPD, development is not merely a function of shifts in linguistic performance, as in the case of Krashen's model, but is also determined by the type of, and changes in, mediation negotiated between expert and novice.

EXEMPLARY STUDY:
ALJAAFREH AND LANTOLF (1994)

The research literature on corrective feedback and its relation to L2 development is substantial. Though findings have been divergent, the bulk of studies have focused on implicit versus explicit input or the amount and type of negotiation involved. Research based in SCT addresses feedback from a different vantage point. Specifically, corrective feedback and negotiation are contextualized as a collaborative process in which the dynamics of the interaction itself shape the nature of the feedback and inform its usefulness to the learner (or learners in the case of more symmetrical peer interaction). There is also a concern with the timing and quality of the feedback as it aligns with the participant's ZPD. The following case study provides a detailed overview of a seminal study in this area.

Aljaafreh and Lantolf framed their study on error correction and feedback within the ZPD. In so doing, they looked at the evolving nature of the negotiation process between learners and their tutor in an ESL context. In their review of the L2 acquisition research literature on the role of negative feedback on L2 development, they assert that findings are mixed and do not explicitly link learning outcomes with particular kinds of feedback procedures. The authors claim that both implicit and explicit feedback impact linguistic development, but that "the relevance of the type of feedback offered (as marked by a learner's reactive response to the feedback) is as important an index of development in second language as are the actual linguistic forms produced by the learner" (p. 467). Development in this context is the internalization of the mediation that is dialogically negotiated between the learner and others that results in enhanced self-regulation. The ZPD in this case forms an activity frame that relates the current developmental level to the potential development that is possible through collaboration with a more competent tutor. The potential level of development is suggested by the kinds of assistance needed to carry out the activity and the visible ability of the learner to utilize forms of external assistance.

Aljaafreh and Lantolf identify a number of "mechanisms of effective help" relating to intervention within the ZPD. Assistance should be *graduated*— with no more help provided than is necessary because the assumption is that over-assistance decreases the student's ability to become fully self-regulated. At the same time, a minimum level of guidance must be given so that the novice can successfully carry out the action at hand. Related to this is that help should be *contingent* on actual need and similarly removed when the person demonstrates the capacity to function independently. Graduation and contingency are critical elements of developmentally productive joint activity. This process is *dialogic* and entails continuous assessment of the learner's ZPD and subsequent *tailoring* of help to best facilitate developmental progression from other-regulation to self-regulation.

The participants in the study are three English-as-a-second-language (ESL) learners enrolled in an eight-week early-intermediate ESL writing and reading course, at level 2, where 6 is the highest level. The learners volunteered for one extra tutorial session a week that would focus on their required weekly composition. Although other usage problems were also addressed in the tutorial sessions, Aljaafreh and Lantolf analyzed interactions around four frequently recurring grammatical problems: articles, tense marking, use of prepositions, and modal verbs. Before each session, the tutor would familiarize himself with the essays. As described earlier, however, interactions within the actual tutorial sessions were emergent in the way they played out as the need for quantity and quality of assistance changed within and between sessions.

At the start of each session, the learner was asked to read through her essay and to identify any problems or mistakes. The tutor–tutee pair would then read through the essay sentence by sentence. When either the tutee or tutor observed a problem, they would stop for discussion. Though each interaction was variable, assistance usually took the form of tutor-initiated prompts that began at a very general level, such as "Do you notice any problem?" or "Is there anything wrong in this sentence?" (p. 469). Should this strategy fail, the tutor would become progressively more focused and specific, such as "Is there anything wrong with this segment?" or "Pay attention to the tense of the verb" (pp. 469–470). If yet more help was needed, the tutor would explicitly point out the problem, give clues as to necessary corrections, or ultimately provide the learner with the correct answer and, if appropriate, a grammatical explanation. Analysis of the interactions showed changes in grammatical competence that illustrated learners were moving from the need for other-regulation provided by the tutor to the partially or completely self-generated capacity to notice and correct errors in written production. Aljaafreh and Lantolf describe ESL development as a process of moving from other-regulation to self-regulation through a series of stages, each of which is characterized by differing abilities to notice and correct an error, and in the quantity and quality of assistance needed to do this.

A principle challenge to research based on educational interventions is the issue of how to operationalize the quantity and quality of assistance. Unstructured and/or entirely emergent assistance may provide the essential help needed for a learner to carry out a task that he or she is unable to manage alone, but such conditions are problematic in two ways: a) tutors may inadvertently over- or underprovide assistance, and b) qualitative and quantitative differences in assistance and their precise correlations to learner performance cannot be consistently documented. To address these issues, Aljaafreh and Lantolf developed a thirteen-point "regulatory scale" that models tutor behaviors ranging from broad and implicit leading questions to explicitly phrased corrections. This scale was used to code observable behavior with particular attention to qualitative differences in assistance provided by the tutor. Level 0 (zero) marks independent functioning on the part of the learner (independent reading and marking of errors/problems in the essay). Levels 1–12 describe collaborative interaction between the tutor and learner, and the higher the number on the scale, the more explicit the assistance provided by the tutor. As Aljaafreh and Lantolf argued, however, even Level 0 is "social" in that the learner is reviewing her essay at the request of the tutor and would do so in ways that reflect her understanding of the nature of the task. In other words, her behavior, although carried out with minimal or no temporally immediate assistance from the tutor, is still inscribed by the acculturation processes that influence her construction of what independent reading and error detection entails.

Changes in the category and quantity of feedback were tracked over time for each of the three participants in the study as they engaged in the tutorial. An important finding is that, though the three learners in this study demonstrated similar proficiency on a placement exam, according to Vygotsky's formulation of the ZPD, one "cannot arbitrarily assume that any two learners who attain identical scores on a test are necessarily at the same stage . . . if all we assess is their actual developmental level. It is imperative to assess the learners' potential level of development as well" (p. 473). Through a discussion of use of the definite article, Aljaafreh and Lantolf show that the same error made by different learners represents different problems. Though neither of the learners appropriately used the definite article with "U.S." (for example, in regard to travel to *the* U.S.), in one example occurring over 36 turns at talk, a learner needed explicit intervention that concluded with the tutor eventually providing the correct form, while a second learner immediately produced the definite article only after being asked to read aloud and think about what might be missing from a particular sentence in her essay. At the surface level, both learners had omitted the same obligatory linguistic feature, but their need for qualitatively different assistance to remedy this problem indicates that they required qualitatively different mediation in order to develop increased grammatical sophistication and accuracy.

At the start of the interaction cycle, Aljaafreh and Lantolf note that the novice's linguistic performance is mediated and enhanced by the tutor. Over time, both within a session and across sessions, each of the participants demonstrated that they had internalized aspects of assistance and gained a greater ability to function autonomously. Importantly, "for this to happen . . . the expert must relinquish control (itself dialogically negotiated) to the novice at the appropriate time. There can be no real development otherwise" (p. 480).

Another critical issue is that all feedback has the *potential* to be relevant for learning, "but their relevance depends on where in the learner's ZPD a particular property of the L2 is situated" (p. 480). The hierarchy of regulation captures the dynamic character of feedback when it is organized and interactionally deployed within the pedagogical framework provided by the ZPD.

EXPLANATION OF OBSERVED FINDINGS IN SLA

In this section we will consider if and how SCT addresses the observed phenomena in SLA raised by the editors in the first chapter of the present volume. As a preamble to this discussion, however, we would like to point to a fundamental difference between the observed phenomena taken as a whole and how SCT approaches the learning process. It is clear that the ten phenomena taken together are predicated on a theoretical assumption that separates individuals from the social world (in our view, and in the view of many other researchers, scientific observations are never theory free). In other words, the phenomena assume a dualism between autonomous learners and their social environment represented as linguistic input—a concept closely linked to the computational metaphor of cognition and learning. As we have argued throughout this chapter, SCT is grounded in a perspective that does not separate the individual from the social and in fact argues that the individual emerges from social interaction and as such is always fundamentally a social being. This includes not only obvious social relationships but also the qualities that comprise higher-order mental activity that is rooted in semiotically mediated social interaction. With this as a background we will briefly address each of the ten observations from an SCT perspective.

Observation #1. Exposure to input is necessary for SLA. Since the social world is the source of all learning in SCT, participation in culturally organized activity is essential for learning to happen. This entails not just the obvious case of interaction with others, but also the artifacts that others have produced, including written texts. It also includes Ohta's (2001) "vicarious" participation in which learners observe the linguistic behavior of others and attempt to imitate it through private speech or dialogue with the self. Learning is always an active engagement; the engagement may be overt, as in the case of social dialogue, or it may be covert as in the case of private dialogue.

Observation #2. A good deal of SLA happens incidentally. Here we believe a bit of clarification is in order. From the perspective of SCT, what matters is the specific subgoal that learners form in which the language itself becomes the intentional object of their attention in the service of a higher goal. Thus, looking up a word in a dictionary, asking for clarification or help, or guessing at the meaning of a word when reading a text for comprehension may not constitute an activity conducive for optimal learning of the language. This is because reading a text is itself not normally a primary goal. We normally read, write, talk, and listen in the service of higher goals—for example, to write a research paper, to pass a test, to find our way through an unknown city, and so on. In order to achieve the higher goal, we form subgoals along the way. This process reflects the tool function of language—that is, the use of language to achieve specific concrete goals. It is analogous to learning how to shift gears when learning to drive a car. It would be odd for shifting gears to be the primary goal, but it must at some point in the process be the focus of the learner's attention and therefore at least a temporary and intentional goal that serves the higher goal of moving the car. Thus, what is called incidental learning is not really incidental. It is intentional, goal-directed, meaningful activity. From the SCT perspective, there are no passive learners and there is no incidental learning.

Observation #4. Learner's output (speech) often follows predictable paths with predictable stages in the acquisition of a given structure, and Observation #9. There are limits on the effects of instruction on SLA. In order to consider these observations, it is important to distinguish between learning in untutored immersion settings and highly organized educational settings. The evidence reported in the L2 literature supports the developmental hypothesis position in the case of untutored learners. There is also research that shows that learners follow the same paths in classroom settings. This research, however, did not take into account the ZPD, as far as we are aware. In other words, it provided a uniform intervention for all learners and did not engage learners in the type of negotiated mediation demanded by the concept of ZPD. Unfortunately, the research that has been carried out so far on learning in the ZPD has not focused on features of the new language that are supposedly acquired in stages. Until this research is conducted, the matter remains empirically unresolved.

Observations #5. Second language learning is variable in its outcome, and *Observations #6. Second language learning is variable across linguistic subsystems.*   As we have shown in our discussion of the ZPD, variability in the development of any given learner and across learners is a characteristic of L2 acquisition. In addition, the evidence shows that learners variably acquire different subsystems of a new language depending on the type of mediation they receive and the specific goals for which they use the language.

Observation # 8. There are limits on the effect of a learner's first language on SLA.   From an SCT perspective it is important to distinguish form from meaning when addressing this observation. While L1 forms may have a limited effect on L2 learning, it is clear from the kind of evidence considered with regard to observations on variability that L1 meanings continue to have a pervasive effect in the L2 learning. In addition, as we saw in our discussion of L2 private speech, L2 users have a difficult time using the new language to mediate their cognitive activity, notwithstanding high levels of communicative proficiency.

Observation # 9. There are limits on the effects of output (learner production) on language acquisition.   In this case it is important to distinguish between the use of the L1 to mediate the learning of the L2 and the effects of L1 on L2 production. Because our first language is used not only for communicative interaction but also to regulate our cognitive processes, it stands to reason that learners must necessarily rely on this language in order to mediate their learning of the L2. This was our response to the previous observation. However, there is also evidence showing that social speech produced in the L1 and the L2 also impacts on L2 learning. In a continuing series of studies, Merrill Swain and her colleagues have documented how classroom learners of second languages, including immersion learners, push linguistic development forward by talking, either in the L1 or L2, about features of the new lan-

guage (Swain, 2000, 2006; Swain & Lapkin, 2002). In addition, recall our discussion of the function of imitation in the internalization process. Learners
clearly rely on L2 imitative production (albeit in their private speech) as a
means of acquiring the new language.

CONCLUSION

In this chapter we have outlined the primary constructs of SCT, namely mediation and regulation, internalization, and the zone of proximal development
(ZPD), and have considered how they inform the study of SLA. Mediation is
the principle construct that unites all varieties of SCT and is rooted in the observation that humans do not act directly on the world—rather their cognitive and material activities are mediated by symbolic artifacts (such as languages, literacy, numeracy, concepts, and forms of logic and rationality) as well
as by material artifacts and technologies. The claim is that higher-order mental functions, including voluntary memory, logical thought, learning, and attention, are organized and amplified through participation in culturally organized activity. This emphasis within the theory embraces a wide range of
research including linguistic relativity, distributed cognition, and cognitive
linguistics. We also addressed the concept of internalization, the processes
through which interpersonal and person–environment interaction both forms
and transform one's internal mental functions, and the role of imitation in
learning and development. Finally, we discussed the ZPD, the difference between the level of development already obtained and the cognitive functions
comprising the proximal next stage of development that may be visible
through participation in collaborative activity. We emphasized that the ZPD is
not only a model of developmental processes but also a conceptual and pedagogical tool that educators can use to better understand aspects of students'
emerging capacities that are in early stages of maturation.

Because of its emphasis on praxis, SCT does not rigidly separate understanding (research) from transformation (concrete action). While SCT is
used descriptively and analytically as a research framework, it is also an applied methodology that can be used to improve educational processes and
environments (see Thorne, 2004, 2005). SCT encourages engaged critical inquiry wherein an investigation would lead to the development of material
and symbolic tools necessary to enact positive interventions. In other words,
the value of the theory resides not just in the analytical lens it provides for
the understanding of psychological development but also in its capacity to
directly impact that development. Although certainly not unique among theoretical perspectives, SCT approaches take seriously the issue of applying research to practice by understanding communicative processes as inherently
cognitive processes, and cognitive processes as indivisible from humanistic

issues of self-efficacy, agency, and the effects of participation in culturally organized activity.

DISCUSSION QUESTIONS

1.   Both Lantolf and Thorne's and Gass and Mackey's approaches are "in-
     ternactional" in nature. How are they different?
2.   What is private speech? Thinking on your own language learning expe-
     riences, can you relate any instances in which private speech has played
     some role?
3.   In the exemplary study, learners produce a target linguistic feature with
     assistance from an expert speaker. Lantolf and Thorne appear to equate
     this production with acquisition. How does this view of acquisition dif-
     fer from other approaches?
4.   If you were to adopt a sociocultural approach, what implications would
     this have for conducting classroom SLA research? How would it com-
     pare with research using any other approach you might adopt?

SUGGESTED FURTHER READING

Lantolf, J. P., & Thorne, S. L. (2006). *Sociocultural theory and the genesis of second language development*. Oxford: Oxford University Press.

   This book presents an in-depth introduction to sociocultural theory and
   to research carried out on L2 development within this framework. It also
   includes two chapters that focus on how SCT principles can be implemented in second language classrooms.

Lantolf, J. P. (2006) Sociocultural theory and second language development:
State-of-the-art. *Studies in Second Language Acquisition, 28*, 67–109.

   This article presents a critical survey of research conducted on L2 learning from the perspective of sociocultural theory over the past decade.

Thorne, S. L. (2003). Artifacts and cultures-of-use in intercultural communication. *Language Learning & Technology, 7*, 38–67.

   This article provides an overview of the concept of mediation and describes three case studies of Internet-mediated intercultural foreign language learning.

Thorne, S. L. (2005). Epistemology, politics, and ethics in sociocultural theory. *The Modern Language Journal, 89*, 393–409.

   This article describes the history of Vygotsky-inspired research, provides
   a select review of L2 investigations taking this approach, and outlines
   recent conceptual and methodological innovations.

REFERENCES

Aljaafreh, A., & Lantolf, J. P. (1994). Negative feedback as regulation and second language learning in the zone of proximal development. *The Modern Language Journal*,
78, 465–483.
Arievitch, I., & van der Veer, R. (2004). The role of nonautomatic process in activity regulation: From Lipps to Galperin. *History of Psychology*, 7, 154–182.
Centeno-Cortés, B. (2003). Private speech in the second language classroom: Its role in in-
ternalization and its link to social production. Unpublished doctoral dissertation,
Pennsylvania State University. University Park.
Chaiklin, S. (2003). The zone of proximal development in Vygotsky's analysis of learning
and instruction. In A. Kozulin, B. Gindis, V. Ageyev, & S. Miller (Eds.), *Vygotsky's
educational theory in cultural context* (pp. 39–64). Cambridge: Cambridge University
Press.
Diaz, R., & Berk, L. (Eds.). (1992). *Private speech: From social interaction to self regulation*.
Hillsdale, NJ: Lawrence Erlbaum Associates.
Dunn, W., & Lantolf, J. (1998). Vygotsky's zone of proximal development and Krashen's
i + 1: Incommensurable constructs; incommensurable theories. *Language Learning*,
48, 411–442.
Ellis, R. (1997). *SLA research and language teaching*. Oxford: Oxford University Press.
Frawley, W. (1997). *Vygotsky and cognitive science: Language and the unification of the social
and computational mind*. Cambridge, MA: Harvard University Press.
Frawley, W., & Lantolf, J. (1985). Second language discourse: A Vygotskyan perspective.
Applied Linguistics, 6, 19–44.
Gillette, B. (1994). The role of learner goals in L2 success. In J. Lantolf & G. Appel (Eds.),
Vygotskian approaches to second language research. Norwood, NJ: Ablex.
Hoffman, E. (1989). *Lost in translation: A life in a new language*. New York: Penguin Books.
Kozulin, A. (1990). *Vygotsky's psychology: A biography of ideas*. Cambridge, MA: Harvard
University Press.
Krashen, S. (1982). *Principles and practices in second language acquisition*. Oxford: Pergamon.
Kuczaj, S. (1983). *Crib speech and language play*. New York: Springer Verlag.
Lantolf, J., & Genung. P. (2002). "I'd rather switch than fight": An activity-theoretic
study of power, success, and failure in a foreign language. In C. Kramsch (Ed.), *Lan-
guage acquisition and language socialization: Ecological perspectives* (175–195). London:
Continuum.
Lantolf, J., & Thorne, S. (2006). *Sociocultural theory and the genesis of second language
development*. Oxford: Oxford University Press.
Lantolf, J., & Yáñez, C. (2006). Talking yourself into Spanish: Intrapersonal communica-
tion and second language learning. *Hispania*, 86, 97–109.
Luria, A., & Yudovich, F. (1972). *Speech and the development of mental processes in the child*.
Harmondsworth, UK: Penguin Books.
Meltzoff, A. (2002). Elements of a developmental theory of imitation. In A. Meltzoff &
W. Prinz (Eds.), *The imitative mind: Development, evolution, and brain bases* (19–41).
Cambridge: Cambridge University Press.

Meltzoff, A. N., & Gopnik, A. (1989). On linking nonverbal imitation, representation, and language learning in the first two years of life. In G. Speidel & K. Nelson (Eds.), *The many faces of imitation in language learning* (23–52). New York: Springer Verlag.

Ohta, A. (2001). *Second language acquisition processes in the classroom: Learning Japanese.* Mahwah, NJ: Lawrence Erlbaum Associates.

Ratner, C. (2002). *Cultural psychology: Theory and method.* New York: Kluwer/Plenum.

Saville-Troike, M. (1988). Private speech: Evidence for second language learning strategies during the "silent period." *Journal of Child Language, 15,* 567–90.

Speidel, G. (1989). Imitation: A bootstrap for language to speak? In G. Speidel & K. Nelson (Eds.), *The many faces of imitation in language learning* (pp. 151–180) New York: Springer Verlag.

Speidel, G., & Nelson, K. (1989). A fresh look at imitation in language learning. In G. Speidel & K. Nelson (Eds.), *The many faces of imitation in language learning* (pp. 1–22). New York: Springer Verlag.

Stetsenko, A. (1999). Social interaction, cultural tools and the zone of proximal development: In search of a synthesis. In S. Chaiklin, M. Hedegaard, & U. J. Jensen (Eds.), *Activity theory and social practice: Cultural historical approaches* (pp. 235–253). Aarhus: Aarhus University Press.

Swain, M. (2000). The output hypothesis and beyond: Mediating acquisition through collaborative dialogue. In J. Lantolf (Ed.), *Sociocultural approaches to second language research* (pp. 97–115). Oxford: Oxford University Press.

———. (2006). Verbal protocols: What does it mean for research to use speaking as a data collection tool? In M. Chaloub-Deville, C. Chapelle, & P. Duff (Eds.), *Inference and generalizability in applied linguistics: Multiple research perspectives.* Amsterdam: Benjamins.

Swain, M., & Lapkin, S. (2002). Talking it through: Two French immersion learners' response to reformulation. *International Journal of Educational Research, 37,* 285–304.

Thorne, S. (2000). Second language acquisition theory and the truth(s) about relativity. In J. Lantolf (Ed.), *Sociocultural approaches to second language research* (pp. 219–243). Oxford: Oxford University Press.

———. (2003). Artifacts and cultures-of-use in intercultural communication. *Language Learning and Technology, 7,* 38–67.

———. (2004). Cultural historical activity theory and the object of innovation. In O. St. John, K. van Esch, & E. Schalkwijk (Eds.), *New insights into foreign language learning and teaching* (pp. 51–70). Peter Lang, Frankfurt.

———. (2005). Epistemology, politics, and ethics in sociocultural theory. *The Modern Language Journal, 89,* 393–409.

Tomasello, M. (1999). *The cultural origins of human cognition.* Cambridge, MA: Harvard University Press.

———. (2003). *Constructing language: A usage-based theory of language acquisition.* Cambridge, MA: Harvard University Press.

van der Veer, R., & Valsiner, J. (1991).*Understanding Vygotsky: A quest for synthesis.* Oxford: Blackwell.

Vygotsky, L. (1978). *Mind in society: The development of higher psychological processes* (Ed. by M. Cole, V. John-Steiner, S. Scribner, & E. Souberman). Cambridge, MA: Harvard University Press.

———. (1981). The genesis of higher mental functions. In J. Wertsch (Ed.), *The concept of activity in Soviet psychology*. Armonk, NY: M. E. Sharpe.

———. (1987). *The collected works of L. S. Vygotsky, volume 1: Problems of general psychology*. R. Reiber & A. Carton (Eds.), New York: Plenum Press.

Weir, R. (1962). *Language in the crib*. The Hague: Mouton.

Wertsch, J. (1985). *Vygotsky and the social formation of mind*. Cambridge, MA: Harvard University Press.

———. (1998). *Mind as action*. Oxford: Oxford University Press.

Winegar, L. (1997). Can internalization be more than a magical phrase? Notes toward the constructive negotiation of this process. In C. Lightfoot & B. Cox (Eds.), *Sociogenetic perspectives on internalization*. Mahwah, NJ: Lawrence Erlbaum Associates.

Wood, D., Bruner, J., & Ross, G. (1976). The role of tutoring in problem-solving. *Journal of Child Psychology and Psychiatry, 17*, 89–100.

Yaroshevsky, M. (1989). *Lev Vygotsky*. Moscow: Progress Press.

12

Second Language Learning Explained? SLA Across Nine Contemporary Theories

Lourdes Ortega

University of Hawai'i at Mānoa

As a field, second language acquisition (SLA) is young but strong. It began in the late 1960s with a few key initial developments during the decade of the 1970s, followed by a prodigious expansion in research and theorizing during the 1980s and 1990s. The field of SLA is also decidedly interdisciplinary, both in its origins and its development. It interconnects with four related fields, some of them also relative newcomers in academia: language teaching, linguistics, child language acquisition, and psychology. SLA has developed more recent interdisciplinary ties with other disciplines, notably bilingualism, cognitive science, education, anthropology, and sociology. Most scholars agree that the coming of age of SLA as an autonomous discipline happened some time at the end of the 20th century, after some 40 years of exponential growth. The first decade of our new century is, therefore, an opportune time to reflect on the theories that offer the most viable explanations about the human capacity to learn additional languages (henceforth L2) besides the first (henceforth L1).

The editors of this volume, VanPatten and Williams, offer ten observations based on well-established empirical findings in SLA (see chapter 1, this volume). They reason that these agreed upon "observed phenomena" need to be explained by any viable theory of second language acquisition, or at least incorporated into them in some formal fashion. For the sake of economy, the ten facts can be combined into five central areas that have occupied the attention of most SLA researchers in the past four decades: the nature of second language knowledge, the nature of interlanguage development, the contributions of knowledge of the first language, the linguistic environment, and instruction. Table 12.1 presents these five areas and associated observations that VanPatten and Williams offer in chapter 1.

In keeping with the overall purpose of the collection to introduce uninitiated readers to SLA theories, I have two goals in this closing chapter. First, I hope to help readers review their understanding of the nine contemporary theories of SLA presented in this book. To do so, I will contrast and compare the position each theory takes with regard to the five key areas outlined in Table 12.1. My second goal is to pique readers' intellectual curiosity and encourage them to pursue further study of SLA. To achieve this goal, I will conclude the chapter with a small glimpse of some of the exciting but complex challenges that theories in SLA will likely have to tackle in the future.

THE NATURE OF LANGUAGE
KNOWLEDGE AND COGNITION

Each of the theories featured in this book offers a different take on the nature of L2 knowledge depending on the view about human language cognition that

TABLE 12.1.
Ten Observations That Every SLA Theory Needs to Explain

Central Focus	Specific Observations
Knowledge and cognition	#2. A good deal of SLA happens incidentally.
	#3. Learners come to know more than what they have been exposed to in the input.
Interlanguage	#4. Learner's output (speech) often follows predictable paths with predictable stages in the acquisition of a given structure.
	#5. Second language learning is variable in its outcome.
	#6. Second language learning is variable across linguistic subsystems.
First language	#8. There are limits on the effect of a learner's first language on SLA.
Linguistic environment	#1. Exposure to input is necessary for SLA.
	#7. There are limits on the effects of frequency on SLA.
	#10. There are limits on the effects of output (learner production) on language acquisition.
Instruction	#9. There are limits on the effects of instruction on SLA.

Note: Text taken from VanPatten & Williams, chapter 1, this volume.

they espouse. Figure 12–1 offers a summary of the key differences and similarities in this area across the nine theories.

Universal Grammar theory (UG) and Autonomous Induction theory (AI) are affiliated with the field of generative Chomskyan linguistics and therefore adopt a linguistic view of language cognition. Both theories offer the following logical argument: If L2 learners possess abstract knowledge of ambiguity and ungrammaticality that could have never been derived from the linguistic

The Theory	Cognition	Learning	Representation
Universal Grammar Theory	linguistic: nativism, modularity	implicit abstract deduction	symbolic and unconscious
Autonomous Induction Theory			
Associative–Cognitive CREED Framework	psychological: general cognitive architecture	implicit induction, association	unconscious
Skill Acquisition Theory		explicit deduction, automatization	declarative, then procedural
Input Processing Theory	psychological, underspecified	explicit–implicit interface?	UG? functional universals?
Processability Theory		unspecified	functional universals
Concept-Oriented Approach			
Interaction Framework		explicit–implicit interface?	both conscious and implicit
Vygotskian Sociocultural Theory	social: relational, situative	conscious, goal-driven, mediated	conscious, inter-mental, then intra-mental

FIGURE 12–1. The nature of language knowledge and cognition in nine SLA theories.

input available in the environment or from their L1 knowledge alone, we must assume that the knowledge was already there, in some initial form at least, independent from experience. That is, the two theories are committed to nativism. Furthermore, in both theories learners are thought to be constrained (in the positive sense of "guided") in their learning task by this preexisting initial grammatical knowledge they possess. Proponents of both theories are also committed to modularity. In other words, they believe language is distinct from other forms of cognition; it is a separate faculty, an organ of the mind. (In the specialized literature, the terms "language-specific" and "domain-specific" are also used to refer to this same notion.) Finally, in both Universal Grammar theory and Autonomous Induction theory, language knowledge is thought to be symbolic. This symbolic knowledge is posited to be formal, highly abstract, and unconscious or tacit, represented in our mind in the form of principles and parameters (in UG) or features and categories (in AI). It follows that according to these two theories, core grammatical knowledge (of an L1 or an L2) unfolds incidentally by deduction from the innate abstract knowledge. The instantiated rules of the specific L1 or L2, once acquired, remain implicitly represented.

In sharp contrast stand two theories that also make the nature of L2 knowledge central to their explanations: the Associative–Cognitive CREED framework and Skill Acquisition theory. Both have their roots in the field of contemporary cognitive psychology and thus both offer a psychological view of cognition. In them, language is thought to be learned and used through the same cognitive architecture we have at our disposal for the acquisition and use of other kinds of knowledge (e.g., knowing about history and biology; or knowing how to cook, how to play the piano, tennis, or chess; or knowing how to solve mathematical equations or do computer programming). The Associative–Cognitive CREED explains language learning as, by and large, an implicit inductive task and, therefore, is committed to incidental learning and unconscious representations. That is, human language capacities are thought to result from the extraction of statistical patterns from the input. This extraction is fueled by an innate general predisposition of the brain to learn and be shaped by experience, and it is further pushed by communicative needs as the organism interacts with the environment. The extraction of associative patterns is also driven implicitly and ineludibly by the human brain's predisposition towards probabilistic learning: "A general property of human perception is that when a sensation is associated with more than one reality, unconscious processes weigh the odds, and we perceive the most probable thing" (Ellis, chapter 5 this volume, p. 78).

By contrast, Skill Acquisition theory focuses on the prototypical case when a skill or expertise is approached through formal instruction as the starting point, for example when people avail themselves of a manual or a tutor to get started with learning tennis, computer programming, chess . . . or a foreign language. Therefore, the theory is committed to conscious processing, deliberate learning, and explicit representations with an interface that allows for the conversion of this explicit knowledge into eventual expert performance. As DeKeyser (chapter 6 this volume) puts it, learning to become an expert (in language as in anything else) is viewed as a process of turning knowledge into behavior (p. 98). It should be clear, then, that the Associative–Cognitive CREED and Skill Acquisition theory, while sharing the same basic psychological view of language, differ greatly in the relative importance they accord to implicit and explicit knowledge in explaining SLA.

Four other SLA theories in this book also hold a psychological view of cognition, but they are much less specific than the previous two theories about the assumptions they may make regarding the nature of language knowledge and the architecture of cognition. On one hand, they are ambiguous as to whether language cognition should be understood in psychological or linguistic terms. For example, Input Processing theory assumes that Universal Grammar knowledge probably constrains learners' hypotheses (see VanPatten, 1998), and both Processability theory and the Concept-Oriented approach have explicitly tried to accommodate some version of linguistic nativism in their models, although they do so by drawing specifically on functional rather than formal linguistic constructs. In terms of the nature of knowledge representation, Processability theory and the Concept-Oriented approach appear to side with implicit knowledge, and they remain silent as to how learning actually happens. On the other hand, Input Processing theory and the Interaction approach seem to assume an explicit–implicit knowledge and processing interface, but neither addresses directly the issue of how the interface may work.

Vygotskian Sociocultural theory of SLA stands apart from all the other theories presented in this book in that language cognition is viewed as neither a linguistic nor a psychological faculty of the mind. Instead, SLA sociocultural theorists posit that cognition can best be understood as a social faculty. That is, human cognition is thought to arise from the material, social, cultural, and historical context in which human experience is embedded. Learning (including language learning) is explained via processes by which the mind appropriates knowledge from affordances in the environment. These affordances, in turn, are fundamentally social: They arise out of our relations to others, via tools (including language) that mediate between us and our environment, and out of the specific events we experience. The appropriation of such knowledge itself happens through participation in social events and fundamentally involves consciousness. Indeed, consciousness, agency, and intentionality are central to explaining cognition and learning in this theory.

THE NATURE OF INTERLANGUAGE

How do the nine SLA theories in this book address systematicity and variability in interlanguage? Figure 12–2 summarizes the range of positions on this issue.

Both Universal Grammar and Autonomous Induction understand systematicity as a natural property of linguistic knowledge. Since all human languages are systematic, interlanguages must be too. It is also natural to expect that there will be differences between the grammatical core of a language and everything else (pragmatics, vocabulary, and so on) because only certain properties of a language are thought to fall within the scope of the universal abstract

The Theory	Systematicity	Variability
Universal Grammar Theory	principles and parameters	no theoretical status
Autonomous Induction Theory	features and categories	
Associative–Cognitive CREED Framework	systematicity, variability, and dynamicity in all complex systems	
Skill Acquisition Theory	taken for granted	experiential, cognitive, and developmental sources
Input Processing Theory	no theoretical emphasis on either	
Processability Theory	two sides of the same phenomenon, both derived from functional constraints on processing and/or communication	
Concept-Oriented Approach		
Interaction Framework	congruent with processability and concept-oriented views	congruent with skill acquisition views
Vygotskian Sociocultural Theory	no theoretical emphasis	central to activity and social cognition

FIGURE 12–2.   The nature of interlanguage in nine SLA theories.

linguistic knowledge that all humans share as a species. Both theories leave room for the possibility that certain variability is the result of a quality of "indeterminacy" that may be typical of L2 grammars (e.g., the fact that a learner may reject an ungrammatical string some times and accept it as grammatical other times). However, in both theories much of variability is considered to be theoretically uninteresting on the grounds that it stems from simple short-comings of performance that have nothing to do with genuine L2 grammatical knowledge (for example, the typical experience when a learner remembers to use a rule while writing but forgets to use it in her speech).

The Associative–Cognitive CREED takes for granted that systematicity and variability are two properties of language just as they are of all complex systems. In addition, it introduces a third construct, dynamicity (see Larsen-Freeman, 2002), in order to explain how systematicity and variability can co-exist and arise out of the brain's interaction with its environment. By compar-ison, Skill Acquisition theory focuses little on systematicity (or dynamicity, for that matter) and concentrates instead on explaining variability. Also notewor-thy is that this theory finds the locus of variability in three sources that are ex-ternal to the language system per se. A first source of variability is posited to be experiential. Namely, between-learner variability will arise from differing L2 experiences, as different learners are exposed to (or seek on their own to be exposed to) different amounts, qualities, and sequences of declarative knowl-edge and deliberate practice. A second source from which variability will arise is predicted to be psychological: Certain cognitive abilities differ greatly among people. (SLA research on this kind of variability is also known under the rubric of "individual differences.") A third source of variability pertains to the same learner across contexts and conditions and can be considered cognitive-developmental. Namely, the same learners' performance will vary depending on whether communicative and cognitive stressors are present and overload their current performance capacities. That is, this kind of variability is an in-dication that performance has not yet become automatic in that particular area for that group of learners.

Explaining interlanguage systematicity as well as variability is a major goal of both the Processability theory and the Concept-Oriented approach. Processability theory, in particular, has been instrumental in establishing the basic findings for developmental sequences in a number of L2 word order phe-nomena. This theory posits that learners are constrained (which in this theory is used in the sense of "limited") in systematic ways by what grammatical in-formation they can process syntactically at a given point in development. To process the L2 syntactically in this theory means to hold forms together in working memory for comparison and exchange of grammatical information. Variability is explained as the other side of the same coin, in that these same processing constraints will also determine the sets of alternatives (or variants) that are available to learners (their hypothesis space) at any given point in development. The Concept-Oriented approach, conversely, makes interesting but broader predictions about the interplay between systematicity and variability in interlanguage development, along the additive progression from the realm of pragmatic resources (e.g., gesture, knowledge of the world and the context), to lexical resources (e.g., adverbs as a means to convey time), and finally to the morphosyntactic or grammatical dimension (e.g., verbal morphology as a means to convey time). Existing nonlinguistic concepts and the need to express them linguistically pushes the system to arrive at increasingly complex solutions along the pragmatic-lexical-grammatical cline. Input Processing theory does not appear to make systematicity or variability central to its explanations, although it offers principles that are consistent with the prediction that interlanguage development will not be haphazard but systematic.

The Interaction approach makes broad use of the functionalist explanations for systematicity that the Concept-Oriented approach and Processability theory have put forth and is simultaneously interested in the second and third sources of individual variability posited in Skill Acquisition theory. Proponents of the Interaction approach find it theoretically important to understand the cognitive-developmental variability that is associated with communicative and cognitive stressors operating during communication (for example, different interlocutors or interlocutors of same versus different gender) and with requirements of task performance (for example, a complex versus a simple task). The rationale is that such context and task factors might be manipulated externally so as to enhance processes during interaction that may eventually facilitate development. A second area of increasing theoretical importance in this approach is individual differences in cognitive resources. This focus is natural among interactionists, given that since the early 1990s they have viewed attention as a possible major explanatory construct for L2 learning, and given that it is well established in psychology that humans vary greatly in their attentional capacities.

Sociocultural theory also makes variability the center of study but for very different reasons. Variability is a theoretically important phenomenon in this theory because actions and learning are thought to come about from situative engagement with others and out of affordances from specific contexts. Thus, it is thought that no universal cognitive abilities can be studied in disembodiment from the context and the people out of which they come about. The Zone of Proximal Development (ZPD), the intentional goals that drive learners, and the type of mediation and tools (including language and others) available to them in any given event all conspire to create variability. Moreover, this variability is theoretically interesting because it helps explains why some learners may acquire certain dimensions of language expertise but not others, and why some learners may be unsuccessful in their apparent efforts to learn the L2.

THE ROLE OF THE FIRST LANGUAGE

The nine theories presented in this book afford diverse roles to the L1 in their explanations of SLA, as depicted schematically in Figure 12–3.

Three theories afford the L1 a privileged role in their explanations of SLA. Universal Grammar theory views the L1 as potentially the initial point of departure for L2 acquisition. Indeed, some proponents of this theory posit a large influence for the L1 in the early stages of L2 acquisition, although several other possibilities are also considered and empirically pursued (for an accessible explanation of the range of positions, see Mitchell & Myles, 2004, pp. 84–90). In the end, however, all UG proponents agree that it is impossible to speak of L1 influence as a wholesale phenomenon. As White (chapter 3 this volume, p. 51) describes it, in some areas the contribution of the L1 is fleeting, in

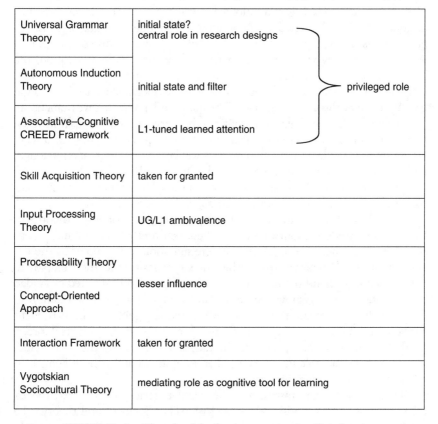

Universal Grammar Theory	initial state? central role in research designs	
Autonomous Induction Theory	initial state and filter	privileged role
Associative–Cognitive CREED Framework	L1-tuned learned attention	
Skill Acquisition Theory	taken for granted	
Input Processing Theory	UG/L1 ambivalence	
Processability Theory	lesser influence	
Concept-Oriented Approach		
Interaction Framework	taken for granted	
Vygotskian Sociocultural Theory	mediating role as cognitive tool for learning	

FIGURE 12–3.   The role of the first language in nine SLA theories.

others long-lasting, and yet in others it may be permanent. Since one important goal in this theory is to determine whether UG knowledge still guides L2
acquisition in ways that are fundamentally similar to the ways in which it is
posited to guide L1 acquisition, it is imperative to tease out the relative contributions of L1 rules versus innate universal linguistic biases across key areas of
linguistic knowledge. Thus, studies are set up to investigate groups of learners
from carefully chosen L1 backgrounds and always by reference to native-speaking baselines for the L1 and L2 involved. Therefore, the L1 holds a privileged
role in this theory not only in theoretical terms but also in terms of actual research practices. Autonomous Induction theory also lends L1 a privileged status
in SLA, in that it accords L1 knowledge the function of a filter during parsing
that will operate automatically (that is, unstoppably) during the moment-to-
moment processing of L2 input. This filter will only give in on occasions when
parsing failure occurs and the language acquisition device intervenes.

The Associative–Cognitive CREED also accords the L1 a privileged role in
SLA, but it does so based on a rationale that is reminiscent of behaviorist un-
dertones: "L1-tuned learned attention limits the amount of intake from L2 input, thus restricting the end state of SLA" (Ellis, chapter 5 this volume, p. 91).
As a result of early years of development, experience, and socialization, the
brain's neurons are tuned and committed to the L1, and any subsequent language learning (of a second, foreign, or heritage additional language beyond the
first) is biased by this *learned attention*. The framework posits that we humans are
hard-pressed to change habits and routines that serve us well. It is as if with the
flashlight of our L1 we were looking in the wrong L2 places for cues about what
we are supposed to learn now. Certain cues will be frequent and salient enough,
and redundant and meaningful enough, that they will be attended to after sufficient L2 experience. More subtle features of the L2 input, however, may completely remain outside our flashlight's beam, perhaps irreparably so.

The place of the L1 in the other five psychologically oriented theories of
SLA is more modest. Input Processing theory currently holds an ambivalent
stance because there is no theoretical determination at this point in the development of the theory as to whether the strategies that learners employ to
parse and comprehend the input ought to be considered L1-filtered or guided
by linguistic universal knowledge (see VanPatten, chapter 7 this volume). In
Processability theory and the Concept-Oriented approach, the L1 is thought
to exert a lesser influence by comparison to robust functional universal forces.
In Skill Acquisition theory and the Interaction approach, on the other hand,
a selectively predictable influence is taken for granted but without being crucial to any of the explanations proposed.

Finally, and by contrast to all other eight theories in this book, the L1
takes on a unique and positive role in Vygotskian Sociocultural theory. The
first language is a mediating tool, voluntarily used by learners to achieve self-

regulation and to enable collaborative engagement in L2 learning events on occasions when using the L2 for higher-level mental activity would be developmentally premature. In essence, the use of the L1 during L2 learning events is viewed not as a subconscious influence that cannot be avoided but as a strategy through which learners can achieve goals otherwise unavailable to them in the L2 (for example, to discuss the L2 as an object of reflection or to clarify how to tackle a difficult L2 task). The L1, in these ways, can contribute to (rather than interfere with) L2 learning.

CONTRIBUTIONS OF THE LINGUISTIC ENVIRONMENT

What are the putative contributions to L2 learning of the linguistic environment to which learners are exposed and through which they interact with others? Each theory stipulates a different weight and role for input, input frequency, and output in explaining SLA. This is summarized in Figure 12–4.

Let us review first the place that L2 input holds across theories. In Universal Grammar theory, input is thought to play only a limited, if necessary, part in acquisition: that of triggering values of knowledge that predate any experience with the linguistic environment. After some relevant part of the linguistic input triggers, for example, our knowledge that the language we are learning is head-final (as in Japanese, where we say "the house to" instead of "to the house" or "I movies like" instead of "I like movies"), our pre-existing knowledge gets reorganized in a domino effect, and a series of other knowledge pieces that "cluster" together around the given value "head-final" also get selected. At the opposite extreme, the Associative–Cognitive CREED posits that language learning is input-driven. Every time constructions and exemplars in the linguistic input are experienced by the learner (through listening, reading, or both), neural connections are fired and strengthened, and memory traces are established until networks of associations emerge into a complex system. That is, of all the ingredients of acquisition, input is posited to play the most central role in this framework.

In all other theories presented in this book, the linguistic input plays intermediate positions between these two extremes. All of them maintain the importance of being exposed to L2 input, but each lends an increasingly large role to other ingredients of the learning process. In four of these theories— Autonomous Induction theory, Input Processing theory, Processability theory, and the Concept-Oriented approach—it is how the learner processes the input, rather than the input per se, that is regarded as truly essential to explain acquisition. The specific theoretical details differ greatly among the four, however. Thus, AIT construes input as the physical material (albeit mostly parsed

The Theory	Input	Frequency	Output
Universal Grammar Theory	triggers deduction of knowledge	no theoretical status	
Autonomous Induction Theory	can trigger processing failure, can afford cues for extraction	already existing L1 feature representations more important	no theoretical status, time lag with comprehension
Associative–Cognitive CREED Framework	associative learning is input-driven	utmost influence, subconscious tallying leads to chunking	confined roles: beneficial only for • summoning consciousness
Skill Acquisition Theory	one ingredient only, necessary but not sufficient	frequency of exposure/practice is important in automatization	• developing fluency • raising awareness of input misinterpretations
Input Processing Theory	how learners processes input during comprehension is important	degree of meaningfulness more important	• only a reflection of what is processable
Processability Theory	developmental constraints or functional processing principles determine what can get processed, which in turns is reflected in production	nature of the grammatical information exchange required more important	• general pressure to communicate intended meanings drives acquisition
Concept-Oriented Approach		subconscious tallying of prototypicality of form-function mappings	
Interaction Framework	one ingredient only, necessary but not sufficient	important but in combination with other factors	causal role: can lead to development
Vygotskian Sociocultural Theory	one ingredient only	no theoretical status	important as social participation (collaborative dialogue, private speech)

FIGURE 12–4. The role of the linguistic environment in nine SLA theories.

through the filter of L1 knowledge) that contains cues for fine-tuning and revising the inventory of symbolic features represented in the given mental grammar. Nevertheless, an essential contribution of pre-existing knowledge is assumed and, as in UG, the input is thought to be underdetermined and impoverished by comparison to whatever L2 knowledge the language acquisition device ends up building. Input Processing theory affords input a rather central role but, most importantly, exactly what part of it feeds into learning (that is, becomes intake) is determined by comprehension, processing, and parsing strategies that learners bring with them and through which the input is perceived.

The Concept-Oriented approach and Processability theory also place the weight of their explanations on how learners process the input. The Concept-Oriented approach predicts that two strategies brought to the task of input processing by learners, the one-to-one principle and the multifunctionality principle, figure prominently in shaping how learners are able or unable to use the L2 input for developing new resources for meaning-making during language production. Processability theory predicts that L2 learners' limited capacity for what can be held momentarily in memory determines what abstract grammatical information in the input (as described in Lexical-Functional Grammar) can be held simultaneously and compared mentally in order to build a formal and meaningful representation of any utterance. It is somewhat ironic that despite the primacy accorded to input in both theories, in the end both find their strongest evidence and make their most interesting predictions with regard to language production, not input: What gets processed is best reflected in what can be generated in L2 production at a given time in development.

The Skill Acquisition theory, the Interaction approach, and Vygotskian Sociocultural theory go much further in construing the input as only one of several ingredients of SLA, necessary but not sufficient, and perhaps not even the most crucial one. Thus, both the skill learning and interactionist explanations lend more importance to other ingredients of the environment, such as explicit grammar explanation and deliberate practice (in Skill Acquisition theory), or interaction, feedback, and pushed output (in the Interaction approach). In Vygotskian Sociocultural theory, on the other hand, the input plays an important but general role for language learning insofar as learners choose to engage with it actively, for example, through goal-oriented vicarious participation when they observe others using the language and through creative imitation of others' utterances in private speech. However, social participation in optimal learning events is thought to be more crucial for acquisition than the linguistic environment per se.

Naturally, because frequency is a feature of the linguistic input (referring in essence to the statistical properties of the input), only SLA theories that stipulate a central role for input afford frequency a high explanatory power. All such theories, however, agree that the workings of frequency in L2 learning can only be understood as a force that affects acquisition in interacting with several others, rather than alone. In the Associative–Cognitive CREED the statistical properties of the input are of foremost importance in explaining

SLA. As humans process language input, they unconsciously compute the relative frequencies with which they encounter forms, constructions, and exemplars; the relative frequency of the surrounding linguistic contexts in which they appear; and the likelihood of the meanings they can refer to. Language knowledge gradually emerges in the learner by constantly tuning itself through every repeated experience to approximate the statistical properties of the experienced linguistic environment. Skill Acquisition theory acknowledges the importance of frequent exposure and practice for enabling automatization and thus predicts that higher frequency forms in the input will be proceduralized earlier than rarely occurring ones.

Work carried out within the Concept-Oriented approach also affords an important role to the statistical and distributional properties of the input in ways that are actually compatible with the Associative–Cognitive CREED. The relative frequency of form-function mappings in the input is predicted to influence the directions in which learners expand their linguistic repertoires. This is particularly well captured in the distributional bias hypothesis (e.g., Andersen, 1990), which posits that certain morphological markings (e.g., imperfective –*ing*) are prototypically experienced in the input in combination with certain lexical meanings (e.g., actions that imply duration, such as "run," "walk," or "sing"). The hypothesis predicts that this bias in the input will be reflected in learners' development. For example, –*ing* may appear first in learner's utterances containing activities like "run" ("Look, a rabbit is running through the grass!") and only later can spread to contexts containing accomplishments like "run a marathon" ("Look, that man is running the marathon barefoot!").

In Input Processing theory, Processability theory, and Autonomous Induction theory, objective frequency in the linguistic input is thought to explain less than other input features, such as the semantic load or degree of meaningfulness (in Input Processing theory), the nature of the grammatical information exchange required (in Processing theory), or the already existing feature representations from the L1 (in Autonomous Induction theory). On the other hand, in the Interaction approach, frequency is understood as only one of a number important influences, several outside the scope of input proper, and in explanations proposed by Universal Grammar theory and Vygotskian Sociocultural theory, frequency has no theoretical status.

Finally, let us review the place that L2 output holds across the theories. Most of the linguistically and psychologically oriented theories afford output a rather confined role. In neither Universal Grammar theory nor Autonomous Induction theory does output have theoretical status, as it occupies no place in the explanations proposed or the evidence sought. On the psychological front, on the other hand, theories often construe output as beneficial for L2 learning but without playing any major causal part in acquisition processes.

Thus, the Associative–Cognitive CREED holds that output is facilitative in promoting self-awareness and conscious processes that enhance learning or in fostering fluency, hence reinforcing chunking and automatization processes that normally happen tacitly during the processing of the input. Skill Acquisition theory views output as "deliberate practice," a special kind of language production activity in which explicit declarative knowledge about language is put to use, first slowly and with effort and later (with sufficient reiteration and deliberate effort) more fluently and accurately. If it is not embedded in the right combination and sequence of explicit rule explanation plus deliberate practice, however, output cannot contribute to learning. Output is afforded an even more limited role in Input Processing theory, because comprehension (meaning extraction) is seen as the driving force in language learning. Output may promote fluency or, at most, allow for extra opportunities to realize that something in the input has been misinterpreted or misanalyzed (if, for example, a lack of understanding caused by such an input miscue is revealed during interaction). Processability theory, in turn, stipulates an even smaller role for output because it predicts that output simply mirrors development (hence the best evidence for acquisition can be gleaned from production data) but can never cause it or drive it.

Only three of the nine SLA theories lend output some theoretical prominence. The Concept-Oriented approach explains language learning as driven by a general pressure to communicate intended meanings. Acquisition proceeds when the means available to the learner do not suffice for conveying the desired functions and concepts in their messages. Vygotskian Sociocultural theory also affords an important role to output, albeit a more general one. This theory reconceptualizes output broadly as social participation and identifies an important learning potential for the productive use of language through collaborative dialogue and imitation in private speech. The Interaction approach is unique in that it accrues to output the status of an acquisition catalyst, an acquisition-expanding force with interlanguage-stretching capabilites (for examples of how this is possible, see Ortega, forthcoming). When learners produce language for and with others, they can rely less on lexical and contextual cues (which often suffice during comprehension) and are forced to draw more on morphosyntactic cues. In addition, they may become more aware of gaps and holes in their linguistic resources, which may motivate them to look for solutions in the available input provided by others, either immediately upon experiencing difficulties or on a later occasion, when opportune timing and resources allow it. It is also through imperfect attempts to produce messages that mutual understanding may be obscured to the point that meaning needs to be negotiated (although of course, depending on the circumstances, mutual understanding could be faked or abandoned altogether). If meaning is negotiated, language is often broken down into more manageable segments, new forms are offered, and implicit and explicit corrections are issued from well-intentioned (or, alternatively, ill-predisposed) interlocutors. In the Interaction approach, output drives acquisition: We learn a language by speaking it, literally, and syntax emerges out of communication, a suggestion first made by Evelyn Hatch in the beginnings of the field (Hatch, 1978).

THE ROLE OF INSTRUCTION

How does instruction interact with natural L2 learning processes? And what are the limits of what can be achieved, and what cannot, with instruction? Of the nine SLA theories in this book, some make claims as to whether instruction is necessary, sufficient, beneficial, or detrimental, whereas only a few go further to make specific proposals as to what features are needed for the design of optimal L2 instruction. The positions are presented schematically in Figure 12–5.

In four theories, instruction can play no substantial role in learning of L2 grammar. Both Universal Grammar theory and Autonomous Induction theory are consistent with this view. Much of a language may be teachable (e.g., vocabulary, stylistic choices, pragmatic preferences) but its morphosyntactic core is not because "conscious processing of grammar is simply not a viable means by which to develop any kind of mental representation of language" (Carroll, chapter 9 this volume, p. 167). Autonomous Induction theory, however, does not discard the possibility that some instruction could be designed successfully to alter the ways in which L2 learners tend to process the input. The Concept-Oriented approach and Processability theory also share the view that L2 instruction can play no large role, although the forces thought to overpower instructional influences are functional rather than formal (see Bardovi-Harlig & Reynolds, 1995, for an example of effective instruction within the Concept-Oriented approach).

Given this view of instruction as peripheral, proponents within these four theories rarely pronounce themselves about the "how" of optimal instruction. Pienemann, however, has addressed the "what" of optimal instruction by urging instructional design that respects the principle of learner readiness. That is, he notes that instruction should target a level above learners' current developmental stage or else it can have negligible and possibly detrimental effects (see Lightbown & Pienemann, 1993; Pienemann, 1984). It is also possible to speculate that optimal instruction that is congruent with Autonomous Induction theory principles would need to recreate natural (incidental, meaning-oriented) language use and would build in some additional conflict for the L1 parser to fail and for the Language Acquisition Device to intervene and operate on relevant L2 cues during the particular processing event.

The Theory	Effects	Optimal features	Instructional design
Universal Grammar Theory	no effect possible on subconscious core knowledge	none offered	none offered
Autonomous Induction Theory		beneficial if incidental processing is carefully flooded with opportunities for the L1 parser to fail	none offered
Associative–Cognitive CREED Framework		explicit instruction that summons consciousness and fosters implicit (bottom up) and explicit (top down) learning interfaces	none offered
Skill Acquisition Theory	beneficial	helping explicit knowledge to become proceduralized	cycles of carefully sequenced explanation and deliberate practice
Input Processing Theory		comprehension exercises designed to short-circuit unproductive parsing strategies and replace them with productive ones	processing instruction
Processability Theory	limited effects, cannot override universal forces	consider developmental learner readiness when choosing targets (the "what" of instruction)	none offered
Concept-Oriented Approach		none offered	none offered
Interaction Framework		attention attracted to language form in the course of meaningful task performance	focus on form, task-based language teaching
Vygotskian Sociocultural Theory	beneficial	learning environments should foster meaningful events and other-assistance, aligned to Zone of Proximal Development	none offered

FIGURE 12–5.   The role of L2 instruction in nine SLA theories.

Another position is that instruction can play an important, if only comple-mentary, role in facilitating L2 acquisition. The Associative–Cognitive CREED envisions a clearly beneficial role for instruction, albeit one that is subordi-nated to input-driven, implicit statistical pattern induction. Without specifying particular pedagogies, proponents of this framework typically offer general prin-ciples for optimal instruction—for example, that L2 input brought into class-rooms needs to be as abundant, rich, and authentic as possible. Instruction can be seeded with any kind of feedback (implicit or explicit) or other elements that help summon awareness because conscious attentional control may help offset the effects of L1-learned attention. Grammar explanations can help, particularly when followed by strategically sequenced exemplars that make hidden patterns more salient to learners (see Ellis, 1993). Repetition and practice are thought to be beneficial too. Vygotskian Sociocultural theory also construes instruction as clearly facilitative: "intentionally designed learning environments (e.g., instructed L2 settings) can stimulate qualitative developmental stages" (Lantolf & Thorne, chapter 11 this volume, p. 207). The theory specifies that instruction should be designed to foster a social and material environment in which two things happen. One, learners are encouraged to negotiate participation in meaningful activities and, two, the quality of assistance from teacher and peers is orchestrated to gauge the appropriate current level, aligned developmentally and contingent to learner needs. If these conditions occur, learners can accomplish valued goals, first through assisted participation and later on their own. In this sense, appropriate L2 instruction should work within learners' Zone of Proximal Development and seek to expand it by enabling qualitative changes in the required types of assistance and negotiated participations.

Three theories of the nine presented in this book take the firm position that instruction can optimize natural learning processes and may even be necessary when the goal is truly advanced levels of proficiency. Proponents of each have articulated full proposals for the design of optimal instruction and have addressed the "how" of instruction. Proponents of Skill Acquisition theory firmly believe that optimal instruction should consist of cycles of explanation and deliberate practice of the various parts of language and language skills to be taught. Learners first need to be given explicit grammar explanations, often pedagogically simplified, and always accompanied by good examples of the phenomenon being explained. This is because they must process this knowledge consciously until they understand the rules well. This must be followed by carefully planned "deliberate practice" activities that enable learners to apply to further examples and cases the rules they have newly committed to declarative memory, first slowly and with high degrees of error, but gradually more fluently and accurately. Thus, learners who are found to make little progress in one (or all) areas of the L2 may lack the relevant declarative knowledge, or they may have engaged in insufficient, nondeliberate, or ill-sequenced practice for those areas. It is through the provision of relevant explanation and practice in the specific areas targeted by instruction that learners can eventually be propelled to advanced levels of L2 competence. However, it is not grammar explanations alone or repetition per se that fuel learning but the fact that the two instructional elements are sequenced in these specific ways and that the learners apply themselves in the conscious processing of knowledge and further practice the target performances through deliberate and conscious efforts (see DeKeyser, forthcoming).

Input processing theorists claim that optimal instruction should alter how learners process the input during meaning-based comprehension. To this end, they have developed a special type of instruction called processing instruction (see VanPatten, 2004), designed to afford high-quality opportunities to process certain aspects of the L2 input in the context of meaningful comprehension exercises and under conditions that short-circuit unproductive L1 or universal parsing tendencies. In this way learners are primed to employ more appropriate parsing strategies in the target language. For example, L2 Spanish learners may be given practice with noncanonical (object-verb-subject) word order examples like *A Juan lo besó María* or literally "As for Juan, Maria kissed him" immediately after being warned it would be misguided to assume that "Juan" is the doer of the kissing just because their L1 English creates the expectation that the first noun in the string will most likely be the doer of any action. (It should be noted that explanations that draw explicit attention to L1–L2 parsing mismatches are thought to help, but they are not posited to be necessary.) With sufficient practice on how to parse strings using Spanish morphological cues rather than word order, learners' internal parsing strategies are expected to attune themselves to the appropriate cues for extracting meaning and making Spanish-sensitive syntactic interpretations. (Farley, 2005, offers good suggestions for how to design a variety of input processing exercises across several target languages.)

In contrast to the sentence-level meaningful practice that is prioritized in pedagogies based on Skill Acquisition theory (via explicit instruction that provides declarative knowledge and opportunities for well-sequenced practice) and Input Processing theory (via interventions that seek to affect implicit processing), the Interaction approach favors task-based activities that afford learner practice with discourse-level language performance and that subtly attract attention to the specific formal features that need to be learned. That is, this approach conceives of instruction as externally orchestrated opportunities to attend to relevant features of the target language in context, precisely when they are embedded unobtrusively in the task at hand, during meaningful comprehension and production activities. A wide array of pedagogical techniques are posited to be facilitative, ranging from most implicit (e.g., recasts) to most explicit (e.g., collaborative negotiation of language problems in group dictation exercises called dictogloss). Instruction is not expected to alter natural constraints and paths of development but to optimize them, and it is posited to be possibly necessary for the development of very advanced L2 capabilities. Currently debated within this approach is what counts as "unobtrusive" attentional manipulation and whether optimal instruction should seek changes in knowledge and processing at more explicit or more implicit levels (see Doughty & Williams, 1998).

SOME FUTURE CHALLENGES FOR SLA THEORIES

The nine contemporary theories that readers find in this book (plus the early ones also reviewed by VanPatten & Williams in chapter 2) are the most widely cited and discussed in the history of SLA to date. They attest to the three characteristics of the field mentioned earlier: youth, strength, and interdisciplinarity. In this final section, I forecast some areas that I believe will likely attract keen attention in future SLA work. In my opinion, future work that ventures in these directions has the best potential to improve our explanations about second language learning.

First, I predict that in the future SLA theories will expend renewed efforts to incorporate views of language cognition and L2 knowledge that are plausible, in the sense of being compatible with cutting-edge knowledge about the workings of human cognition gleaned in the field of cognitive science. Some of the current theories in the field fare better than others on this account. For example, the Associative–Cognitive CREED and Skill Acquisition theory offer fine-grained models of language cognition that draw heavily on contemporary, plausible models of cognition. Several alternatives to traditional Universal Grammar theory, such as Autonomous Induction theory (Carroll, chapter 9 this volume), have originated precisely as attempts to accommodate cutting-edge knowledge of psycholinguistic processing into formal linguistic theories of language acquisition. However, in many SLA theories, a lack of specification of the assumed cognitive architecture is apparent. Indeed, this weakness was identified as a major obstacle for theory development in an oft-cited special issue of *TESOL Quarterly* devoted to exploring the proper scope and form of SLA theories. In it, Schumann (1990, p. 681) noted that claims like the "one-to-one principle" or the "noun-first principle" are useful in expressing observed, external behavior into predictive laws, but they are implausible direct descriptions of any underlying cognitive process or mechanism. More than fifteen years later, the need for better specification of the cognitive architecture assumed in each SLA theory remains urgent.

Discussions regarding the contributions of the linguistic environment and instruction to L2 learning can be particularly muddled by the problem of underspecification regarding the nature of L2 knowledge that is posited in each theory. One illustrative case is the ongoing debate about recasts among proponents of the Interaction approach (see Gass & Mackey, chapter 10 this volume). It remains unclear in these exchanges whether the learning benefits of recasts that are under dispute stem from metalinguistic (conscious) or psycholinguistic (subconscious) levels of processing. If the latter case is to be assumed, valid evidence would have to come from two sources, online processing data and gains resulting from experimental manipulations. By contrast, a commitment to benefits that are metalinguistic and metacognitive in nature would demand that critical evidence be found in learner reports of awareness and documentation of incorporation of recasts in the immediate discourse. Without a theoretically guided agreement on what kinds of evidence can settle the debate, little progress (whether theoretical or empirical) can be made.

The six psychologically oriented SLA theories presented in this book assume an explicit–implicit interface to some extent. Therefore, this area will likely attract much work in the future and stands to benefit greatly from interdisciplinary influences from cognitive science. Several fundamental questions that need to be pursued are:

What constitutes explicit versus implicit knowledge of an L2?

How does each type of knowledge originate?

How and when do they interface with each other?

What are the relative contributions of each to L2 learning?

Interesting research is currently carried out from different psychologically oriented perspectives (e.g., see the recent special issue of *Studies in Second Language Acquisition*, Hulstijn & Ellis, 2005). However, in the future it will be important to investigate the nature and contributions to SLA of explicit and implicit knowledge from a wider range of theoretical SLA frameworks. The first challenge in this direction would be to specify appropriate empirical strategies for investigating the relative roles for implicit and explicit knowledge that can (or cannot) be postulated by a range of theoretical approaches beyond the ones currently engaged in this area. To be sure, each SLA theory will frame the questions regarding explicit and implicit knowledge differently, in ways that are congruent with the rest of the constructs and with the view of cognition entailed in each. However, at this stage of our disciplinary knowledge it would be problematic for any theory of SLA to discard a priori one or the other type of knowledge as irrelevant for explaining L2 acquisition. For one, it is undeniable that L2 learners across formal and informal contexts encounter multiple opportunities to learn from implicit, bottom-up, and subconscious processing, and they also seize opportunities for learning from explicit, top-down, and conscious processing. In addition, all learners experience a "curious disjunction of knowledge" (VanPatten & Williams, chapter 2 this volume, p. 33) so pervasive and striking that the phenomenon begs better theoretical understanding across all possible perspectives.

A second area that will attract future attention involves a complete reevaluation of SLA theories in light of what we know about bilingualism and the nature of bilingual competence. Ironically, the field of SLA takes as prototypical the idealized case of the individual who already possesses a mature monolingual grammar and who subsequently begins learning an L2 with the goal to add on a monolingual-like command of the additional language. This bias is in part reminiscent of the same monolingual orientation in the field of child (first) language acquisition, which exerted a strong disciplinary influence on SLA during its formative years. Indeed, this should come as no surprise because both fields have largely concentrated on studying individuals and groups acquiring an L1 or an L2 in largely Western, middle-class contexts, and in such contexts it is not unusual for people to grow up speaking only one language.

In recent years, however, burgeoning research in the neighboring field of bilingualism has exposed this monolingual bias and has left SLA theories vulnerable to serious critique on this count. Vivian Cook, one of the earliest SLA voices to raise these concerns (e.g., Cook, 1991), notes that the best psycholinguistic bilingual processing evidence tells us L2 competence is fundamentally different from the linguistic competence of a monolingual. To use Cook's terminology, L2 users are not two monolinguals in one. Instead, they possess a psycholinguistically distinct form of *multicompetence*. The validity of key notions in the field of SLA (e.g., interlanguage and ultimate attainment) is called into question when the monolingual native speaker is no longer held to be the norm. Consider, for example, how radically vacuous certain theoretical and empirical statements are if we substitute the notion of "target-like" for the notion of "monolingual-like." Thus, saying that "a given learner has failed to develop target-like competence in a given area of the L2" or that "most L2 learners fall short of the target norm" makes little sense if we mean that a given learner has failed to develop *monolingual* competence in a given area of the L2 or that most L2 learners fall short of the *monolingual* norm. After all, the impossibility for bilinguals to reach levels that are isomorphic with monolinguals would be a nonissue in a world in which bilingualism would be considered the default state of the human language faculty.

When L2 competence is reconceptualized in this way, the attainment of bilingual competence (whether by early or late bilinguals) can no longer be directly compared to the attainment of monolingual competence. Thus, some SLA researchers have begun to consider whether the appropriate comparison for interlanguage data may be data contributed by mature bilinguals rather than data contributed by monolinguals of the given target language.

Other areas of SLA have begun to be transformed by the newly adopted prism of bilingualism. Once monolingualism is not taken as the default starting point for L2 learning, it is also easy to remember that in many cases, people bring knowledge of multiple languages to the task of learning an additional one. This has opened up new questions in the field: How does knowledge of two (or more) preexisting languages influence knowledge of the L3 or L4, and so on (see Cenoz, Hufeisen & Jessner, 2001)? Will the L1 still play a privileged role in such cases? Can knowledge of the L1 be influenced by languages learned later in life? Whatever answers SLA researchers offer to these questions, pursuing them will no doubt affect our understanding of the theoretical explanations we propose in the future. Assuming that these new lines of SLA research continue to thrive, and hoping that a more bilingual outlook on SLA phenomena slowly takes hold across this and other areas of SLA scholarship, we can predict that our existing SLA theories will need to incorporate the new findings and, in the process, will likely be transformed.

The final area for future theoretical development that I would like to forecast here pertains to the need to theorize experience in explanations of SLA. As DeKeyser notes (chapter 6 this volume), different learners are afforded (or seek on their own to obtain) different amounts, qualities, and sequences of experience in and with the L2. Differential experience is thought to be connected to one of the most salient "facts" to be explained by any SLA theory, namely, the large variability and heterogeneity in L2 learning processes and outcomes, which contrast with the moderately variable processes and largely uniform outcomes of L1 acquisition. Of course, all theories of SLA acknowledge this fact and all admit that variable L2 outcomes are related in part to variable life experience across learners and contexts. However, most SLA theories are typically ill-equipped to deal with this reality in theoretically rigorous ways. As a consequence, they trivialize learner experience as anecdotal and outside the systematic scope of empirical or theoretical understanding, divesting it from any theoretical status. The exception is Vygotskian Sociocultural theory (Lantolf & Thorne, chapter 11 this volume), which is specifically designed to investigate cognition and learning as embedded in experience and context, not divested or abstracted from it.

There are, however, other theories originally from the fields of anthropology, education, and sociology that have also been designed to deal with social experience as an object of study rather than as random noise that needs to be eliminated from theory development. These less traditional theories have the potential to help SLA researchers understand a range of social influences on L2 learning processes and outcomes, beyond the dimensions of cognition and language traditionally investigated in current SLA theories. They do so by theorizing learning experience. They draw on alternative social understandings of cognition that are germane to the one proposed by Vygotskian Sociocultural theory. In addition, however, they offer social respecifications of a number of other areas that are important in SLA thinking, including L2 grammar (Schleppegrell, 2004), L2 communication (Markee & Kasper, 2004), and L2 learning (Kanno & Norton, 2003; Pavlenko & Blackledge, 2004; Watson-Gegeo & Nielsen, 2003). Explanatory constructs that cut across this new family of SLA theories are agency, power, and identity.

At the risk of grossly simplifying, just as certain SLA theories have helped us understand that input may be less important than how input is processed by learners, these other theories help us understand ways in which social experience has explanatory power not as externally documented experience or as fixed environmental encounters but as experience that is lived, made sense of, negotiated, contested, and claimed by learners in their physical, interpersonal, social, cultural, and historical context. If, in the future, SLA researchers recognize the importance of theorizing learner experience, it may be possible to achieve a balance between linguistic, cognitive, psychological, and social explanations in our theories.

Explaining how people learn languages other than their mother tongue is the central task of the field of SLA. Scholarship in this area attracts increasing interest and even fascination. This intellectual appeal is not surprising, given that speaking more than one language and being comfortable with more than one culture have become great personal and socio-economic assets to people from all walks of life and from all over the world. In little more than forty years of vibrant existence, SLA has produced a surprisingly varied and healthy number of theories that convincingly explain particular phenomena in L2 acquisition, some times in ways that are similar across theories, on occasion in ways that differ from, and sometimes even contradict, other theories. Naturally, the most progress has been made in the areas where the most effort and attention has been directed to date, namely the acquisition of a linguistic system (mostly defined as morphology and syntax of the L2; see also VanPatten & Williams, chapter 1 this volume). In the future, we can look forward to further theoretical development, innovation, and expansion. Future SLA thinking that continues to be interdisciplinary and that reaps the benefits of advances in cognitive science, bilingual studies, and social theories will be of essence in improving our explanations of second language learning.

REFERENCES

Andersen, R. W. (1990). Verbal virtuosity and speakers' purposes. In H. Burmeister & P. L. Rounds (Eds.), *Variability in second language acquisition: Proceedings of the tenth meeting of the Second Language Research Forum* Vol. 1 (pp. 1–24). Eugene, OR: University of Oregon's Department of Linguistics and American English Institute.

Bardovi-Harlig, K., & Reynolds, D. (1995). The role of lexical aspect in the acquisition of tense and aspect. *TESOL Quarterly, 29,* 107–131.

Cenoz, J., Hufeisen, B., & Jessner, U. (Eds.). (2001). *Cross-linguistic influence in third language acquisition: Psycholinguistic perspectives.* Clevedon, UK: Multilingual Matters.

Cook, V. (1991). The poverty-of-the-stimulus argument and multicompetence. *Second Language Research, 7,* 103–117.

DeKeyser, R. (Ed.). (forthcoming). *Practicing in a second language: Perspectives from applied linguistics and cognitive psychology.* New York: Cambridge University Press.

Doughty, C., & Williams, J. (1998). Pedagogical choices in focus on form. In C. Doughty & J. Williams (Eds.), *Focus on form in classroom second language acquisition* (pp. 197–261). New York: Cambridge University Press.

Ellis, N. (1993). Rules and instances in foreign language learning: Interactions of implicit and explicit knowledge. *European Journal of Cognitive Psychology, 5,* 289–319.

Farley, A. P. (2005). *Structured input: Grammar instruction for the acquisition oriented classroom.* Boston: McGraw Hill.

Hatch, E. (1978). Discourse analysis and second language acquisition. In E. Hatch (Ed.), *Second language acquisition: A book of readings* (pp. 401–435). Rowley, MA: Newbury House.

Hulstijn, J. H., & Ellis, R. (Eds.). (2005). *Theoretical and empirical issues in the study of implicit and explicit second-language learning.* Special Issue of *Studies in Second Language Acquisition, 27,* 129–352.

Kanno, Y., & Norton, B. (2003). Imagined communities and educational possibilities: Introduction. *Language of Language, Identity, and Education, 2,* 241–249.

Larsen-Freeman, D. (2002). Language acquisition and language use from a chaos/complexity theory perspective. In C. Kramsch (Ed.), *Language acquisition and language socialization* (pp. 33–46). New York: Continuum.

Lightbown, P., & Pienemann, M. (1993). Comments on Stephen D. Krashen's "Teaching issues: Formal grammar instruction." *TESOL Quarterly, 27,* 717–722.

Markee, N., & Kasper, G. (2004). Classroom talks: An introduction. *Modern Language Journal, 88,* 491–500.

Mitchell, R., & Myles, F. (2004). *Second language learning theories* (2nd ed.). New York: Arnold.

Ortega, L. (forthcoming). Meaningful L2 practice in foreign language classrooms: A cognitive-interactionist SLA perspective. In R. DeKeyser (Ed.), *Practicing in a second language: Perspectives from applied linguistics and cognitive psychology.* New York: Cambridge University Press.

Pavlenko, A., & Blackledge, A. (Eds.). (2004). *Negotiation of identities in multilingual contexts.* Philadelphia, PA: Multilingual Matters.

Pienemann, M. (1984). Psychological constraints on the teachability of languages. *Studies in Second Language Acquisition, 6,* 186–214.

Schleppegrell, M. J. (2004). *The language of schooling: A functional linguistics perspective.* Mahwah, NJ: Lawrence Erlbaum Associates.

Schumann, J. (1990). Extending the scope of the acculturation/pidginization model to include cognition. *TESOL Quarterly, 24,* 667–684.

VanPatten, B. (1998). Cognitive characteristics of adult second language learners. In H. Byrnes (Ed.), *Learning foreign and second languages* (pp. 105–127). New York: Modern Language Association of America.

————. (Ed.). (2004). *Processing instruction: Theory, research, and commentary*. Mahwah, NJ: Lawrence Erlbaum Associates.

Watson-Gegeo, K. A., & Nielsen, S. (2003). Language socialization in SLA. In C. Doughty & M. H. Long (Eds.), *Handbook of second language acquisition* (pp. 155–177). Malden, MA: Blackwell.

Author Index

Subject Index